OUT THERE

OUT THERE

by George Day
and Herb McCormick

SEVEN SEAS PRESS, INC. NEWPORT, R.I.

To Rosie and Jack Mack

PUBLISHED BY SEVEN SEAS PRESS, *Newport, Rhode Island, 02840*
Edited by James R. Gilbert

Library of Congress Cataloging in Publication Data
Day, George, 1950–
  Out there.
  1. BOC Challenge Race.   I. McCormick, Herb,
1955–   . II. Title.
GV832.D38   1984   797.1'4   84-5293
ISBN 0-915160-59-5

Designed by Irving Perkins Associates
Printed in the United States of America by R. R. Donnelley & Sons

CONTENTS

ACKNOWLEDGEMENTS

ONE OF THE great benefits in covering the BOC Challenge was getting to know the fine people who were associated with the race. There are several people who deserve special recognition.

Murray Davis, the publisher of *Cruising World* magazine, stood behind the race and this project from the outset. Without his enthusiasm and support, this book would not have been possible.

Dale Nouse, Dan Spurr, Bernadette Brennan, and Lynda Morris, all editors for *Cruising World,* were on the docks for the race's start and finish. Their pre-race interviews with the competitors provided an initial base of information. And Dale Nouse tackled the manuscript a final time before it was off to the typesetters. His comments and corrections were especially welcome.

Noreen Barnhart, editorial assistant at *Cruising World,* cheerfully typed (and retyped) the original manuscript.

Jim Roos was hustling the race before the BOC Group knew it existed and opened up his vast files without hesitation. His knowledge of the race's background and the genuine respect he held for the racers were both invaluable.

Nigel Rowe of the BOC Group was behind this book from the beginning, even though his company had already commissioned an "official" account. His blessing made our job all the easier.

Public relations firms on three continents were very helpful in obtaining background material and photographs. We'd like to thank P. R. Associates of Johannesburg, South Africa; Hall and Jenkins of Sydney, Australia; and especially Newsome & Co. of Boston, Massachusetts. Kathy Giblin and Rid Bullerjahn, of Newsome & Co., particularly, are to be acknowledged for their assistance and professionalism.

Bill Rabinowitz of the Cruising Association of South Africa was a fountain of information and stories and always a joy to tap. Race committee members Peter Dunning and Peter Hegeman always were available to answer one more question and have brought the Goat Island Yacht Club a long way since it was better known as the D Dock Chowder and Marching Society.

Barbara Lloyd, a freelance journalist who covered the race from its inception, was a priceless colleague when it came to names, dates and anecdotes and, much more importantly, a great friend.

Andrew Rock and Jim Gilbert of Seven Seas Press deserve and get a hearty thanks.

And last, but certainly not least, we'd like to acknowledge the 17 sailors who accepted the BOC Challenge. To a man, they were more than generous with their time and thoughts. If this book captures even the barest essence of what these men and their race were about, it will have been worthwhile.

Finally, despite all the help we received, the end product is ours alone and we take full responsibility for the material it contains.

HERB McCORMICK and GEORGE DAY
Newport, RI
March, 1984

INTRODUCTION

AT 3:25 P.M. ON APRIL 22, 1969, the world got one notch smaller. That day, British sailor Robin Knox-Johnston sailed into Falmouth Harbour, England, winning the Golden Globe, the first singlehanded around the world race, after a remarkable, non-stop, 313-day voyage of 30,123 miles. Falmouth Harbour teemed with spectator boats. Along the quay, crowds of well-wishers waved little Union Jacks in the pale spring sky. The Mount Everest of sailing had been climbed.

In many ways, the Golden Globe had been a contest as much as a race. In the wake of Englishman Francis Chichester's one-stop singlehanded circumnavigation in 1966–67, for which he was knighted, several individuals began making plans to do the voyage non-stop. When a London newspaper, *The Sunday Times,* became aware of the relatively widespread efforts, they decided to increase the incentive (and capitalize on the publicity) by sponsoring a race. The rules were simple: Entrants had to leave any English port by a specified date, and return to it after rounding the three capes of Good Hope, Leeuwin and the Horn. Two prizes were offered, one for first to finish and one for fastest time.

Of the nine contestants who sailed out separately from England, Knox-Johnston alone completed the voyage. At the age of 30, the strapping young merchant seaman became a national hero overnight. He was made a Commander of the British Empire (CBE). He wrote the best-selling book *A World Of My Own.* And he went on to build and race many more boats with the help of commercial sponsors, all eager to share his limelight. The race around the world transformed his life.

But Knox-Johnston was only the most noticeable of those touched by the first "around alone" sailing race. All the adventurers who had entered the premier race were changed by what they discovered during their lonely months on the open sea. The others were not as lucky as Knox-Johnston. Four sailors, Chay Blyth, John Ridgeway, Alex Carozzo and Loick Fugeron, were forced to withdraw due to damage to their boats and gear. Frenchman Bernard Moitessier, sailing his steel ketch *Joshua,* started after Knox-Johnston but sailed at a rapid pace, and had nearly caught the Englishman by the halfway point. Yet the oceans and months of solitude worked a primitive magic upon him. With the victory his for the taking, Moitessier suddenly turned east again after rounding Cape Horn and made an unexplained second rounding of the Cape of Good Hope. Off Cape Town, South Africa, he contacted a ship with the single message, "I am going away to save my soul." Before finally stopping in Tahiti, he sailed a total of 37,455 uninterrupted miles—one and a half times around the planet.

Another racer, Nigel Tetley, made the first circumnavigation in a trimaran, only to have his great voyage end when his boat, *Victress,* sank 1,100 miles from the finish line. The disappointment scarred Tetley terribly. Less than three years later, he hung himself.

If Knox-Johnston gained fame from the race, Donald Crowhurst achieved notoriety as one of the greatest frauds in sporting history. Also sailing a trimaran, Crowhurst never made the voyage around the world. Instead, he remained in the South Atlantic while the other racers sailed on. Over the radio he faked position reports in a systematic deception that, if carried to its conclusion, could have won the race for the 37-year-old Englishman. But Crowhurst, an intense, intelligent man, was unable to culminate his hoax. His trimaran *Teignmouth Electron* was found on July 10, 1969, drifting quietly in midatlantic. Crowhurst was not aboard, but on his chart table he had left his logbooks, which when pierced together by investigative reporters Nicholas Tomalin and Ron Hall, contained the fantastic record of his deception. In their haunting book, *The Strange Last Voyage of Donald Crowhurst,* Tomalin and Hall conclude that Crowhurst lost his mind and stepped off *Teignmouth Electron*'s stern into the void of the sea.

For all but Robin Knox-Johnston, the race had proven more than a match. But Knox-Johnston had succeeded, and by doing so he extended an open challenge to adventurers and singlehanded sailors everywhere.

It is not surprising that 14 years had to pass before another solo round-the-world sailing race would be staged. Organizing and running such an event requires time and resources usually not available for sailboat races. For most individuals, the three years necessary to prepare for and then sail in a race around the world means that entering necessarily is a once-in-a-lifetime opportunity. But, in the 20-20 vision of hindsight, a second race was inevitable. Too many young men and women had followed the

Golden Globe with awe. Too many had read Knox-Johnston's and Moitessier's books and the Tomalin/Hall report on the Crowhurst tragedy to leave dormant the dream of making the world yet even one more notch smaller.

On August 28, 1982, a new generation of sailors set out from Newport, Rhode Island, at the start of a four-leg singlehanded race around the world. Called the BOC Challenge after the race's sponsor, the London-based BOC Group, the race was conceived by American David White as the ultimate challenge for men or women who sail alone across oceans. Unlike the Golden Globe, the fleet started with and raced against one another. The boats were divided into two classes of monohulls; Class I was for yachts between 45 and 56 feet, and Class II for yachts between 32 and 44 feet, though the smallest boat to enter was 38-feet. A $25,000 prize awaited the winner of each class.

This was the first round-the-world race of any type to originate and finish in the United States, and the first long-distance singlehanded race to run from the East Coast. For anyone familiar with sailing, Newport was an approprate place for the BOC Challenge to start. First, New England was Joshua Slocum's home, and Slocum—who sailed alone around the world from 1895 to 1898—is the grandfather of all solo sailors. Newport also is the terminus of the greatest singlehanded races, the *Observer* Singlehanded Transatlantic Race (OSTAR). The OSTAR was founded in 1960 by Englishmen Francis Chichester and Blondie Hasler. It runs from Plymouth, England, to Newport every four years. Its success has thrust the idea of singlehanded ocean racing into the minds of sailors around the world. During the 1970s, the OSTAR grew into a grand prix of specialized ocean racing that spawned other races like it—the Two-Star (doublehanded transatlantic), the Route du Rhum, the Bermuda One-Two and others. The OSTAR also generated a new breed of boats, equipment and specialized sailors. Singlehanding came of age in the 1970s and in America, Newport was its home.

The development of gear and boats since the Golden Globe was evident in the 16-boat BOC fleet that left Newport on August 28. (Another departed two weeks later.) Unlike Knox-Johnston's 32-foot *Suhali* or Moitessier's *Joshua,* most of the BOC entries were vessels that had been designed specifically for singlehanding. Moreover, three boats, David White's 56-foot *Gladiator,* Tony Lush's 54-foot *Lady Pepperell* and Philippe Jeantot's 56-foot *Credit Agricole,* were built especially for the race. Self-steering devices, considered essential for solo sailing, had evolved from clumsy homemade gadgets into sophisticated, sea-tested designs. Other new gear such as roller furling systems on headsails and self-tailing winches (which automatically roll or unroll sails and lines) acted as another pair of hands for the overworked skippers. Modern satellite navigational receivers (SatNav), weather map facsimile printers, and a worldwide ham radio network aided the racers with electronics unavailable 14 years before. The sport had evolved. It had become more sophisticated and much safer.

The sea alone remained the same.

Ahead of the racers as they left Newport lay a 27,000-mile course around the world with ports of call at Cape Town, South Africa; Sydney, Australia; and Rio de Janeiro, Brazil. The race took a total of nine months (each of the four legs lasting from 30 to 70 days), during which each sailor was responsible for every aspect of sailing his boat. Each man washed his own socks and performed his own celestial navigation. He had to cook meals, wash dishes and dash up on deck to change headsails. When something broke, he either fixed it or learned to live without it. If he got six hours sleep in 24 he was lucky. Often he got none.

The obstacles the skippers faced were the same that centuries before had tested caravelles, clipper ships and whalers. They negotiated the currents and fickle winds of the Atlantic, and then survived the cold gales of the Great Southern Ocean.

If there was one object to it all, one Holy Grail, it was Cape Horn. The rocky promontory at the southern tip of South America was and still is the gale-swept Mecca to blue-water sailors. But earning the title "Cape Horner" and the traditional gold earring proved as difficult for the BOC racers as it had for those in the Golden Globe.

Several months before the start of the BOC race, Knox-Johnston, who had appropriately been named race committee chairman by BOC, predicted that fewer than 10 of the 33 boats then entered would complete the course. His estimate proved pessimistic. Yet he was not far wrong. Of the 17 who sailed across the starting line only 10 made it home. Although no lives were lost, the rest were casualties. Their stories, like those of the men who finished, are remarkable.

For most of the original 17, the BOC Challenge was their once-in-a-lifetime race, never to be repeated. And like the first OSTAR, the first BOC Challenge was conceived and raced by enthusiastic adventurers, whose seamanship and personal integrity made the race a success. The ranks of professionals may crowd out the amateurs in future races, diluting the camaraderie of the fleet with a competitiveness born as much by their will to win as from the corporate sponsors that will make future races possible. Never will there be another round-the-world race like this premier edition. But the traditions established in this first race will continue to nourish racers, offshore sailors and adventurers everywhere for years to come.

The Men And The Boats

CLASS I

RICHARD BROADHEAD, 29, of South Devon, England, worked as a ranch hand in Australia and as a rubber plantation manager in Brazil's Amazon Basin before the race. Although he approached more than 800 companies in search of sponsorship, he failed to get financial backing.

Perseverance of Medina, designed by Britton Chance, was built in 1973 for Sir Max Aitken's participation in the British Admiral's Cup trials. The 52-foot fiberglass yacht was originally a centerboard ketch but was later converted to a cutter with a fixed keel.

NEVILLE GOSSON, 55, of Sydney, Australia, took leave from his building and contracting firm to enter the race. An experienced ocean racing sailor and member of the Cruising Yacht Club of Australia, the BOC Challenge was his first singlehanded event.

Leda Pier One is a 53-foot aluminum cutter, designed by Joe Adams and commissioned by Gosson in 1974 for participation in the Australian Admiral's Cup trials. Gosson sold the boat in 1979 and repurchased it for the race. The yacht was sponsored by Pier One, a waterfront shopping development.

DESMOND HAMPTON, 41, of London, England, took a sabbatical from his position in a London real estate firm for the race. His previous racing experience included the second leg of the Parmelia Race from Cape Town to Perth in 1979, and the 1980 OSTAR.

Gipsy Moth V is a cold-molded staysail ketch commissioned by Sir Francis Chichester, designed by Robert Clark and built in 1970. Chartered

xii   *The Men and the Boats*

from the Chichester family for the race, the boat had a little over a foot removed from her stern to meet the upper qualifying limit of 56 feet.

PHILIPPE JEANTOT, 30, of Le Havre, France, is a former paratrooper in the French army and free-lance commercial diver who shares a world record for the deepest dive ever—501 meters. He had cruised more than 25,000 singlehanded miles before the race.

Credit Agricole is a 56-foot aluminum cutter designed specifically for the race by Guy Ribadeau Dumas; it incorporated several custom ideas by the skipper. The boat, whose namesake is a French bank, was conceived, built, launched and sailed across the Atlantic over a span of eight months before the race began.

TONY LUSH, 33, of Gainsville, Florida, was a veteran of the 1976 and 1980 OSTARs. He worked for Hunter Yachts in Florida for two years following the 1980 race and it was there that he built his radical 54-footer *Lady Pepperell*.

Lady Pepperell, a 54-foot fiberglass cat-ketch, was a modified Hunter 54, originally designed by John Cherubini. Her unstayed rig flew no headsails and was designed for downwind running and easy handling. Her name derived from Lush's sponsor in the race, the West Point Pepperell Corp., of West Point, Georgia.

BERTIE REED, 38, from Simonstown, South Africa, is a naval warrant officer and sailing instructor. Though his country's premier sailor, Reed's first singlehanded race was the 1980 OSTAR. With a partner, he set a monohull record for the Round Britain race just prior to the BOC Challenge.

Altech Voortrekker, the oldest boat in the fleet, is a 49-foot sloop designed by E. G. Van de Stadt and built in 1967 for the 1968 OSTAR (in which she finished second). The wood yacht was sponsored by Altech, an electronics firm.

PAUL RODGERS, 37, of London, England, has been a trichologist (a scientist who studies the causes of baldness), newspaper editor and book author. He sailed a 38-foot trimaran in the 1980 OSTAR.

Spirit of Pentax is a 55-foot centerboard schooner in which Rodgers spent 251 days at sea while circling the globe one and a quarter times in an unsuccessful quest for a double circumnavigation. Despite the name, *Pentax* was unsponsored for the BOC race.

DAVID WHITE, 38, of Sarasota, Florida, was a co-founder of the BOC Challenge. A seasoned singlehanded sailor, White spent two years organizing the race and building a boat for the event. He was formerly a salesman for Colter Electronics, a California computer firm.

Gladiator is a 56-foot fiberglass cutter designed specifically for the race by Alan Gurney. She was unsponsored.

CLASS II

GUY BERNARDIN, 38, of Brittany, France, sold his restaurant to enter the race. In 1979, Bernardin was at sea for 125 straight days while trying to better Robin Knox-Johnston's non-stop round the world record of 312 days. An equipment failure forced him to turn around off Cape Town, South Africa.

Ratso II, at 38 feet, was the smallest boat in the race. Her skipper and his father finished off the fiberglass cutter from a bare hull. Her name, spelled backwards, is OSTAR, in which Bernardin sailed her in 1980.

DAN BYRNE, 53, of Santa Monica, California, retired in 1979 as an editor from the *Los Angeles Times* to devote more time to real estate interests and sailing. The Singlehanded Transpac from California to Hawaii in 1980 was his first singlehanded race.

Fantasy is hull number one of the popular Valiant 40 line of cutter-rigged cruising boats. Designed by Robert Perry and first built in 1975, more than 160 of the fiberglass yachts have been sold since.

GREG COLES, 26, of Cape Town, South Africa, was the fleet's youngest starter. Originally from New Zealand, Coles' qualifying sail from South Carolina to Newport was his first singlehanded voyage. He started 12 days behind the fleet.

Datsun Skyline, with a single wing spar that moved fore and aft on a track and a hydraulic keel, was the fleet's most radical boat. The 44-foot carbon fibre boat, which weighed a mere 4.5 tons, was designed by Richard Glanville.

JACQUES DE ROUX, 43, of Toulon, France, was a submarine commander and instructor at the French Navy school for submarine navigation before the race. His sailing experience included stints as navigator for Eric Tabarly and as crew for an attempt on the transatlantic speed record in 1980.

Skoiern III, his 41-foot aluminum cutter, was designed by Dominique Presles. The flush-decked yacht was built in 1979 for a race from Lorient, France, to Bermuda.

RICHARD KONKOLSKI, 39, of Bohumin, Czechoslovokia, circumnavigated the globe between 1972 and 1975 aboard a 24-foot yawl which he designed and built himself. He was a well-known author and celebrity in his homeland but announced his defection the morning the BOC race began.

Nike III was built by her skipper in 1978 and raced in the 1979 Parmelia Race and the 1980 OSTAR. The husky 44-foot fiberglass cutter was specifically laid out for singlehanded sailing.

TOM LINDHOLM, 57, of Hidden Hills, California, was the oldest starter in the race. In 1978, the lawyer and former Los Angeles vice squad detective, sailed in the Singlehanded Transpac and finished first in his division.

Driftwood, an Ericson 41 that was one of three production boats in the race, was designed by Bruce King. The fiberglass sloop was built in 1968.

RICHARD MCBRIDE, 38, of Christchurch, New Zealand, is a former dog sled driver, bulldozer operator, copywriter and photographer. His first offshore voyage in a sailing yacht was his qualifying sail for the race.

City of Dunedin is a 42-foot steel staysail schooner, designed by Colin Childs, that McBride built in his spare time over a period of five years. The venture was sponsored in part by contributions from New Zealand businessmen.

FRANCIS STOKES, 56, of Moorestown, New Jersey, is a yacht broker in Annapolis, Maryland. One of the more experienced racers, Stokes' sailing background lists five Atlantic crossings, including two OSTAR's and three Bermuda One-Two races.

Mooneshine is a William Garden-designed Fast Passage 39 built by the Tollycraft Corporation. The only difference from the standard production version of the double-ended fiberglass cutter was oversized standing rigging.

YUKOH TADA, 53, of Tokyo, Japan, is a taxi driver, abstract artist, amateur jazz musician and Zen Buddist. A veteran of several Pacific singlehanded races, Tada was also support leader for a 1978 North Pole expedition.

Koden Okera V is a 44-foot fiberglass and carbon-fiber sloop fitted with a full array of marine electronics that were donated by a partial sponsor, Koden electronics.

1

The Gladiator and the Lions

THE MOMENT HAD come. David White, alone at the helm of his 56-foot cutter *Gladiator,* saw the puff of smoke from the starting gun and heard the report. At 3 p.m. on the brilliantly clear afternoon of August 28, the race was underway. He trimmed his genoa and mainsail and within moments the big red boat charged forward toward the starting line. Around him, the spectator fleet, several hundred boats strong, crowded in to watch the 16 singlehanders begin the voyage around the world. It was difficult steering through the traffic.

Ahead of White, closer to the line, Frenchman Guy Bernardin aboard *Ratso II* wrestled alone with his genoa, unable to get it set. Near Bernardin, Czech sailor Richard Konkolski aboard his white-hulled *Nike II,* hauled in his sails and triumphantly crossed the starting line first. His white sloop heeled slightly in the light afternoon breeze as Konkolski led the way out of Rhode Island's Narragansett Bay. Konkolski had announced that morning his defection to the United States from Czechoslovakia, and the spectator fleet cheered him on with air horns and sirens.

But White was close on Konkolski's heels. He sailed by Bernardin, crossed the line second and steered his boat toward the open sea. A bear of a man, White sat on the leeward side of his boat, one hand on the wheel, the other raised in salute to the crowd of well wishers. With his blonde beard and steely gaze, he brought to mind the image of a modern-

1

day Viking bravely setting out onto an uncertain sea toward regions unknown.

Two miles from the starting line, *Nike II* passed through the mouth of Narragansett Bay and sailed into the rolling swells of the Atlantic Ocean. It was just beyond the stout, Castle Hill lighthouse at the harbor heads that David White overtook Konkolski and took the lead. Close behind came Philippe Jeantot's sleek, black *Credit Agricole* and Bertie Reed's white sloop *Altech Voortrekker*. And behind them, the rest of the 16 starters tacked slowly into the afternoon breeze, sailing in the throng of spectator boats toward the solitude of the sea.

For David White, taking the lead at the mouth of the bay was the culmination of three years of hard work. He had placed himself and *Gladiator* just where he wanted and planned to be—first. Ahead lay the first night alone at sea, cold and black and rough. Beyond was the inaugural leg of the great race around the world—the ultimate test of a lone sailor, perhaps of any athlete. White and the fleet had 7,000 miles of open ocean to cross before making their first port in Cape Town, South Africa. It would take the larger boats an estimated 40 to 50 days. The smaller and slower boats could expect to be at sea for as many as 70 days. Beyond Cape Town were two long legs in the Great Southern Ocean, with a stop at Sydney, Australia, and a rounding of the most famous cape of all, Cape Horn. Then, after a layover in Rio de Janeiro, Brazil, the fleet would come home again, having sailed some 27,500 miles, through three oceans over a period of eight or nine months.

Sailing into the closing dusk of the clear August evening was one of the most thrilling experiences of White's life. He was striding out into the ancient coliseum of the sea to do battle with the lions of wind and wave and weather. To survive the race would be a great accomplishment in itself. BOC Race Committee Chairman Robin Knox-Johnston, who had been the lone finisher of the only other race of this type, the Golden Globe in 1969, said before the start, "To win this race you have to finish, and everyone who finishes will have achieved a marvelous victory whether he comes in first or not."

White wanted to survive the journey around the world. But more important was his need to return victorious. So, on the first night, at the head of the fleet, that is what he set out to do—to slay the lions.

The first hours of sailing assured White of one thing. *Gladiator* sailed like a bat out of hell. By the afternoon of August 29, with 24 hours of sailing under his belt, White announced over the radio to the race committee at Goat Island and anyone else who might (he hoped) be listening, that he had covered a remarkable 200 miles. He was averaging 8.3 knots (or roughly 10 miles an hour) and none of the other boats, with the exception of Jeantot, who did not report his position at all during the first week, were able to keep up with him. *Gladiator* had the speed to win.

Much of the sailing during the first few days of the race was in rough conditions and under a gray sky. It was not storm sailing, but aboard *Gladiator,* sailing at more than eight knots to windward, the strain on the boat was persistent and wearing. Time after time the big boat hurdled a wave only to crash into the trough beyond.

Incredibly, the wear on *Gladiator* already was beginning to show. On the second day out, White noticed the foredeck flex under the strain. By the third day, it was worse. The flexing foredeck had created several stress fractures in the interior plywood bulkhead supporting the deck. Under the full press of sail and charging into the waves to windward, something terrible was happening to the big red boat. White realized *Gladiator* was beginning to break apart.

The race around the world had belonged to David White from the start. He thought it up in 1979 as he sailed home on the second leg of a short race from Newport, Rhode Island, to Bermuda and back, known as the Bermuda One-Two. After the race, he and a group of fellow racers were tipping a few bottles of beer in Newport's Goat Island Marina Pub (the unofficial home of singlehanding in the United States) when White proposed the new race, the ultimate race.

David's point was simple. The sport of singlehanded offshore racing had its roots in the great voyages of such American sailors as Joshua Slocum, who was first to circumnavigate the world alone in 1895; Harry Pidgeon, who sailed twice alone around the world in the 1920s and 30s; and more recently, young Robin Lee Graham, who rounded the world in a five-year passage (1965–70), beginning when he was just 16. However, the modern champions of the sport were not Americans, but Englishmen and Frenchmen. American sailors had made famous and superb voyages around the world, but always at cruising speed. This was the age of racing and, in White's view, it was time for Americans to shift up to racing speed. How better to show the world what American sailors were made of than to stage and win a singlehanded around the world race?

For those present at the Pub that afternoon, the idea sounded delightful, if a little daft. But being fresh from the sea and full of beer, those around the table let the conversation roll enthusiastically into the night. Routes were planned, rules devised, new boats conceived. It was a classic "BS" session that in the cold light of the next morning looked to most of the group to be nothing more than a vast, impractical idea that would be almost impossible to organize. One by one, the other sailors climbed aboard their boats and sailed away from Newport.

Only White remained aboard his 32-foot cutter *Catapha* that lay tied to the pier at the Goat Island Marina, not 100 yards from the Marina Pub. At 36, he was single and had the time and the money to spend a few months enjoying Newport's famous good life. He was biding his time. But in the back of his mind the idea of the race around the world continued to burn.

Life had not always been offshore racing for David White. He had come to the slow speed of sailing out of the fast track. Born in California in 1944, White joined the Navy after high school and served as a seaman aboard the aircraft carrier *Shangri La*. After his tour, he spent four years getting an engineering degree from Temple University and the University of Colorado. From there, this big garrulous man, whose voice booms like a ship's horn, went to work as a salesman for the Coulter Corporation, a high tech electronics firm. He was good at his work. By the time he was 30 he had acquired the sales managership of the western half of the United States, a large income and a bleeding ulcer.

In the early 70s, he read an article in *Time* magazine on the new popularity of the Westsail 32 cutter and the allure of the cruising way of life —tropic isles, palm trees, native girls. The article hit White right in the ulcer. He knew he had to get out of the fast lane and go sailing. Before long, he did just that. Naturally, he went aboard a Westsail 32, *Catapha*. In 1974, he sailed from San Francisco to Mexico and then set off across the Pacific to French Polynesia. After a sojourn in the South Pacific, he sailed alone non-stop from Tahiti to San Francisco, covering 4,700 miles in 41 days. A new passion was born—singlehanding.

Always energetic and competitive, White began entering singlehanded races. He competed in the 1975 San Francisco to Okinawa, Japan Singlehanded Race, a passage of 6,500 miles. He sailed in the 1976 Observer Singlehanded Transatlantic Race (OSTAR), the 1978 singlehanded Trans-Pac (San Francisco to Hawaii) and the 1979 Bermuda One-Two. The races were organized adventures for White. His short, squat 32-foot cutter was not designed to race, nor was it fast.

Through the summer of 1979, White played in Newport and pondered the next step. With more than 70,000 miles of singlehanded racing behind him, he had become one of America's top solo sailors. But he was unknown to most sailors and his sport never had been reported in most of America's newspapers. White needed to take the next step, a step that would loft himself and American singlehanders onto a racing platform level to that of his English and French counterparts. He wanted to become the Joshua Slocum of the racing age.

In October, 1979, White made his decision. He would found a race he called Around Alone and he would build a boat to win the race. To get the race off the ground, he needed to secure a base of operations where

n time, host a fleet of racing boats. The
al facility so White's next job was to ignite
a's property manager, Jim Roos. Roos, an
ely was attracted to the grand sporting con-
believed the race would be excellent public
a partnership and a non-profit corporation
World, Inc.) were formed. White had his
and he had a partner in Roos, who, as race
the hundreds of details involved in organiz-
nile race.

le date: September, 1982. That left White two
iild a boat and organize the race. It should have
wasn't. Two pressing problems faced White in
problems that defied simple solutions. He had
to sponsor and underwrite the cost of running
believed would be approximately $200,000. And,
he had to find ~~~~~~~ r for his world-beating boat.

In 1980, trying to squeeze sponsorship for a sailing event from an
American corporation was like squeezing blood from a stone. Roos and
White spent the next 18 months knocking on doors, writing letters and
press releases, and trying to stir the interest of public relations directors
of corporations across America. They were enthusiastic but disorganized.
Even White's prodigious sales acumen could not turn the deaf ears.

To attract European companies accustomed to sponsoring offshore
singlehanded races, White and Roos set class sizes in conformance with
those of the OSTAR—32 to 44 feet for Class II and 45 to 56 feet for
Class I. (The BOC limits were changed in 1983 to conform with the new
OSTAR limits of 40 to 50 feet for Class II and 50 to 60 feet for Class I.)

But their efforts seemed futile. Companies like Anheuser Busch,
Miller, Coca Cola and Pepsico were not interested. Sailboat racing, the
public relations spokesmen said, did not appeal to mass audiences as do
football or tennis or auto racing. Finally, John Wilcox, executive pro-
ducer of the ABC network's "American Sportsman", spelled it out.

"Utlimately," Wilcox explained, "sailboats are dull to look at on television. If you want a major sponsor, you'll need a national media event. It
all comes down to air time."

Finally, in the summer of 1981, Rolex, the Swiss watch manufacturer,
expressed tentative interest in the race. The company had been involved
with sailing for many years and had the positive European attitude toward sponsorship. But the company moved slowly on its decision and, as
it happened, events intervened. Also in the summer of 1981, Richard
Broadhead, a young Englishman eager to enter the race around the
world, contacted several major British corporations seeking personal

sponsorship. His brochure landed on the desk of Nigel Rowe, the executive director of corporate communications for the London-based BOC Group, a multinational conglomerate whose main products are industrial gasses and health care products. Rowe was in the process of looking for a vehicle to link the corporation's subsidiaries around the world in a common undertaking. On its face, a race around the world seemed tailor-made for his needs; it didn't hurt matters either that Richard Giordano, chief executive officer of BOC, was an avid sailor. Unfortunately for Broadhead, the company was more interested in the prospect of sponsoring the entire race, rather than an individual competitor.

Through the fall of 1981, BOC negotiated with White and Roos, as both groups sought to maintain control of the event. Finally, in February 1982, only six months before the start, Roos and White agreed to BOC's terms, which technically turned ownership of the race over to the neutral Rhode Island State Yachting Commission. David White had lost control of the race—now called the BOC Challenge—but at the same stroke he had assured that the race would in fact occur, with or without him. The dream would come true.

In February of 1982, White also realized that he could not be both the race organizer and a participant. No matter how much he wanted to originate the race around the world, his greater desire was to win the race. He had found it impossible to acquire sponsorship for his personal effort. For two years, he had carried on a low-key campaign to secure a large lump of sponsoring cash. He had been offered relatively small amounts, less than $50,000. He turned them all down. White was damned if some corporation was going to get full credit, and publicity, for a fraction of the more than $200,000 of his own money that he already had put into the boat. And, he believed a major sponsor would still come forth—as the West Point Pepperell Corporation had for BOC entrant Tony Lush—after the BOC Group took over the race. But no sponsor appeared.

Sponsor hunting had taken too much of White's time during the time he had allotted himself to prepare for the race. In the summer of 1980, he had laid the keel of a 56-footer, designed by Alan Gurney. But the building process did not go smoothly. Paying for the vessel out of his own pocket, White tried to keep expenses down while still creating a boat that would survive the toughest punishment the sea had to offer. He argued with his builder until the two finally parted company. He also disagreed with his designer until Gurney simply threw up his hands. White was too busy chasing Roos into boardrooms around the country, too distracted trying to persuade corporations to sponsor his race or his boat and too busy trying to nail down the race's rules and procedures to do any one job thoroughly. The boat suffered.

Launched in March, 1982, *One*, as the big red boat was christened for want of a sponsor's logo, proved to be a problem child. On her maiden voyage south from Newport to North Carolina, the deck flexed noticeably and, on the second day out, the fin keel began to work loose from the hull. (Had the keel fallen off, the boat would have sunk immediately.) At Wrightsville Beach, North Carolina, White had *One* hauled. He spent the next three months rebuilding the keel fastenings, reengineering the framing system attached to the keel and completing the interior furniture.

Three months before the start of the race—which had been shifted by the race committee chairman Robin Knox-Johnston from September to August so that the fleet would sail in the Southern Hemisphere at the height of its summer—White found himself with a boat that was not only unsponsored and unfinished, but also unfit for the sea.

It was a hot, airless day in late July when the BOC Challenge's founder sailed back into Newport amid a buzz of controversy. His boat had been renamed *Gladiator*, which expressed White's romantic appraisal of what life was going to be like out there on the open sea. (White had asked the race committee if they would allow him to name his boat *Death Wish*. The committee politely suggested he search for something more suitable.) Beyond the new name, there was concern among race officials that White's keel might not be strong enough. And, as a third morsel for the media and wharfsiders to chew, White handed in a ship's log for his qualifying run (each competitor had to sail his boat 1,000 miles alone to qualify for the race) with several entries referring to motoring the vessel. Running under power during a qualifying run was strictly forbidden, yet the race committee and race director Jim Roos approved the log and permitted White to enter the race. There was never an official comment. None was required. White had dreamed up the race and made it real. There would be little justice served to bar him from the event for so small an infraction.

"Hell, I was sailing," White later quipped. "The *Queen Mary* 'sails' with her engines on, doesn't she?"

At Goat Island Marina, White joined the growing fleet of sailors who had managed to find the time, money and organization to enter the race. All the 16 other skippers who arrived in Newport prior to the start (South African Greg Coles aboard *Datsun Skyline* did not get to Newport until a week after the start) had had prerace ordeals similar to White's, and each had managed to overcome them. It was a strange assortment of men, hailing from eight countries and sailing a wide variety of boats.

Five Americans had entered the race, the largest delegation, and that pleased White. This was an American event and he hoped to have American winners in both classes. Francis Stokes, who had been at the brainstorming session in 1979 when the race was conceived, was there in his 39-foot cutter *Mooneshine.* Two of White's fellow Californians, Dan Byrne and Tom Lindholm, had made it to Newport; neither was truly a veteran singlehander, but both were able and game sailors. And Tony Lush, an OSTAR alumnus, had brought his new specially built *Lady Pepperell,* a unique 54-foot ketch that carried no headsails and an unstayed cat-ketch rig. Of the group, Stokes, who already had sailed alone across the Atlantic four times, held promise as a Class II winner, while Tony Lush's lightweight downwind machine might give White competition in the Southern Ocean. Like White, Lush was not ready for the race when he arrived in Newport. His boat was unfinished and he had been forced to complete his qualifying run without his complete sailing rig.

Three French boats and three English boats made up the other two competitive contingents. But, to White and BOC's surprise, none of the well-known singlehanders, those who had made their names household words in England and Europe, had entered. From France, there was Guy Bernardin in *Ratso II,* who was a seasoned singlehander but was sailing, at 38 feet, the smallest boat in the fleet. The two others, Philippe Jeantot, in his specially built 56-footer, *Credit Agricole,* and Jacques de Roux in his 41-foot cutter, *Skoiern III,* were unknown quantities. But, *Credit Agricole* was tied up next to *Gladiator* and White and everyone else who stopped to look at the two yachts guessed early on that these would be the pace boats. Like White, Jeantot was still fitting out his boat hours before the starting gun.

Among the English, there was one famous boat. Desmond Hampton, an OSTAR veteran, had chartered Sir Francis Chichester's last boat, *Gipsy Moth V,* from Chichester's son, Giles, and had entered the 56-foot staysail ketch in the race. The old ocean racer originally had been 57 feet long. To make her conform to the race rules, Hampton had had a foot of her stern lopped off. The boat was the grand dame of the fleet, lending the event a touch of history and class.

The other two English sailors were from the other end of the spectrum. Richard Broadhead, the youngest skipper, sailed into Newport with the unwieldy 52-foot sloop *Perseverance of Medina.* The boat, a well campaigned racing boat requiring a crew of 11 men, looked fast but difficult to sail singlehanded. Paul Rodgers aboard *Spirit of Pentax* was in worse shape. He recently had returned from a failed effort to make a double, non-stop circumnavigation. He was out of money and his boat was in disrepair.

Making up the rest of the fleet was a broad sampling of offshore sailors. South African Bertie Reed in his 49-foot *Altech Voortrekker* was a formidable presence. A Navy man who was virtually a professional sailor, his reputation for singleminded toughness preceded him. Australian Neville Gosson had sailed halfway around the world to enter the race in his 53-foot cutter, *Leda Pier One*. New Zealander Richard McBride appeared in his black, 42-foot steel staysail schooner; McBride looked more like an extra for a pirate movie than a racer. Czech Richard Konkolski, who had already made a singlehanded circumnavigation, was there in his 44-foot cutter, *Nike II*, and he seemed a top contender to win Class II. Lastly, Yukoh Tada had sailed from his home in Japan to enter his 44-foot sloop, *Koden Okera V*, in the race.

Tada and White were, in fact, an unlikely pair of old friends. They had first met as rivals at the outset of the 1975 race from San Francisco to Japan. But it was at the conclusion of the race that their allegiance was forged. As White was finishing the race he ran aground, seriously damaging his boat. Tada, a practitioner of Zen Buddhism, introduced White to Kiochior Sato, a Buddhist monk who offered the stranded American the hospitality of his temple south of Tokyo. White lived there while he and Tada repaired the boat. When Tada came to Newport for the start of the BOC race, Kiochior Sato followed soon after. Several days before the start, the two Buddhists visited nearly every competitor's boat to bless each sailor and his vessel before they headed out to sea.

Tada soon became a favorite of not only his fellow sailors but the media as well. His simple philosophy was an extension of his spiritual beliefs, and balanced the scale heavily weighed down by White's bravado. "My boat is named *Okera*," Tada said. "In Japanese that means 'empty pockets.' I am good for this race. I have no money but I am in good physical condition. I am a vagabond."

But Tada's understated confidence, like that of the other sailors busy in their pre-race preparations, did not make up for an overall lack of experience in the type of sailing that faced them.

Only Konkolski and Rodgers already had sailed around the world and only two others, Hampton and Reed, knew the wild wind and sea of the southern ocean.

To David White, at the outset, Jeantot and Reed appeared his closest rivals in Class I. But Gosson, Broadhead and Hampton had big, fast boats and, given the right circumstances, they too could be contenders for top honors. What bothered White about all of the other boats in his class, including Jeantot's *Credit Agricole*, was that they all were better prepared for the event than he was.

"I'm not ready. I'm just not ready," was White's mournful refrain in the last weeks before the start.

Yet when the press lined up to interview him, the race's founder and predicted winner, White more or less had to submit to their questions.

His remarks, as always, were salty and jaunty and optimistic. "I've sailed a lot of offshore races just to finish them," he explained time and again. "But this time, I'm going for all the marbles."

The day before the start, White went through a short ceremony of his own. As the cameras clicked, he took off his Topsiders, leaned over the side of the boat and slapped them on the dock. "This is an old tradition among seamen," he said. "Just to make sure I come back."

Off camera, the public image faded. He confessed to friends that he had never been so unprepared for sea, let alone a race. He had doubts and fears. But they did not stop him or slow him down. He had created what he called the "ultimate race" and had built a boat to make sure that he, an American, would win it. He was not about to let that grand plan fade in a cloud of doubt.

He had to find out just how good he was. He had to find out if he could slay the lions.

It wasn't to be.

On the third day out from Newport, grave doubts gathered like storm clouds over *Gladiator*. Wave by jarring wave, the foredeck flexed farther and the bulkhead below deteriorated.

What to do? White was 60 miles ahead of Tony Lush and, as far as he knew because of Jeantot's silence, he was leading. The island of Bermuda was less than a two-day sail away, but White knew that if he diverted and stopped for repairs, he would lose the lead, perhaps forever. Gambling, White pressed on.

On the second day out from Newport, another of the racers in a smaller and older boat faced a similar decision and came down on the other side of the fence. Tom Lindholm, a 57-year-old lawyer from California, sailing his old Ericson 41, *Driftwood,* had been battered badly by a series of squalls that ran through the BOC fleet on the first night. His roller furling genoa ripped, he lost all his spare parts for his wind vane self-steering device and he burned out his engine, leaving his batteries flat. With 7,000 miles to go and possibly 70 days at sea, Lindholm threw in the towel and headed back for Newport. A proud man unaccustomed to failure, he returned with his tail between his legs, having conquered only 200 of the 27,000-mile course.

Lindholm's decision set a tone for similar decisions throughout the race. Despite his disappointment, he knew that going on would have been foolish. The decision to turn back was a model of clear thinking, of prudent seamanship, a decision the other skippers admired. What Lindholm did in the race's first hours was to open the option of retiring, an option that simply had not existed earlier for some of the skippers.

Count David White among them.

Aboard *Gladiator,* White continued to drive hard toward the equator. The big red boat was proving herself to be a true thoroughbred capable of high speeds, but also a vessel that had been too lightly engineered for the task at hand. On the seventh day, September 4, the damaged bulkhead cracked all the way through, leaving the bow and foredeck without the necessary transverse support. The damage needed to be repaired but White had only material enough to build a temporary splint. Such a splint never could be expected to hold up the 6,000 remaining miles to Cape Town.

As the bulkhead weakened, so did White's resolve. No doubt preying upon his mind as he studied the damage were an accumulation of omens and disappointments—his dispute with his boatbuilder and naval architect, his failure to obtain a sponsor, the damage to the keel, the questionable qualifying run and his lack of preparation. The seventh day of the race was a dark one for White. After committing three years of his life, more than a quarter of a million of his own dollars and, after sailing out to a commanding lead, David White quit.

That afternoon, he came up on the radio to Jim Roos at Goat Island. "*Gladiator* to Goat Island, *Gladiator* to Goat Island. The lions have won. Repeat. The lions have won."

Then he altered course for Florida.

2

The Riddle of the Atlantic

LOSING DAVID WHITE at the end of the first week was a blow to the fleet. The skippers who monitored the race committee's radio frequencies chatted about the withdrawal and collectively sent White condolences. White had boasted that he would lead them all around the world. Now they had to find the way themselves.

All the racers knew the first leg was going to be the most difficult to navigate. The trouble was not storms or tricky routes through islands. The trouble was the Atlantic Ocean itself. From Greenland in the north to the tiny island of Tristan de Cuna in the south, the ocean is a maze of quickly mutating weather patterns and currents. At the middle of both the North and South Atlantic sit high pressure systems around which the racers were obliged to sail to find the wind, because the centers of the highs were notoriously windless. Between these two systems were two bands of trade winds, the northeast trades above the equator and the southeast trades below, which are themselves separated by a windless band of doldrums. Complicating this picture was the hurricane season in the Northern Hemisphere (August through November), which made the western side of the route to Cape Town dangerous. (See map in photo insert and Appendix One for more on routes and weather.)

As the skippers headed out from Newport, they sailed into a complex navigational riddle: What was the best route from Newport to Cape Town?

What made the riddle interesting was the paucity of information. This was the first fleet of boats ever to race from the east coast of the United

States to Cape Town. There were no logbooks from which to crib, no sailing narratives relating hints of how best to round the highs and cross the doldrums and no wharfside scuttlebutt.

Was it best to sail east around the North Atlantic high, or to go west of it and chance an encounter with a hurricane? In the South Atlantic, should the skippers circle west of the South Atlantic high toward Brazil, or should they try to shorten the route by going east into the uncertain winds near Africa on the high's east side? Or, was the fastest route straight down the middle?

No one knew.

The only information available to the skippers was in an old sailing volume first published in 1895, nearly 90 years before the start of the race. *Ocean Passages For The World,* published by the Hydrographic Office of the British Royal Navy, was the sailing bible passed down from the great age of sail in the last century. The sage advice in *Ocean Passages* for the 7,000-mile voyage was contained in five, terse paragraphs. The best route from the east coast of the United States ran east of the North Atlantic high, south through the doldrums, and then west around the South Atlantic high until meeting the westerly winds in the southern ocean that would carry the sailors into Cape Town. The course configuration resembled a large, backward S.

The advice in *Ocean Passages* had been accumulated by naval and commercial captains for 300 years, so those five paragraphs rang with authority. Yet, there were those among the fleet who thought they had better ideas.

It is not surprising that different men, sailing different types of boats, chose very different solutions to the riddle of the Atlantic. As might be expected, their qualities as men, as planners and gamblers, had as much effect on their success as did the winds and currents. In general, the fleet broke into two camps, those who followed the beaten path, and those who didn't. Human nature does not change much, even hundreds of miles at sea.

Of the 17 who crossed the starting line (including Greg Coles on *Datsun Skyline* who started a week after the fleet), 11 chose to play it safe. The *Ocean Passages* route was the route of consensus. Among its takers were the two men many considered the best sailors in the fleet—South African Bertie Reed on *Altech Voortrekker* and Frenchman Jacques de Roux on the Class II boat *Skoiern III*. Both Reed and de Roux were Navy men and both brought very "by-the-book" attitudes to the choice of routes.

After leaving Newport, they headed southeast in order to skirt around the eastern side of the North Atlantic high, thus avoiding the hurricane threat near the Caribbean Sea and the windless areas of the high. Relying on the speed of their boats and their skill instead of radical routes, in the first two weeks they both moved quickly enough to lead the herd that also had chosen the conservative path.

Also following the advice of *Ocean Passages* was American Tony Lush on the 54-foot *Lady Pepperell* and Englishman Desmond Hampton on the 56-foot *Gipsy Moth V*. The two skippers played a safe solution to the Atlantic, for reasons very different from those driving Reed and de Roux. Both Lush and Hampton sailed boats that fit the sailing profile of the 19th century ships for which *Ocean Passages* had been written. *Lady Pepperell* was a thoroughly modern boat with unstayed two-masted rig, known as a cat-ketch. Although fast off the wind, Lush's boat was not efficient into the wind. And, the *Ocean Passages* route was intended by its authors to be a reaching and running route.

Like *Lady Pepperell*, *Gipsy Moth V* had been designed to run free before the wind and was not at her best slogging into the weather. Carrying a two-masted staysail ketch rig over her conservative and heavy hull, *Gipsy Moth V* held the promise of good performance in the storm tossed waters of the southern ocean in the legs ahead. But in the Atlantic, she needed reaching and running winds to power her along. Competitive and intelligent, Hampton knew that slow speeds and a conservative route through the Atlantic were the penalties he had to pay for a sleigh ride later. Hampton's route was foist upon him by his boat, not the other way around.

If any of the skippers were suited in boat and temperament to take a safe path through the Atlantic, it was Francis Stokes. The 57-year-old family man and yacht broker from New Jersey brought a constitutionally conservative approach to the riddle at hand, just as he brought a heavy conservative cutter, *Mooneshine*, to meet the rigors of the sea.

With the 10 others who followed the *Ocean Passages'* route, Stokes struck off to the southeast aiming for the northeast trades and the narrow band of doldrums promised in the hallowed five paragraphs. But Stokes and the others found that the book did not hold all the answers.

Two weeks into the race, Stokes and his conservative companions sailed straight into a wide band of doldrums that slowed them to a crawl before they finally emerged to the south into the fresh 15-knot breeze of the southeast trades in the South Atlantic.

For Stokes, who has a fine eye for life's little ironies, the experience was both frustrating and, ultimately, humorous.

"Looking back," he said, "I think we all wasted a lot of time trying to sail so far to the east. None of us found the doldrums where we thought they would be and then the southeast trades didn't fill in when the book *(Ocean Passages)* said they would. I spent one whole day in the southeast trade wind belt rolling around in absolutely no wind at all. The clouds weren't even moving."

Like the others who had been let down by the only traditional advice they could find to decipher the code of the Atlantic, Stokes was at his wits' end that becalmed day. It was like discovering the truth about Santa Claus. Stoke's response to the disappointment was to do something active. He had a strong urge to get off *Mooneshine*. He needed a break in the rhythm of sailing and a different perspective of the little vessel that was his sole hope in the wide ocean. It is not an uncommon longing for singlehanders. Men alone at sea have been known to drag on lines from the sterns of their boats or to swim free when becalmed. This appealed to Stokes. He had read in *A World Of My Own,* Robin Knox-Johnston's account of the Golden Globe Race, how Knox-Johnston had jumped overboard on his journey, swimming under *Suhali*'s keel and surfacing just in time to catch a trailing line as the little ketch sailed by. What an extraordinary thrill to take such a gamble.

But Stokes, soft-spoken and narrow-shouldered, is not exactly the type to strip off his clothes and hurl himself into the deep. Instead, he blew up a small inflatable boat he carried, assembled the plastic oars, hung his camera carefully around his neck and set off for a row around the becalmed *Mooneshine*.

He took a few photos and admired his 39-foot cutter's salty lines and graceful bow. He rowed lazily around to get a shot or two from the stern. And then, as if someone had thrown cold water in his face, he realized that *Mooneshine* was sailing away from him much faster than he expected.

"I don't know if there was a breath of air I couldn't feel or if the swells were moving *Mooneshine*. But whatever it was, all of a sudden I realized she was going on without me. There I was in the middle of the ocean in this silly little toy boat rowing frantically with those little oars trying to catch my boat. I was getting more and more paranoid all the time."

The thought of finishing the race in the inflatable boat was enough to spur him on. He made it back aboard and put the little boat away for the rest of the race.

The turning point for the skippers who chose the *Ocean Passages'* route came when, one by one, they broke free of the doldrums and sailed into the southeast trade winds. Bertie Reed on *Voortrekker* was leading the contingent, having pushed his 49-footer to its limit even in the frustrating calms. In Class II, de Roux had begun to build a lead over the others in his class, seeming always to find a breeze that eluded the rest. Stokes was behind the leaders, but still doing well. Yet he was beginning to have doubts about his choice of routes. Via the daily and weekly position reports radioed from race headquarters in Newport, it appeared that those who had chosen to forego the advice of the centuries—Philippe

Jeantot on *Credit Agricole* in particular—had found a better route with better wind.

Before he could ponder his postition in the fleet after the disaster in the doldrums, Francis Stokes had to face the first real crisis of his voyage. When the southeast trades filled in, the time came for Stokes to begin his long swing west—according to the advice of *Ocean Passages*—that would take him safely around the windless South Atlantic high. He jibed onto the port tack and happily settled down to the pleasing task of making his cutter move again in a fresh breeze. After the calms, the trade wind seas seemed lumpy and uneven. But *Mooneshine* had experienced much worse and he was not worried. Then, on the morning of September 27, five weeks out from Newport, he looked up at his mast and saw a wide crack in the port spreader. If if failed, the mast would tumble into the sea.

Without a firm plan, he lowered his genoa and double reefed the main to take the strain off the top of the mast and the spreader. He set up the running backstays and then sat back to assess the problem. His prospects for finishing the race looked bleak. At 12:15, he tuned up his ham radio to see if Bertie Reed, Yukoh Tada and Dan Byrne—all of whom Stokes spoke to regularly—were at hand. They were and the discussion with the other skippers prompted Stokes to try to make some type of repair.

For the next five hours, Stokes struggled. To get to the broken spreader he had to tie rope steps, or ratlines, to the stays and then climb them. Once up the mast, he drilled holes in the aluminum spreader and spreader mount and inserted bolts to hold the spreader in place. In all, he used five heavy bolts, yet he managed to accomplish the job without dropping a single washer, despite the bucking motion of the mast 20 feet above the deck.

At dusk, the job was complete. He had made the repairs and, with full sail hoisted again, he set off for Cape Town. It had been a narrow escape from a dismasting, all because the aluminum spreader had only been tack-welded and not finished by the builder. With a sigh of relief, Stokes set his wind vane on course and went below to the cabin for a well deserved ration of rum.

Stokes was back in the race. In the weeks that followed, as he made his way to Cape Town, he had time to reflect on his route and on the puzzle of the Atlantic, the riddle that had first becalmed him and then nearly dismasted him.

"As I was sitting out there, I realized that the routes recommended by *Ocean Passages* are really for boats that can sail no closer than 80 degrees to the wind, the old clippers and square-riggers. For close-winded boats like *Mooneshine* and the others, there had to be a better way to get to Cape Town."

Stokes had weathered calms, winds and gear failure. Yet he freely admitted he had not come up with a good solution to the riddle.

If the *Ocean Passages'* route was not the best way to get to Cape Town, as Stokes surmised, then what was the best route?

The six skippers who chose to try a novel approach all had considered the problem and each came up with a different solution, although, in the end, only one of the six would find a way that worked. The traditional route had been devised for square-riggers. But modern boats could sail so much closer to the direction of the wind, that, perhaps, one could sail the wrong way around the high pressure systems into the wind, and thereby shorten the overall distance to be covered?

Neville Gosson aboard the 53-foot *Leda Pier One* was the first to launch into a radical route and became the first to learn the consequences of miscalculation. Gosson even began badly; he was late for the start. He was the last of the initial 16 starters to arrive in Newport, after a 12,000-mile passage alone from his home in Sydney, Australia. He spent the 10 days remaining refitting *Leda*. It was a mad scramble to the end. The morning of the race a new fuel tank was installed, a job that took longer than it should have. When the 3 p.m. gun sounded, Gosson was still at the fuel dock at Goat Island pumping fuel into the new tank.

With the tank topped off, he was towed to the starting line and, 10 minutes after the others, set off for Cape Town. Almost at once everything began to fall into place. He was sailing again and that felt good. The long-dreamed-of race was no longer a dream, reason enough for high spirits. What made Gosson happiest was the rate at which he was catching the boats ahead. By the time he had reached the lighthouse at Castle Hill, at the heads of Narragansett Bay, he had passed most of the boats in Class I.

This was why he had come 12,000 miles. But little did he know that this actually was to be his first test in the racing game of the Atlantic. Gosson trimmed the headsail carefully and adjusted the helm. He was sailing the boat for all it was worth. Sailing into the dusk, his main competitors still were ahead of him, but the gap was closing. That was particularly pleasing because he had modified *Leda* by trimming well over a ton of ballast from her keel. His intention was to improve her performance downwind, while sacrificing some upwind performance. According to the books, the race around the world promised to be a downwind slide. But here she was, walking up on the fleet to windward. They could be caught. They could be beaten.

Night overcame the fleet in the ocean beyond Block Island as they sailed east. It was not a good night. The wind backed into the north and brought with it a series of ugly rain squalls and a fresh wind. It was the kind of weather all passage makers dread for a first night out because in the first 48 hours of an offshore passage, a sailor's equilibrium is off kilter, he hasn't yet found his sea legs or fully developed the necessary cat-like night vision.

The sea became lumpy and several times Gosson had to go forward to change sail. He did so without lighting a deck light or carrying a flashlight, moving from line to winch by feel and by habit. He was still fresh from the sea after his long run from Australia and he still had his sea legs under him.

The others at the front of the fleet were not as lucky. That night, Gosson saw them all, one by one, each wrestling with their lack of equilibrium and fatigue. He passed Richard Broadhead who had his spreader lights blaring on the foredeck as he tried to wrestle a wet genoa back onto the deck of *Perseverance of Medina.* He saw David White, flashing a flashlight at his sails, searching the darkness for clues to sail trim that might give him more speed. And he watched as Philippe Jeantot moved slowly and purposefully in a three-point stance, like a simian, to sort out a tangle of lines and sails after a hectic sail change.

Gosson was in the groove and running "blacked out." It was the hour of triumph he had hoped for but really had not expected so soon. He had shown the speed to run by them all. It was now, he believed, only a question of how big a lead he could establish.

There is nothing as intoxicating as the first whiff of a brilliant, unexpected dash to an early victory. And no hangover so ugly as learning it is an illusion. That's the hangover to which Gosson awoke the next morning. Having sailed out to what he thought was an early lead nearly 200 miles from Newport, he pulled out his charts and tried to decide what he was going to do with it.

One, he reasoned, can never be certain when or where the winds will be favorable. So the best strategy is to sail as fast as possible and to stay close to the straightest line between the two ports, keeping the distance sailed to a minimum. The rhumb line route was a novel idea. Besides his offshore experience, Gosson was an old yacht club buoy racer. His game plan stemmed from the standard tactic during an upwind leg of a buoy race in changing, fickle breezes: Stay in the middle of the course, thereby being hurt the least by an unexpected wind shift. It was cagey and it was dead wrong for the North Atlantic at the end of August.

After charging triumphantly through the fleet, Gosson sailed *Leda Pier One* straight into the windless North Atlantic High. It was like hitting a sandbank. On his second day out of Newport, Gosson sailed 12 miles. On the third, he managed 22. Meanwhile, those who had chosen the conservative route—Reed, de Roux, Lush, Stokes and the seven others—were reporting 170-mile days. David White (still in the race at that point), Richard Broadhead, Paul Rodgers and Jeantot had disappeared west of the rhumb line and were reporting up to 200-mile days.

It was a sobering moment. Later Gosson said, "Three days after I took the lead, I was behind the entire fleet. I finally realized the race is not about boat speed at all. It's about being in the right places and the right weather patterns, with the right sort of gear. You've got to find the wind."

Gosson's poor start led to a long and difficult passage. While he had been unprepared to solve the first problem in the riddle, the other unknown skipper who looked at the start to be a threat in Class I found himself unprepared to solve the middle of the course. Englishman Richard Broadhead aboard the 52-foot *Perseverance of Medina* sailed out quickly and, following his instinct to sail upwind, headed west of the rhumb line. With White and the others who did not heed *Ocean Passages*, Broadhead made good progress in the first week and was sailing near the head of the fleet. But then White dropped out, Rodgers turned radically west of the route (for his own illogical reasons) and Broadhead found himself alone, heading toward the hurricane region just east of the Caribbean. He did not know that at the time he was close on the stern of *Credit Agricole*, because Jeantot was reporting his position only once a week as required in the race rules. Feeling himself out on a limb, he altered course to the east to join the rest of the fleet.

"I was beginning to go down south," he said, "but the combination of hurricanes, not knowing where *Credit Agricole* was and, seeing everyone else going the other way made me change my mind. I figured that if everyone was going east and we're all becalmed, then I've still got a chance of making it up. But if I go one way and get becalmed and everyone else has wind, then I'm totally screwed."

The decision to alter course to the east was one Broadhead would come to regret. But peer pressure can be a powerful force. Moreover, as he turned east, he found himself engaged in a duel with Reed on *Voortrekker*. It should have been a good match, because their boats were of similar size and speed. But it wasn't. Broadhead, after changing his mind once, changed it again.

As the two skippers sailed through the doldrums just north of the equator, Reed held a slim 60-mile lead, less than half a day's progress in moderate wind. It was at that point that Broadhead decided once again to forego the advice of *Ocean Passages* in order to play what he hoped would be his trump card. He decided to split tacks with Reed and, instead of turning south in the southeast trades, he continued east in search of a favorable slant of wind that would carry him to Cape Town. It was a high-stakes gamble, one usually reserved for close quarter buoy racing. It failed.

"As *Voortrekker* continued south, I figured that was the time to get my easting," Broadhead said. "My original idea was to go to windward through the southeast trades, find the South Atlantic high and beat around it to the east. That way, I'd be making as short a voyage as possible.

"I still had Bertie on the radio at that point. He picked up the southeast trades almost immediately and began a series of daily runs over 200 miles each day. I was beating into light winds and getting only 100 miles a day. I wanted to go farther east, but the winds were against me so I changed my plan again because I figured I'd never catch Bertie that way. So, I tacked and got pushed back to the west instead of going straight to Cape Town. I eased off a bit to get the boat moving but right at that point my weatherfax (satellite weather map printer) crapped out and it was like driving in the country without a bloody road map. I had no reports of any highs and sailed right into one. My progress for the next five days was pathetic."

Indecision, lack of a workable plan and peer pressure sent Broadhead wandering through the Atlantic, frustrated at every twist and turn of the weather patterns. Although later in the leg he would find himself once again in the running with Bertie Reed, at mid-passage to Cape Town, Broadhead was thoroughly stymied by the mysterious ocean.

If those who sailed the *Ocean Passages'* route moved like a flock and those who wandered were the lost sheep, there were in the fleet three foxes who had new and radical ideas about how to get to Cape Town. Philippe Jeantot, who had become an enigma to the rest of the skippers during the first weeks of the race because of his radio silence, was the first to solve the riddle of the Atlantic. His solution was touched with genius. Like such strokes of insight, the solution was not altogether rational and was fraught with danger. A seasoned offshore racer would never have dared it. But this was Jeantot's first race. An older man might have shied away from the risk, but Jeantot was a deep-sea diver accustomed to extraordinary rigors—such as living in a diving bell for two weeks at a time.

A traditional man would have balked at the technology involved, but Jeantot was young and modern and able to put his faith in satellites, ham radio and weather facsimile printers. The latter device gave him pictures of local weather systems taken from orbiting weather satellites. The result was a course through the North Atlantic that took him west of the North Atlantic high and straight into the area of the western trade winds, which in that season are not only the main thoroughfare for hurricanes bound for the Caribbean, but also tend to blow from the east and south of east. Only a state-of-the-art boat that could sail as close to the wind as *Credit Agricole* could even consider the route.

"I had on board *Credit Agricole* a copy of *Ocean Passages* and I believe it is a good book," Jeantot said, "but it is a century old and the directions are for old sailing ships."

Unencumbered by tradition, Jeantot watched the printout from his weatherfax, studied the pilot charts, listened over his radio to the advice of friends in France and took his chances. As he approached the North Atlantic trade winds, he made a decision that in effect stole the race. Ahead of him to the south his weather charts showed two hurricanes moving westward, one behind the other, on an intercept course with *Credit Agricole*.

To sail knowingly into the fury of a tropical storm would be foolishness. Yet between the two storms was a gap wide enough for Jeantot to consider sailing through, a window that might allow him to sneak into the South Atlantic without making the end run to the east called for in *Ocean Passages*. Following his instinct and putting his faith in his weatherfax and in the ability of his boat to handle heavy weather if need be, Jeantot decided to go for the window, to go for the chance to win.

It paid off. Hurricane Beryl, the second major tropical storm of the hurricane season, trundled by to his south as he watched on his weatherfax. The long, rolling ocean swells, harbingers of a gale at sea, rose and fell under *Credit Agricole*'s bow. But the wind remained moderate and the sky clear. He had avoided the first storm and now had a second, Hurricane Debbie, to watch out for. This was the moment of risk. Although Debbie was more than 500 miles to the east and moving west 100 hundred miles a day, Jeantot still had to clear the trade wind belt before it passed or risk a hard lashing on his backside. If the wind had failed, or if he had damaged his rig and been unable to make a good average speed, he could have found himself strapped to the rails as the locomotive ran over him. But he pressed on, his decision made, the die cast. His luck— and the trade winds—held and he managed to make one 200-mile day after another. He sailed through the window without even tucking a reef into his mainsail. When Jeantot hit the equator, he was told by his ham radio contacts in France he had a 200-mile lead over Reed and Broadhead.

"They told me 200 miles, but I did not believe them. Then, five days later they say it is 600 miles. Impossible. Sixty maybe, but never 600."

Unlike Richard Broadhead, who had been on *Credit Agricole*'s heels until he had lost his way in the maze, Jeantot gambled heavily, stood firmly behind his wager and reaped a jackpot. And his 600-mile lead would continue to grow as the fleet sailed through the southern Atlantic. Bertie Reed, the skipper who was closest in speed to Jeantot, had relied on the traditional, *Ocean Passages* approach and could only listen to the weekly position reports for the French boat and marvel as the gap widened between *Voortrekker* and *Credit Agricole*. All Reed could say was, "Philippe did everything against the book and got lucky."

Two others in the fleet, Guy Bernardin and Richard Konkolski, had strong urges to gamble on their routes, yet came to a very different decision that ended with very different results. In the preceding 12 years, several crewed races had been run from England and France to Cape Town and further on to Australia, among them three Whitbread Round The World Races, two of which had been won by Cornelius van Rietschoten aboard boats named *Flyer*. Another was the Parmelia Race from England to Perth, Australia, which Konkolski had sailed aboard *Nike II*. In the course of running these races, skippers and navigators had come up with a fresh solution of best handling the South Atlantic high. Go east of it. The route to the west of the weather system is recommended by *Ocean Passages*, but it is 500 miles longer. The new route is shorter but involves a lot of windward sailing through variable winds. In every race so far, the winner has been the boat to cut closest to the African coast while staying clear of the northerly currents and out of the dead airs in the middle of the high. The course is a tightrope and those who fall off fall into a wind hole deeper than any found in the open sea. Unlike Jeantot's route to the west, those who went east risked calms, not hurricanes. And there are many sailors who swear that calms are dreaded more than gales.

Bernardin, a Frenchman who sailed in the 1980 OSTAR, and the Czech, Konkolski, who already had made one singlehanded circumnavigation, took the chance. Both had small boats that behaved well in light airs and to windward. Neither could hope to catch the larger boats on a reach or run. For them, the easterly gamble made sense. More than simply making sense, the easterly route held for both Bernardin and Konkolski an allure that other men see in rock climbing without belaying lines, or in diving to great depths under the sea or in hang gliding off sheer cliffs.

Bernardin, a restaurateur from Brittany, sailed 50,000 miles alone offshore before starting the race. He brought to the sea a very Gallic sensibility. His plan for the Atlantic was a complicated long shot. He sailed farther north than the rest of the fleet after leaving Newport and then carried on farther east than the others before turning south to the equator. Once he crossed the doldrums and set off southward, he steered east along the coast of Sierra Leone, Liberia and the Ivory Coast. He had intended to hurry eastward as fast as possible and then join the Whitbread route from England to carry him to Cape Town. But, when he arrived off the Ivory Coast, he did not find the winds that had propelled *Flyer* south. Instead, he found a contrary current and little or no wind. In the next two weeks, Bernardin wandered through a personal pilgrimage of despair unlike any he had known at sea. He was frustrated at every turn by lack of wind. Squalls carried him ahead quickly for an hour or two only to leave him once again becalmed. The concept of the route was bold, yet it failed. Somehow, perhaps by sailing too far east, Bernardin fell off the tightrope. He would arrive in Cape Town far behind those in his class whom he had believed he would beat.

"It was the worst, most frustrating sail of my life," he said.

Frustrating, but not a complete loss. Bernardin did not enter the around the world race to win, as did White or Jeantot. He was on a more personal mission. The success and failure of any leg was not measured in how many boats he beat but in how well he and his 38-foot *Ratso II* handled the challenges the sea offered. He said before leaving, "A sailor must always realize there might come a situation in which there is nothing he can do. Those are the times when he will know whether or not he was born under a good star."

The star over *Ratso*'s masthead on the way to Cape Town was an ill one. Yet Bernardin and *Ratso* overcame the difficulties and found their way out of the windless labyrinth. Bernardin was exhausted, frustrated and maddened . . . but not beaten. And that was his point.

For the Czech, Richard Konkolski, the choice of the easterly route, the gamble on a brilliant solution to the riddle of the Atlantic, was part of a grander drama that was to change his life forever.

3

On a Race for Freedom

THOUGH EVERY ENTRANT had made personal sacrifices to compete in the race, Richard Konkolski laid more on the line than anyone. When it became apparent to Konkolski just months before the start that the Czechoslovakian government was not going to grant him permission to participate, he put into motion a longstanding contingency plan he hoped he'd never have to use. With his wife and son, he slipped across the Czechoslovakian border and left his homeland forever.

From the outset of the race, Konkolski knew the publicity from his defection from a Warsaw Pact country would make him more closely-watched and controversial than the others. For many of the sailors, the BOC Challenge was the high point of their lives. For Konkolski, it was the first step into a future full of question marks. For him, successfully solving the riddle of the Atlantic went beyond simply doing well in a sailboat race. To the country he left behind, and to the one he hoped to adopt, he felt he had something to prove.

Konkolski had an aim like Guy Bernardin's when he sailed east of the course prescribed by *Ocean Passages*. He, too, wanted to find the seam the Whitbread boats had mined on their way south. Before leaving Poland on *Nike II* for the passage to the start in Newport, he had worked on routes with technicians at the Polish Technical Institute in Gdansk. Konkolski fed the Whitbread and Parmelia race routes into a computer along with information from pilot charts and relevant weather and oceanographic data. He had crossed the Atlantic four times and already had sailed once alone to Cape Town during a previous solo circumnavigation.

24

He had the data and, once processed, it told him what his instinct already had whispered. "Go east. Sail to the Cape Verde Islands and then follow *Flyer*'s route south."

So after the start, he sailed with the fleet on the course north of the Atlantic high, the course followed by Stokes, de Roux, Reed and several others. But when they turned south he continued on almost to the African coast, until he made a landfall on the island of Santa Antao in the Cape Verdes. What happened next almost ended his voyage. He took a compass bearing on the tip of the island as night fell and then sailed on into the darkness, confident that he was in open water. He wasn't.

"I was watching out for a lighthouse on the next island," he said, "and sailing along under the big number one genoa. I couldn't really see what was down to leeward. Suddenly, behind the genoa, I see some shadows and I say to myself, 'What is this thing?' It was a boat at anchor lying right ahead of me. I almost hit her. And then I see little boats all around me. I steered by one and another one. Then I saw the surf on the beach and I knew I was almost on it. I turned the boat and then I see another fishing vessel. I pass it and finally I see the lighthouse. It was nothing. Maybe a 25-watt bulb. But by then I could feel the ocean swell under me again so I was pretty sure I was okay. I very nearly finished the race right there."

After squeaking through the Cape Verdes, Konkolski turned south, trying to follow the track his technical analysts had worked out for him. Yet, like Bernardin, Konkolski did not find the wind. For 17 days in a row, he made runs of but 45 to 60 miles a day. With the prevailing current against him, his actual progress along his course was worse.

Day after day, he hanked on as much sail as possible. At times he would have two spinnakers set. Below these he flew the genoa and a staysail as well as the mainsail. *Nike II* looked like sailmaker's laundry hanging in the sun to dry. The sails hung slack in the blazing, skull-baking sun, with no wind to cool the cheek or fill the sails or give the boat a sense of life. Konkolski, a man in whose presence one senses continuous motion and enthusiasm, was completely becalmed. Stalking the decks of his motionless vessel, there was no outlet for his deep frustration. Considering the extraordinary events that had brought him there, it was a fate that was just not fair.

Along the border that separates Czechoslovakia and Poland is a 20-foot strip of plowed earth marking the boundary between the two communist countries. The tilled land is not farmed but lies fallow to record the footprints of anyone who crosses the line without authorization. The strip is largely symbolic. The guns in the hands of the soldiers who guard it are not.

Near Bohumin, Czechoslovakia, a 300-foot bridge over a river connects the two nations. Gates and a guardhouse stand at Poland's side of the span. Richard Konkolski and his family lived only three miles away. In the early hours of July 6, 1982—less than eight weeks before the race start—Konkolski, his wife, Miki, and 12-year-old son, Richard Jr., drove over the bridge, bluffed the guards with seemingly contradictory documents and then headed into Poland. It was Konkolski's 39th birthday, and the last time he or his family would ever cross that bridge.

It was also another anniversary. Exactly 10 years earlier Konkolski had set sail in Plymouth, England, aboard *Nike,* a 24-foot yawl he designed and built himself, to begin the 1972 OSTAR. Dismasted soon after the start, he returned to port, effected repairs and managed to restart two weeks later. He went on to finish 41st out of 60 boats.

That transatlantic crossing was the first leg of a historic voyage that lasted three years and circled the globe. During the 33,500-mile solo circumnavigation, Konkolski became a skilled offshore sailor and the first and only Czech to sail alone around the world. He had been a topflight dinghy racer and brought the same competitive edge to offshore sailing. He quickly become proficient at the many tasks needed to guide a small boat alone across oceans.

A lot of what he learned during those three years away from home had nothing to do with the sea. To complete his circumnavigation, Konkolski learned to manipulate the government bureaucracy to his advantage.

Originally, he was granted official permission to compete only in the OSTAR. After a four-year application campaign and numerous refusals, he was given a six-month visa—enough time to sail the race and return directly home. But after his dismasting, he was granted an extension on the six months. And once in Newport, he cabled party officials and requested yet another extension because the hurricane season was approaching and he could not immediately sail back. The excuses and extensions came one after the next for the duration of the voyage.

Konkolski's triumphant return in 1975 was well-publicized, although by the letter of Czech law his voyage called for a reprimand. But his accomplishments could not be denied and Konkolski was quick to capitalize on his notoriety. He had ventured into waters unknown before by any Iron Curtain sailor. He had become the Czechoslovakian Chichester.

Books, lectures, regular television appearances and several national sporting awards followed. Konkolski, by nature an outgoing, gregarious man, basked in the attention. Bearded and burly (he looks like a barrel-chested Kris Kristofferson) with sparkling, expressive blue eyes framed by deep lines formed from plenty of hard laughing and squinting into the bright sun, he was well suited to life in the public eye.

Not one to rest on his laurels, Konkolski entered the 1976 OSTAR and sailed an exemplary race, finishing second on handicap in the 125-boat fleet. Upon returning home, his popularity among the people of his country was greater than ever. But if he was loved by his people, he was only tolerated by many members of the communist party. Konkolski had been educated in communist schools and had once been a party member himself. But back in 1968, after Russian tanks rolled into the capital city of Prague, Konkolski was forced out after making public his support of the party leader, Alexander Dubcek, whose liberal policies instigated the invasion and occupation.

He knew his books and lectures walked a fine line between approval and censure. Not only was he an ex-party member, he was also an off-shore sailor who lived in a landlocked country, a solitary sportsman whose singular success was celebrated by the masses. Fortunately, he was as well a born diplomat. He knew his voyages would continue to be allowed only if something politically justifiable came from them. So, as a construction engineer by profession, he arranged to give slide shows and lectures on behalf of his factory, with its banner prominently displayed on the podium beside him.

By 1977, Konkolski was becoming personally independent of the political system. Though he and his wife both held demanding jobs, the books and lectures provided the extra income necessary to finance further sailing adventures. It became apparent that to continue his success he would need a larger, faster boat. But official permission to build a new boat was denied on several occasions. Such was the bureaucratic game. Konkolski rarely received permission to do anything the first time he asked. In this case, as in the past, his perseverance eventually overwhelmed the dissent.

Over the next two years he built *Nike II,* a sturdy 44-foot cutter that he sailed to Newport in the 1980 OSTAR, in the fine time of 21 days and 6 hours. After finishing, he met David White and Jim Roos and pledged his entry for the Around Alone race. Roos worked up several formal invitations for Konkolski to show to the authorities back home.

While sailing back to Czechoslovakia, Konkolski devised a four-year plan of races in which he hoped to compete, including the short overnight Singlehanded Baltic Race in the summer of '82, as well as the BOC Race and the 1984 OSTAR. It was an ambitious schedule. He knew from experience that obtaining permission for the races would be tedious and time-consuming, but certainly not impossible. He'd meet the problem as he had in the past—through the system, if possible, or around it, if necessary. In late 1980, he began the weary, relentless process of seeking official approval and backing.

The documents Konkolski required were exit visas for himself and for his family and a crewmember (who were accompanying him to the start).

From the outset, he found obtaining them more difficult than ever. He believed there were two reasons, the first being plain jealousy by the government bureaucrats who envied his freedom to travel. But even more crucial, he felt, was the matter of his public image.

"My level of activity had become too high," he said. "I was too public a figure. My slides showed an alternative. They showed another way of life. The government didn't like that."

Even so, Konkolski was a proven performer in his sport. The fact that he was prohibited from participating in prestigious competitions, for which he held legitimate papers and credentials, was a poor sign indeed. As the starting date for the BOC race drew nearer, he had exhausted every possible avenue in an attempt to get exit visas. The only race for which he secured a permit was the short race in the Baltic. He felt sure that his career as a sailor, his reason for living, was being stifled. At that point Konkolski knew he would sail in the BOC race, with permission or without.

"They thought they could end my sailing," he said. "I knew some day it would happen. It always had been fine, as long as they let me do my job, my sailing. I loved my country and always came back. But they knew, when they stopped me, I would go.

"I did not escape for a better life. We had a good life in Czechoslovakia. We escaped for freedom. If they could take that from me, they could take it from my son. Now he will live his life as he wishes."

On Friday, June 6, 1982, with the August 28th race start just 10 weeks away—and his own deadline for departure much closer—Konkolski traveled to Prague, the capital of Czechoslovakia, in a final attempt to obtain official exit visas.

Initially, no one with authority in the Czech government would speak to Konkolski. But, late in the day, he wrangled a meeting with the chairman of the central committee of sport, a member of the communist party's inner circle. After listening to Konkolski's plea and examining the invitation by Jim Roos, the chairman said that he could not grant the visas himself, but he would not refuse them either.

With this absence of a refusal, Konkolski was allowed to fill out the appropriate applications. More importantly, he was able to telex a message directly to the Polish Sailing Union to authorize papers for his crewman, 29-year-old Fredek Brodzinski.

Konkolski left Prague that night feeling more at ease than he had in months. His satisfaction was a mirage. The following Monday, the application was considered by the appropriate committee and immediately revoked.

Konkolski returned to Prague on June 16 to pick up his papers and only then did he learn that the visa had been denied. Enraged, he flew into the chairman's office, where he was refused a meeting and diverted to a vice chairman's office. The vice-chairman, like his senior, could not grant a visa himself and would not commit his approval to writing.

As a last resort, Konkolski stole some paper with the letterhead of the Federal Sailing Union. On this, he drafted his own vaguely worded document that could be read in two ways. On one hand, it appeared to be a request to the committee for an unspecified number of persons to sail to America for the start of the race. On the other it could be conceived as a blanket agreement allowing the Konkolskis to sail.

Either way, it was an illusion, a smokescreen never meant for the eyes of the committee. Konkolski took this to an F.S.U. secretary, who in turn read it to the chairman over the phone. Remarkably, he authorized her to sign it in his name. This gave the "forged" document its one redeeming quality: It looked like it had been authorized by the Federal Sailing Union. Later, he filled in his wife's and son's name.

In the weeks before he left, Konkolski took pains not to cause suspicion among his neighbors and co-workers. No one knew of his problems seeking permission. His entry, they were sure, was a foregone conclusion. By Monday, July 5th, Konkolski knew it was time to make his move.

It turned into a long day. Miki left early to meet with the district police and finalize the arrangements for her exit visa. With her, she carried the document that Konkolski had drafted and the union secretary had signed. Its power was derived from its letterhead and its address; it was a weighty message in the border town far from Prague.

The Konkolskis had saved this piece of business for the last possible moment. If the district police were to cross-reference their files, which they were sure to do before long, it would be apparent that there was a discrepancy in the paperwork. Miki, en route to the BOC race, was sailing with her husband to an event in which he was denied permission to compete. The lowest clerk would realize that the sailor and his family were escaping.

Richard spent the day conspicuously busying himself about the house. From his neighbor's point of view, he was a man readying the place for the months while he was away. He did nothing to give the impression that he was leaving his home behind.

Miki returned in the afternoon with papers for herself and Richard Jr. She'd had no trouble. After all, everyone knew her husband was sailing in the great race and wasn't he supposed to be in Newport already?

But the Konkolskis were hardly home free. Konkolski kept his boat in the seaside city of Szczecin, Poland. He traveled there often, but rarely with his family. The justification for his exit visa was the overnight race in the Baltic, while his wife's papers listed her destination as the United States to deliver the boat for the BOC Challenge. That wasn't the only problem. Widespread strikes in Poland, backed by the Solidarity labor union, had led the government to establish martial law some six months earlier. With its institution came the suspension of all sporting activity. Not only was there a discrepancy in the family's exit papers, but Richard was leaving for a local race that no longer existed.

Shortly after midnight on the morning of the sixth, the Konkolskis loaded the car and made the short drive to the border bridge. The guards were cordial but businesslike; they had come to know Konkolski well. They confiscated all the papers, permits and passports—a normal procedure—and ran them through the computer. Everything checked. Konkolski explained that the dissimilar papers were a technicality, that he was just visiting the boat and would have to return to Prague to pick up his papers for America, which were still being prepared. Though Konkolski was anxious, the situation seemed under control.

The guards, bored at the quiet outpost, made small talk. "How are things? How is the boat? We see you have a birthday today. Something to drink?"

Konkolski reminded himself to be patient. "Like always."

He grabbed a bottle of whiskey and glasses from the rear of the car and poured drinks for himself and the guards. He was well aware of the bleak irony of the situation and it did not strike him in a trivial way. Even as they drank, some government clerk or policeman could be discovering the exit visa error. With a simple check, it would become apparent that no papers were waiting for Konkolski in Prague. Even now, someone might be reaching for the phone and calling the border. His dreams, and the ones he held for his son, would be shattered.

Konkolski could barely believe his ears. "I have a cake," Miki said. "Richard, you cut your cake."

And so, the sailor and guards drank Scotch and ate cake and celebrated.

"Have a good race," they said after the brief party. When Konkolski was finally out of sight, he put the gas pedal to the floor. He knew the roads and he knew the radar traps. He made it to the coast in just over eight hours.

Day was breaking but safety was still far, far away. He first went to his small house on the water and dropped off Miki and Richard Jr. Next he went to the local shipyard where he picked up his boat, took on fuel and water, and returned with it to the pier alongside his house. He started loading the gear and provisions he would need.

There were lots of people on the docks and Konkolski was careful not to load anything that would make his departure seem suspicious. In the late afternoon, Fredek Brodzinski stopped by. Konkolski quietly told him there'd been a change of plans, to gather his gear and say his goodbyes. They would be leaving very early the next day.

With darkness, he felt comfortable enough to begin loading the personal belongings he'd hidden away in his house. They were packed and ready for this occasion, though Konkolski had hoped it would never come. Films, books, cameras, manuscripts and clothes were brought aboard. He worked all night. Brodzinski arrived in the early morning. When the sun came up, they cast off the lines.

To reach the Baltic, some 45 miles away, first a river and then a lake had to be crossed. One final obstacle remained, a guarded jetty lying off the port city of Swinoujscie, Poland. Any boat venturing into the Baltic Sea, be it for one hour or one month, had to clear immigration and customs there before sailing into the open waters beyond.

Konkolski knew what to expect; he'd crossed the checkpoint, legitimately, many times before. He knew how long the procedure would take and what make of rifles the soldiers carried.

At the jetty, Konkolski handed over the exit visas—his short-term and his family's long-term—along with passports, ship's papers and a crew list he'd prepared long before. Two officers remained on board. He expected that he would be gone in 20 minutes, if all went well. But from the beginning he sensed trouble. He thought to himself, "Something is not good."

The tension grew. Konkolski, who had not slept for almost three days, realized he must remain composed. Miki and Richard Jr. had gone to sleep. Konkolski had to concentrate hard to stay awake. He felt if he fell asleep he would awake in custody. He could not give the authorities the luxury of time.

An hour passed. The officers who had remained on board accepted an invitation to come below. Soon they were joined by another, who did nothing to relieve the pressure. Konkolski was now convinced something was very wrong, but struggled to remain calm. The jokes and the liquor, which the guards expected as a matter of custom and deference, flowed freely. Another hour passed.

Instinctively, Konkolski decided it was time to take the initiative. In an outburst, he began screaming about the crippling strikes in the country and the pigheadedness of the bureaucracy.

"Look at the crew list," he demanded. "It has the names of several other crewmembers on it. I must return to pick up crew and go to Prague to get my papers. I'm on a sea trial. My wife has papers. My crewman has papers. They would give papers to them but not to me. That is crazy!" Then he blamed the shaken officers for delaying him from the race start, and promised that if he was late there'd be hell to pay.

When Konkolski was done, one officer beat a hasty retreat. He returned within 15 minutes, with *Nike*'s full set of processed papers under his arm. Konkolski left almost immediately and once in the Baltic he raised full sail in the light winds, added full power from his diesel engine and set a course for West Germany. He had a long stretch of East German coastline to pass, and wanted to do so quickly. In just over 18 hours, he was at the Kiel Canal.

As he entered the gates to the canal, he popped the cork on a bottle of champagne. Only then did he bring Richard Jr. on deck to explain how their lives had changed. "We are leaving but we can never go back," he said. And then he explained why.

In the steel light of dawn, headed for a future filled with uncertainty, the father and son toasted a new life with tears streaming down their cheeks. For the son, they were tears of loss. For the father, they were tears of hope.

In his heart, Konkolski knew he was doing the right thing.

Konkolski knew that, like other Eastern sailors, he would find sanctuary at the Transoceanic Club in Cuxhaven, West Germany. "It's one place where sailors from the East don't have to pay to stay. It's one place we are understood."

While in Cuxhaven, Konkolski drafted a letter to over 2,000 friends and influential citizens in Czechoslovakia explaining his actions.

"People always thought that I never had a problem with the government," he wrote. "It wasn't true." He explained in his message how he had written letters every ninth day for almost two years requesting permission to enter the race and had never been answered. He told of the trouble seeking permission for past races. He said that he had committed all his money and effort for several years to just one goal and now he was going to realize it. And to make sure there were no repercussions, he was taking his wife and son with him.

So that his letters would not be detected by the censors in the International Exchange Office, he mailed them identical-looking letters, only theirs were simply regards from the BOC race. As all the letters arrived in bulk, there was no reason to believe their letters were different from any other. They were circulated throughout the country.

Nike II sailed on to Plymouth, England, and after a brief layover crossed the Atlantic in 25 days, arriving just five days before the race began. Konkolski granted many interviews with the press but never alluded to the fact that his presence at the start was ever in question.

Nike II was first across the starting line on August 28th. The front page headline on the next morning's *Providence Journal* from Providence, Rhode Island, broke the story of Richard's secret: "Setting Out On A

Race For Freedom—Czech defects, begins global sail as U.S. weighs asylum request."

Drifting along the coast of Africa several weeks into the race, Konkolski wondered if it had all been worth it.

Day after day, the airborne dust from the Sahara Desert settled on board *Nike II*, fine as powdered chalk. It collected in the tops of winches, in the corners of the cockpit, in Konkolski's beard and eyes and nostrils. *Nike II* felt dead beneath him as the glassy swells rolled slowly by, their mirror surfaces unsullied by creases of wind. As the boat rolled, the mainsail flopped back and forth banging against its sheets and blocks, the clatter an insolent reminder of his helplessness. He worked the sails until he could work them no more. He toasted Neptune with rum. Nothing worked.

"I didn't get wind for 17 days. I have all the courses from the Whitbread boats and others who have come this way. I have their daily progress charts. Nobody was ever becalmed here. Nobody but me. For 17 days.

"When I left Newport I was really ready to do my best, to put all of my energy and force into this race. I wanted to show everyone that I could sail fast, show my government that I am somebody and show the American government that I'm somebody. It was just bad luck that finished me."

Before the ordeal was over, before the wind picked up and brought new hope, Konkolski sat down on the deck of *Nike II* under the limp sails. Drifting alone in the midst of a friendless, mirrored sea, he begged for wind and cried into his hands when it didn't come.

4

Birth of the Tribe

AT THE OUTSET of the race, no one common denominator linked the 17 men who had come to test themselves against the sea—other than the solitary quest itself. But during the race, the collection of 17 individuals was transformed into a community unique in the annals of sailing, perhaps in any field of adventure. The reasons for the emergence of this ocean sailing community run as deep as the deepest river of human nature. Yet it was made possible by the age in which they were sailing, the age of microcircuits and instant radio communications. During the first leg, an informal communications system, involving a worldwide network of amateur radio operators (hams), evolved among the skippers. As the race progressed, the system grew and took solid shape, until the skippers became not a collection of individuals but a fraternity of kindred souls.

This did not happen all at once. Nor, at first, was it universal throughout the fleet. But slowly, the reliable radio network instilled in the racers a sense of camaraderie that had not been evident ashore. By sharing their troubles, joys and fears with one another over their radios, the group assumed an identity that went beyond their own limited individual horizons. Their solo journeys became intertwined; they became a tribe.

As with previous offshore races, such as the Whitbread, the official radio link for the BOC race was originally the single sideband (SSB), which is the standard for commercial radio traffic and monitored in every seafaring nation along the race's route. The race rules regarding communications were simple: Each racer had to state his position to race headquarters once a week. Nine of the racers planned on doing so with SSB radio.

Fourteen boats, however, carried ham radios. Before the start, one ham enthusiast, Rob Koziomkowski of Portsmouth, Rhode Island, visited Goat Island to inform the sailors that an amateur network would be monitoring the race and at their disposal. By chance, Koziomkowski met Yukoh Tada and the two agreed to follow a daily schedule. Word got out to Dan Byrne and Francis Stokes, who in turn informed Bertie Reed, David White, Greg Coles and Guy Bernardin. The daily talks among the group became known as the "chat show." Position reports, meteorological information and other matters pertinent to the race—as well as plenty of casual talk—were discussed.

The land-based Koziomkowski, a 38-year-old Vietnam veteran, more or less adopted the BOC fleet. He used his 28 years of experience and his powerful broadcasting and receiving system to keep a keen ear on things for the race committee in Newport. Koziomkowski, with a partial disability from the service, had his own version of solitude with which to deal. His basement radio shack in Rhode Island was his window on the world. To the good fortune of the fleet, he opened it to them while they were at sea. Later, the fleet would reach out for help from Koziomkowski, who became one of the backstage heroes of the entire event.

Stokes, one of the most competent seamen, proved more than once to be a vital link in the emerging tribe. Dan Byrne, who looked up to Stokes, spoke daily with his hero on the ham chat show. He said, "He's such a nice guy. There are at least five things he helped me fix over the radio. He explained how to repair the autopilot, since we both carry the same type. And, he told me how to stop the leak that was squirting in around the packing gland on *Fantasy*'s shaft. He used to own a Valiant 40 and he told me to break the packing nut loose with a hammer. Well, I tried it and it worked. He was forever helping me out."

Although Stokes would cringe at the nickname, in the first leg he became the fleet's "St. Francis," because he patiently extended help to everyone around him. When Bertie Reed's temperamental alternator died several weeks into the leg, leaving the South African with no way to charge his batteries other than the small solar panels on his afterdeck, Stokes became his link to the race committee, which did its best to help. In Newport, Jim Roos and Peter Dunning, manager of Goat Island Marina and active in the race organization, found an alternator like Reed's. They figured out how to rewire the unit and passed the information on to Koziomkowski in Portsmouth, who then passed the information to Stokes who was still in the North Atlantic. He, in turn, transmitted the instructions on to Reed, then sailing off the coast of Brazil.

At the end of this chain knelt Reed, with a wrench in one hand and a microphone in the other, as he tried to bypass his voltage regulator in order to charge his ship's batteries directly.

The picture is remarkable. Astronauts in orbit communicate this way, but this was something new for offshore racers. The pains everyone took to help Reed solve his problem—just to enable him to talk over the radio as often as possible—underscored the importance to each sailor of their radio kinship.

While all found good use for their radios in the first leg, not all were dependent on each other. Philippe Jeantot, for instance, was unaware of the chat show frequency, so he could not speak to the other racers throughout the first leg. Jeantot did keep a regular schedule with a ham in France, who dutifully passed along *Credit Agricole*'s position to race headquarters on the required weekly basis. But because of his silence, Jeantot was considered a "lone wolf" by some racers who felt that the Frenchman was playing his hand extremely close to his chest. In fact, his silence did have its advantages. In the early weeks, he set off to the south without anyone knowing. His novel route and incredible progress was not discovered until it was far too late to make up for it tactically.

Limited radio contacts, however, were better than no contact at all, as Richard Broadhead discovered. By the fourth week, Broadhead had lost the use of his engine, thereby losing his prime electrical generator. This meant limited radio contact of any kind and few, if any, calls to race headquarters or the maritime ham network.

When Broadhead lost his ability to communciate hundreds of miles at sea, he found himself living the single most potent nightmare for lone offshore sailors—gravely ill with only limited radio capacity to call for help. Broadhead developed ulcers on the back of one leg. Later, he admitted that he did not worry about them at the time and did not bother to clean them, thinking they would simply go away. But the ulcers didn't go away. As he sailed *Perseverance of Medina* into the southeast trade winds south of the equator, the ulcers turned septic.

"I've never felt so weak in all my life," he said. "I'd go on deck to take a morning sight and I'd do the sun all right and write down the figures. But I just didn't have the strength to go down and sit at the chart table to work out my position. I had to go to bed for an hour and then try later to work out the sights."

The ulcers gave him a case of blood poisoning, including a high fever that knocked him into his bunk for four days while his 52-foot cutter sailed on more or less without him. His mind suffered and his thoughts wandered. Not only was no one aware of his predicament, he was incapable of calling for help, even if he had thought to cry out.

Strange things happen to sailors when they are sick and alone. In 1895, Joshua Slocum, during the first months of his circumnavigation in *Spray*, had a similar experience soon after departing the Azores for Gibraltar. Caught in a northerly gale, he fell sick after eating white goat's cheese and fresh plums he had been given as a bon voyage present in the islands. He became delirious and at one point awoke to find a strange man at the helm of his little sloop. The vision, who looked like a pirate, introduced himself as "the pilot of the *Pinta,* one of Columbus's crew," and ordered Slocum back into his bunk. The old Yankee obeyed. Strangely, when he really awoke hours later he found *Spray* steady on her course despite a high wind and sea.

Broadhead did not have a spectral visitor but he did lose touch with reality. As he lay sweating with fever in his bunk, he dreamed about sailing *Perseverance* to the Seychelle Islands, one of the few remaining unspoiled tropical paradises. There was one hitch with the plan, however. The Seychelles lay 5,000 miles away on the other side of Africa. At best the plan was improbable, at worst, delirious. Later, he said, "I know it sounds stupid, but at the time I was completely out of it."

After four days of solitary sickness, the fever passed and, gradually, Broadhead's health returned. But the ulcers did not clear up entirely and he experienced flare-ups later in the race. It is remarkable that throughout the ordeal, Broadhead kept his boat moving. Little did he know, his problems were far from over.

No skipper was more interested in regular communication with his fellows and with the race committee in Newport than Desmond Hampton aboard *Gipsy Moth V.* So there is a measure of irony in the breakdown that nearly robbed him of his voice. In Cape Town, he recalled the incident.

"It was October 3 and I was on deck at 0100 GMT. I was about to read the log, when I suddenly noticed that the main and mizzen forestays had gone very slack and the mizzen was creaking horribly. I looked up to see the backstay gone. It was hanging over the side. In a panic, I dropped all sail except the mizzen, which I reckoned was acting as a backstay and keeping the mizzenmast standing. That left us effectively hove to."

It took Hampton only four hours to clear up the mess of sails and line on deck, then rig temporary backstays with the spare halyards on the mizzen and finally fit another permanent backstay. As it happened, an old backstay was coiled in the bow of the boat.

"Luckily there was a full moon," he wrote in his log, "so I could see what I was doing at the top of the mast without a torch. When I got down, I had to struggle to make the new stay meet the bottle screw at the deck, but managed it eventually. After tightening it up, I set all sails again and was underway by 0405. Finally, I had a large whiskey and a bit of sleep."

Hampton is a real estate broker from England with the dashing good looks of a Royal Air Force fighter pilot. A boyish lock of black hair hangs over his forehead and he wears a trim mustache, like the Errol Flynn of *Dawn Patrol*. So, at 41, he seemed well suited to hard scrambles up and down the mizzen in the early hours of the morning. His main reason for such a double-time repair was to keep the mast from falling down and to keep *Gipsy Moth* in the race.

But he had another motive as well.

The backstay was the aerial for his single sideband transmitter. Without it, he was cut off from the rest of the fleet, from race headquarters and from his wife, Kitty, and two daughters in England. He had to get it back up there. But the spare backstay was not insulated and could not be used to receive or transmit. He had to improvise.

"In the morning," his log continued, "I rigged up the old backstay using the mizzen topping lift. I then was able to tell Tony Lush, who was quite near at hand, the whole saga and with his help I was able to rig the aerial in an effective way from the mizzen. The system worked that night during the evening chat show. What a relief. The next day I anchored the old stay permanently. That concluded the most exciting 24 hours I have had in a long time."

All the racers shared Hampton's fear of complete silence and all went to great lengths to meet the daily radio schedules and tune into the daily chat show. As long as they had access to the airwaves, they could maintain the notion that help might arrive if called for. Without their radios, each man's nightmares were his, alone.

In the seventh week of the race, Jim Roos and the race committee declared Neville Gosson aboard *Leda* overdue and perhaps missing. Gosson had had his share of bad luck and trouble along the first leg. Near the Cape Verde Islands, his forestay parted and dropped on deck leaving his mast supported only by the much shorter staysail located below the forestay. Later, he damaged a cap shroud that runs to the masthead. Now he was out of contact. His radio problems stemmed from his long voyage to Newport before the race began, trouble that Newport's electronics experts were unable to fix. On leaving for Cape Town, he was unable to transmit over any great distances.

Gosson said, "When I started the race the only way I could 'get out' (over the radio) was to have Desmond do the work for me. That system worked well until we reached the halfway mark and then Desmond decided to go the long way around the South Atlantic high and I decided to go down the rhumb line. So we parted and my radio link ended. I asked Desmond to tell the race committee that I would be having trouble getting through. They understood and that's why they didn't panic when they didn't hear from me for more than three weeks."

In Newport, Roos was monitoring the progress of the fleet and staying in touch with the boats. He felt he and the race committee had Gosson's situation under control, as best as they could.

"We knew he was having radio difficulties," Roos said. "That information was passed to us via *Gipsy Moth* on the 28th of September and we had Neville's position plotted on that day. We had been following his track all along, we knew his intention to sail the rhumb line and we tried to keep a log of where he ought to be. When he didn't come up at the end of the next week we talked about it, looked at the weather patterns for the area and decided that we would give him another week to try to report before we notified authorities."

Gosson was doing his best to communicate. As he sailed the rhumb line course through the South Atlantic, following Philippe Jeantot who was nearly 1,000 miles ahead, he found mostly light head winds that slowed his progress. As he passed St. Helena Island, he diverted course significantly in an effort to raise St. Helena radio.

"I got so close I could have thrown a stone on the roofs of the buildings, but the guy on the radio there could not make out my message. I think we had a language problem. Anyway, that was the end of that. I tried Cape Town radio but couldn't get through to them at all."

Back in Newport two more weeks passed and the race committee came to the end of its tether. On October 18, 20 days after Hampton had informed them that Gosson might be sailing out of range, the race committee issued the "all ships alert" through Lloyds of London. Its decision was based on silence. No news from Gosson, in this case, did not mean good news. It meant that every possible mishap that Roos or the other members of the race committee might dream up for Gosson, out there alone and out of contact, might be true. They just didn't know. As the weeks passed, their need to know grew stronger until they were impelled to act. It was not information that motivated them. It was a fear of the void.

Ready to play on that fear was an Australian public relations man named Rodney Jenkins who was working for BOC's affiliate in Sydney, Commonwealth Industrial Gas. On learning of the all ships alert from Lloyd, Jenkins issued a press release declaring, in effect, "Australian Sailor Lost At Sea." It was a catchy lead evoking all the primal fears of drowning, so the Australian newspapers picked up the report and ran with it, despite the release's skewed emphasis. Gosson was out of touch, but he was not missing. Within three days of the Lloyd's alert, he was sighted by a passing freighter and his position was relayed to area headquarters.

Found or not, Gosson still had no voice and he longed to speak. As *Leda* limped toward Cape Town, trailing the other boats in Class I by a wide margin—after leading so boldly for the first night—Gosson tried to raise anyone who might be monitoring the radios. Finally, he switched onto the frequencies used by the maritime mobile net run by a sugar planter, Alistair Campbell, from Durban, South Africa, and his voice was heard. Gosson said, "Alistair picked up my signal and really persevered. He couldn't make out anything I was saying and had to invent a special code to get my latitude and longitude."

Campbell joined the ham network soon after the BOC fleet crossed the equator. He made it a habit to speak with Koziomkowski in Rhode Island daily. Koziomkowski informed him of Gosson's predicament and the South African took up the cause.

"Cape Town radio had been receiving garbled signals for a while," Campbell said. "It was from an unknown source, so I monitored it and once I heard that it was, indeed, a voice, I spoke back."

Campbell broke through, "I can hear you. If you can hear me answer with three beaps for yes and one beep for no."

The answer was three.

"Are you a BOC boat?"

Three beeps.

"Are you *Leda Pier One?*"

Three beeps.

Hurrah!

The process was painfully slow, but as rewarding to Campbell as watching the eyelids of a stroke victim signal that all is clear behind the frozen face. Within half an hour of first contact, Gosson had beeped out his position and had established voice contact for the first time in 23 days. From there, as he closed the coast of South Africa, Gosson and Campbell communicated regularly, using their special code at first and gradually, moving into straight voice communication.

"We stayed in touch," Campbell said, "and with a little instruction in knob twirling, I was able to show Neville how to tune his set a bit better. By the time he reached Cape Town, I was able to understand about half of what he was saying. The rest we got with threes and ones."

Gosson sailed into Cape Town on November 1, 1982. It had taken him 64 days to limp the 7,100 miles from Newport, but he had made it, and those who had watched his progress carefully, the race committee and the hams, made it with him.

After a sea voyage, the land holds a special allure. Yet when landfall is made and the goal of the passage has been achieved, a certain melancholy often falls over a boat and crew. Left behind is the simple and solitary sea while ahead are all the conflicting pressures of society. After two months at sea, that transition is even more dramatic. Society fits like a coat one has outgrown.

Before the start of the race, the press speculated at length about how the men and the boats would stand up to the rigors of such a long race. News stories quoted eerie passages from *The Strange Last Voyage Of Donald Crowhurst* in order to call up images of deprivation and hardship for their audiences. If the racers were not sunk by whales or lost to the gales of the Southern Ocean, the journalists said, then certainly some among the fleet would lose their minds.

Yet, none of the racers coming into Cape Town suffered, either from the strains of the sea or from reentry. There is no doubt that the close ties established among the fleet via radio played a large part in that success.

In Cape Town during the layover before the second leg, the racers and the race committee—with cooperation and advice from Koziomkowski in Rhode Island and Campbell in Durban—established the maritime ham network as the official communications system of the BOC Challenge. Tony Lush commented later that it was "the organization and discipline of the hams, Alistair in particular, that made the ham network successful."

For Stokes, who finished on October 29, the ham radio community is a fact of offshore life. He and his teenage son, Arthur, took classes and received their operating licenses together before the 1980 OSTAR, so they could talk to one another during the race.

Soon after arriving in Cape Town, Stokes said, "I had no real problems, no deprivation or hardship. I didn't set out with Spartan living in mind, or to make this an endurance contest. I set out to have an adventure. I think it was important for all of us to stay in contact through the two months it took to get here. In a sense, I lost part of the full reason for being out here, which was to experience the solitude. I lost that, a bit, but I gained the contact with everybody and that was valuable. The radio schedule became part of the day, like the morning cup of coffee and the noon sight. It's something you can look forward to and build your day around. When you're alone for two months, you need that.

"Two months is an incredibly long time to be out there. When you look ahead, it seems a long time and then you look back and the time seems so short."

For Stokes and the other members of the chat show, the communications network established in the first leg was not just a central clearinghouse of position reports and weather information. It was also a base camp, a reliable place in time where one could return daily to briefly share the common experience that each had undertaken alone.

For Broadhead and Richard McBride (who also experienced engine trouble), who had little radio contact, establishing a workable shipboard system once in Cape Town became a priority of the highest order. Everyone in the fleet took careful note of frequencies and assigned schedules, and all made vows to continue conscientious communications.

In the relatively calm conditions of the first leg, the ham radio fostered a sense of community among the racers that had not been possible in the last hectic days in Newport. It brought them together. In the uncertain oceans that still lay ahead, it would keep them that way, and would, ultimately, save the lives of two skippers.

5

The French Imperative

FOR PHILIPPE JEANTOT, the last two weeks of Leg I were as difficult as any he had experienced in his 35,000 miles of ocean sailing. They were the weeks that galvanized the young Frenchman's will.

As he sailed through the trade winds of the South Atlantic and rounded the South Atlantic High, cutting the corner to save miles, he experienced one gear failure after another.

The first problem was the most dramatic. Off the coast of Brazil his main water tank ruptured, spilling most of his drinking water supply into *Credit Agricole*'s bilge. Out on the open sea, far from land, freshwater is as important to sailors as it is to Arabs crossing the desert. The ability to carry ample freshwater always has been a key to ocean crossing. The Horse Latitudes, the windless regions lying in the middle of the North Atlantic High, got their name in the 16th century because it was there that Spanish galleons bound for the New World exhausted their water supplies and had to jettison the heaviest drinkers aboard, their horses.

For Jeantot, losing his water was a problem severe enough to put him out of the race, if he was unable to come up with a solution. "I first thought about stopping at the island of Trinidad," he said. "But I had a lead on Bertie (Reed in *Voortrekker*) that I wanted to keep, so I pressed on. I wanted to be sure that I had half a liter of water a day, so that's what I set for a ration. And that's what I drank all the way to Cape Town."

It was a risky choice. He collected a small amount of rainwater in his inflatable dinghy and distilled seawater in his pressure cooker. Had he suffered a serious gear failure, such as losing his mast, he could

43

have run out of stove fuel and thus water long before help could have arrived.

He was not without other troubles as well. As he sailed eastward for Cape Town into the strong winds of the South Atlantic, his Aries self-steering vane began to malfunction. The British-made device, rated by the racers as the best wind-vane steerer available, developed worn bearings and the shaft bent. The alternative to sailing under the guidance of a wind vane was either hand-steering—a forbidding prospect to a single-hander who also must be crew, navigator, cook and chief steward—or using an electronic auto-pilot.

Jeantot carried two autopilots manufactured by Combi Autohelm, another British company. With two systems, Jeantot had the kind of redundancy that ought to have prevented serious trouble.

But one unit never worked properly. Soon after leaving Newport, the device began to lead *Credit Agricole* on a weaving tour of the Atlantic that is more the style of a cruising vessel than a racer. For many other sailors in the fleet, this would not have seemed a major problem; for Jeantot, it was disastrous. He abandoned the first unit for the second and relied on it until he reached the South Atlantic. Ten days before reaching Cape Town, it too ceased to function properly when the last rubber drive belt, part of the steering mechanism, snapped. Jeantot was left with no option but to hand-steer. Hand-steering exhausted him.

Low on water and tired from long watches at the wheel, he nearly lost his mast over the side when the block holding a running backstay, a temporary rope support for the mast that is advisable in strong breezes, broke and fell to the deck. The mast shuddered under the strain of too much canvas in too much wind. But it stood straight and did not fall ignominiously into the sea. With such luck on his side, coupled with fine seamanship and the ability to capitalize on given opportunities, Jeantot was alone in more ways than one when he crossed Cape Town finish line in first place.

His victory was stunning. He was an unknown sailor who had never competed in a major singlehanded race. Yet he sailed the 7,000 miles from Newport to Cape Town in a remarkable 47 days and finished 900 miles in front of Bertie Reed. For the more than 100 well-wishers on the pier to greet this new hero in Cape Town, led by the French Consul General, Jeantot had risen like a bright star. He was whisked off to a local French bistro and feted royally.

There was no questioning Jeantot's initial success; however, many of those following the race closely doubted his ability to maintain the lead through the whole event. Yet when Jacques de Roux sailed *Skoiern III* into Cape Town 12 days later winning Class II, everyone realized the two Frenchmen were sailing, metaphorically, on a different ocean than the rest of the fleet. De Roux, a demure career naval officer and navigation instructor—a submarine commander when not sailing his 41-foot sloop —sailed a perfect, textbook course to Cape Town. His route from Newport was to the letter the route recommended in *Ocean Passages For The World*. Yet he managed to beat his closest rival, Yukoh Tada, by two days, and his natural rival, Richard Konkolski by a week. He even beat two Class I boats (the 53-foot *Leda Pier One* and the 56-foot *Spirit of Pentax*) that theoretically, he should have been nowhere near.

At 43, de Roux was an experienced ocean racer and had sailed as navigator with the legendary French sailor, Eric Tabarly, on long-distance offshore races. But he did not have the singlehanded experience of his main rivals, Konkolski or Francis Stokes. He was an unknown factor to many at the start of the race, yet the voyage to Cape Town proved the boat was fast and her skipper tough enough to keep her going for weeks on end.

The French sailors were doing it differently. Even Guy Bernardin, who did poorly on the first leg, had tried to split tacks with the fleet in order to look for a better slant of wind to overcome the natural handicap of sailing the smallest boat. Like Jeantot slipping between hurricane systems in the North Atlantic or chancing he would collect enough water to last until Cape Town, Bernardin was willing to take large risks.

To the French sailors, winning was all important. In France, singlehanders are among the sporting elite. They are rewarded with fame and money and adoring sponsors. Such carrots might be incentive enough to drive French sailors to excellence. But, in characteristic French fashion, they have devised a second level of the game. In it, challenges are encountered, like mountain peaks, for their own sake—because they are there. A solid financial support system has grown to spur these sailors on in their quest—physical and philosophical—of solo adventure. Together, the money and the philosophy form the French imperative.

But, as Jeantot and the others knew, the race and the adventure began long before the August 28 starting gun. "This is really a race with five legs, one preparing and four actually racing," Jeantot observed.

For Jeantot, the race began only a short eight months prior to the start when he sent the race committee (Jim Roos and David White, at that point) the $400 entry fee. Originally, he planned to race his 44-foot steel cutter, a boat he had sailed across the Atlantic four times singlehanded.

Jeantot is the consummate man of action. At age 18, he decided to forego college and instead joined the French Army and became a member of an elite squad of paratroopers. After the army, he took up professional deep-sea diving and was a member of the diving team that set a world depth record of 501 meters (1,644 feet).

But sailing was his passion. The round the world race was a rare opportunity. He would take his old cruising boat if that was the best he could find. But in January, when the rumor got out that BOC was going to sponsor the race, Jeantot convinced Credit Agricole, one of France's largest banks, to sponsor him. His deal with the bank was not elaborate. In exchange for half the cost of a new boat, roughly $116,000, Jeantot would campaign *Credit Agricole* for four years, after which he would become its sole owner. To raise the rest of the cash he sold everything he owned. In Newport, before the start he said, "I sold my house. I sold my car. The bank account, it's in the bilge. I have nothing. I must win to recoup!"

In January 1982, after signing the contract with Credit Agricole, Jeantot went to the Paris boat show and there met naval architect Guy Ribadeau Dumas. At 30, Dumas was one of the young wizards of the French racing circuit. Among his successful boats, he had designed *Antares,* the 62-footer that won the 1981 Seahorse maxi-boat series in England. The boat that Dumas drew, incorporating many of Jeantot's design ideas, was a specialized singlehander's machine, suitable for sailing in every extreme from the Horse Latitudes to the Roaring Forties.

Dumas said of the boat, "Philippe was looking for a 50-footer, alloy (aluminum) construction and he didn't want to go over 50-feet as he didn't want to overtake his budget. He was right, but the maximum length was 56 feet. I knew that David White and others were preparing special maxi boats, so I was not able to prevent my hand from sliding with the first sketches."

Once he saw the design, Jeantot wanted the boat, even though building a 56-footer would cost more than he had to spend. Money was one problem, finding a builder who would consider constructing the vessel on such short notice was another. In March he finally found a builder, Nautalu, willing to take on the project. Three months later—a third of the time usually required to build such a boat—*Credit Agricole* was launched in Toulon. She was not finished, but Jeantot could wait no longer. In July, with several of his diving comrades aboard to help him install interior furniture, electronic equipment and sailing systems, *Credit Agricole* departed Toulon and made a very quick passage across the North Atlantic to Newport, arriving only 10 days before the start of the race. It took Philippe 20 days to cross the Atlantic, a time that would have been good enough to win all but one of the six previous OSTARS. (American Phil Weld aboard his 50-foot trimaran *Moxie* won the 1980 OSTAR in just over 17 days, setting a race record.) The crossing was a very satisfactory shakedown. The boat was fast, easy to handle, and strong.

By comparison, White's *Gladiator* had taken more than two years to complete (at a cost very close to the quarter-million dollars spent on *Credit*

Agricole). Yet, all that time and money had not enabled White to build a boat that would stand up to the rigors of the sea. In the end, White did not bring to his boatbuilding project the intensity of purpose that motivated Jeantot. The difference in their efforts was obvious within a week of the start.

Jeantot's intensity was not a spur-of-the-moment enthusiasm. It was an abiding passion. When he was 15, he read Bernard Moitessier's *The Long Way,* an account of the 1968 Golden Globe race, in which Moitessier dropped out and sailed on from Cape Horn to Tahiti instead of turning north to Europe to finish and probably win the race. It was then that the slender young man from Quimper in Brittany vowed he too would someday sail alone around the world. Fifteen years later he got his chance.

During that decade and a half, singlehanding had gone through a renaissance in France sparked by one man, Eric Tabarly. The crusty "iron man," as he has been called, gained fame in his homeland when in 1964 he challenged Frances Chichester, Blondie Hasler and the other English sailors who had founded the OSTAR, and won. Tabarly became a national hero. He was offered sponsorship, sold his name in endorsement contracts and took the life of the highly paid professional athlete. There had never been anyone quite like him. It may be difficult for an American to grasp the kind of hero Tabarly became in France because Americans pay little attention to sailing and sailors. For an American, comparable heroes might be baseball player Pete Rose or football player Earl Campbell—stocky, no-nonsense working-class-types who make their avocation their profession.

But those men are team players. Tabarly performs his feats of skill and daring hundreds of miles offshore, alone, without witnesses, racing against a fleet of other loners, who together are racing over the same indifferent sea. When he returns from his trials, Tabarly is greeted by an avid public, the media, eager sponsors and politicians. But he also is greeted by a generation of young sailors who have followed his example —Marc Pajot, Florence Arthaud, Alain Gabbay and many others—who have made singlehanded offshore sailing a national obsession.

Jeantot explains the phenomenon.

"You see, French people are not very good at team sports," he said. "We can never agree on anything and so our teamwork suffers. We are best at things we do alone, like singlehanding."

It is not surprising that after building *Credit Agricole* in only three months, sailing it across the Atlantic in nearly record time and then sprinting out to a wide lead in the first leg of the race, that Jeantot would soon be compared to his own hero, Eric Tabarly.

Of the generation of young solo racers that followed Tabarly, one, Alain Colas, burned with a brighter flame than the rest and gave himself more completely to the imperative of the sea . . . until it consumed him. To know what drove Jeantot, Bernardin and de Roux, you must know Colas, for they all carried Colas' saga with them.

Colas accomplished more in his one decade of racing than most of his contemporaries will achieve in their lifetimes. He epitomizes the passion and philosophy that lie at the heart of the French imperative. Like Moitessier, Colas helped create the vocabulary of singlehanding in France so that the experience of running alone before the terrifying seas of a southern ocean gale could be comprehensible not only to the general public but to the racers themselves. He was the consummate, articulate, French adventurer/philosopher.

A short wiry man, Colas was not born to the sea. The son of a potter, he had done well in school and gone to the Sorbonne, from which he was graduated in 1966. He was 22, restless and impatient. On a whim, he flew to Australia where he taught French at the University of Sydney. Crewing for friends and reading basic texts on sailing, he quickly discovered that he possessed a lot of natural sailing talent. At Christmastime in 1967, Tabarly brought *Pen Duick III* to Sydney to sail in the Sydney-Hobart race, where he met and befriended the young fellow Frenchman. Still footloose and restless, Colas gained a mentor. He tossed his professorship to the wind, joined the crew of *Pen Duick III* and spent the next three years sailing and working with Tabarly.

In 1970, after cruising through the Pacific with Tabarly, Colas got the chance to buy Tabarly's aluminum trimaran *Pen Duick IV*. He jumped at it, although it meant a sizeable loan for which he had no collateral but the boat. Tabarly went back to France to build a new *Pen Duick V* and Colas departed to wander through the Pacific looking for topics for the articles he was now writing for French sailing magazines.

In 1971, after marrying a Tahitian woman, Teura, he decided to test his new skills in the championship arena. He entered the 1972 OSTAR, Chichester's and Tabarly's race. He was a long way from the halls of the Sorbonne.

"We are a special brand of maniacs," Colas told a *Sports Illustrated* reporter, William O. Johnson, for a story that appeared in that magazine. "We derive our pleasure from our own lonely actions instead of performing in a gymnasium or a pool or a stadium. Our sport involves long hardship and strange times, but it makes us very happy."

The 1972 OSTAR made Colas very happy. His 69-foot trimaran won the race in a time of 20 days, 13 hours and 15 minutes. It was Colas's first race, but he had shown the qualities of a great offshore sailor. His victory brought fame and livelihood at home—one of his books sold 200,000 copies—giving him the luxury of time to decide his life's next challenge. He had met one. Another lay ahead.

Cape Horn.

In September 1973, Colas departed Saint-Malo, France, for Sydney, Australia. On the chart table of *Manureva* (*Pen Duick IV*'s new name) were charts and logbooks from the days of the great clipper ships of the mid-19th century, in particular, those from *Cutty Sark*. His aim was to break the old ship's record to Australia and then sail on around Cape Horn. It took him 79 days to reach Sydney, 10 slower than *Cutty Sark*'s best time but breaking all singlehanded records for the trip. After a stop of a month, he set off on December 30 for Cape Horn, "rubbing minds with the ancient mariners."

He sailed more like a pilgrim than a blowhard. There was something personal to be won at Cape Horn. He needed another rite of passage to give more meaning to all that had gone before. In the early pages of his book *Around The World Alone* he wrote, "I've already spent a number of years questioning the sea, and I count myself lucky if, in all these thousands of miles, I have enjoyed a few passing moments of understanding."

And a few lines later, "There are many elements that make up a victory, and the human element is not the dominant one. In the final analysis, I know very well that a victory over the sea is not 'won' through a struggle. It is given by default, as it were; and the true master of the situation remains, as always, the sea itself."

The voyage from Sydney to Cape Horn passed quickly, although the weather in the southern ocean was hostile and difficult. As he rounded the Horn, the weather turned light and he ghosted on a fair breeze past the rock that had played such a leading role in his own mythology.

The rite of passage over, Colas turned northward toward home and made a remarkably fast passage back to Saint Malo. Although he did not break *Cutty Sark*'s record for the around-the-world run, he did set a new singlehanded record of 169 days at sea that would stand for a decade. He had become one with the old Cape Horners.

He could have rested on the mountains of laurels that were tossed his way, but he had another plan. During the long run through the southern ocean he had begun to dream of a modern but singlehanded clipper ship. He wanted speed and that required waterline length.

The boat he had in mind was a 236-foot, four-masted schooner, with a revolutionary fore-and-aft rig. It could fly 14,000 square feet of sail, displace 280 tons and would cost at least $1 million. Moreover, he planned to build the boat in time for the 1976 OSTAR, two years away. Applying his abundant energy to the project, he began to raise money and gather support. Finally, the Club Mediterranee resort agreed to underwrite the cost of the bare hull, roughly $600,000, and the project was underway.

Then on May 19, 1975—one year from the start of the OSTAR—disaster struck that would provide a test more demanding than rounding the Horn. While out for an afternoon sail with friends aboard *Manureva*, the mainsail became stuck at the masthead as Colas was steering into an anchorage. He ran forward to drop the anchor. As the rope ran overboard, his right foot became snarled in the line. The line rapidly sawed through the flesh, the muscle and then the bone of his right ankle. By the time he was able to cut the anchor line, all that held his foot to his leg was his Achilles tendon. He said, "I fished the foot up by the tendon and I knew enough to press the artery in my leg to slow down the rush of blood."

Colas was rushed to a hospital in Nantes 85 miles away, and there a team of doctors successfully reattached the foot. Over the course of the next year, he had 22 operations reattaching tendons, blood vessels and nerves. When *Club Mediterranee* was launched in the spring of 1976, he still had to wear a specially designed boot to give his right leg support and he had very little feeling in the foot. But medical concerns were secondary to his consuming desire to race his singlehanded clipper ship in the OSTAR. Colas achieved the larger part of his dream when he sailed *Club Mediterranee* across the starting line off Plymouth, England, bound for Newport.

Despite his determination, there was nothing Colas could do about the gales that swept over the OSTAR fleet that year. Of the 125 boats that started, five sank and 37 others ran for cover. Two skippers were lost. Colas' giant boat sped eastward in the strong winds, but with only one lame man to tend gear, she suffered breakdowns that forced Colas to stop briefly in Newfoundland for repairs. He sailed into Newport with a time of 24 days, 3 hours and 36 minutes, including his layover in Newfoundland. But he finished second. Eight hours earlier, Eric Tabarly had sailed the 73-foot *Pen Duick VI* across the finish line to win his second OSTAR.

Disappointed and still not fully mended from the accident, Colas left the Atlantic behind and retreated in his giant ship to Tahiti, where he ran day trips from the Club Med in Moorea. His exile did not last long. In the winter of 1978, a new singlehanded event, the Route du Rhum race—from Saint Malo, France, to Guadeloupe in the Caribbean—was announced. Colas' intention was to sail the race in *Manureva*, and then continue on to Tahiti, where he would retire.

It wasn't to be. On the night of November 16, 11 days after the fleet of 37 boats had started from Saint Malo, Colas radioed a French coastal station that he was west of the Azores, all was well and he was making good progress. But later that night an unpredicted gale ravaged that region of the Atlantic. That night, ham radio operators from Norway to Lisbon picked up a frantic Mayday call and a request for "immediate assistance" from an unidentified vessel—no name, no position.

Three weeks later, all the boats in the fleet had sailed into Guadeloupe . . . all but Colas. The French Navy spent 450 hours over the next four weeks combing a five-million-square-kilometer region between the Azores and the Guadeloupe. No trace was ever found. The sea that was his mistress claimed Alain Colas once and for all.

That was the philosophical heritage that Jeantot, Bernardin and de Roux carried with them as they sailed away from Newport. The stakes for them were higher than for sailors from other nations, for they had both the promise of fame and wealth if they won, and the imperative to push to the very limit of their capacity. Ahead always lay an unknown from which they might not return. That simple fact acted as the spring that drove them on to take risks, to push harder, to win.

Yet it would be wrong to conjure a somber picture of the French imperative. It is a hard road, yet at it's end there is relief and repose.

Colas wrote at the end of *Around The World Alone*, "I had driven myself, and driven myself hard; I had worked and worked hard; from day to day I had done my best to fulfill the mission that I had assigned to myself. And now, I suddenly realized how good it was to have done what I set out to do."

After sailing hard and sailing well, after winning their classes on the first leg, Jeantot and de Roux were beginning to appreciate what Alain Colas meant.

6

Landfalls

LANDFALL IS WHAT sailors dream of and dread. It is the reward at the end of a passage across an ocean, but it is also the most dangerous part of the voyage. Tired, eager to finish, uncertain of precise navigation after days and weeks at sea, more sailors lose their lives closing the land than at any other time.

For the BOC fleet, the landfall on the southwestern tip of the African continent brought them upon a rocky, windswept coast largely unmarked with navigational aids. Few yachts come that way. Few small boats fish or patrol along the shore. The waters off Cape Town—the "Cape of Storms"—are notoriously the roughest and stormiest in the world. Waves roll untamed from Cape Horn to the Cape of Good Hope and there climb into the shallow waters of the Agulhas Bank, where they rise into top-heavy monsters that tumble crazily forward, smashing anything in. their path. The effect is compounded by the Benguela Current; its northerly set along the southwest African coast presents another hazard to the sailor who does not take it into consideration. Cape Town has seen its share of wrecks and lost seamen. It was a landfall that promised to be difficult.

As Richard Broadhead closed with the coast of South Africa, he had little idea where he stood in the fleet. His voyage had been depressing. Because of his engine problems, he had been out of radio contact for long stretches in the South Atlantic. The longer he sailed in silence the more he longed to transmit his position and to learn his competitors' whereabouts. His health was improving but he was still weak. Worst of all, he had begun the voyage feeling that his boat was perhaps the best-suited of all for the light head winds he expected to encounter and while *Perseverance* was still a front-runner, Broadhead was convinced he'd not done better due to his own poor strategy.

There was one factor Broadhead had not taken into consideration when writing off the entire first leg to experience. While his average speed was not great, he was still sailing a shorter course than Reed and the majority of racers who had followed the *Ocean Passages* route.

On his final approach to Cape Town, steering due east with his destination less than 400 miles away, Broadhead made an incredible open-ocean rendezvous and learned a startling piece of news. The boat he met was a husky, Colin Archer-style wooden ketch—a sturdy, 45-foot double-ended cruising yacht especially designed and built for long-distance voyaging. Broadhead came alongside, luffed his sails, and rounded the boat twice. He called out to the lone sailor on deck that he was a sailor in the BOC race, and that his radio was out.

He asked the ketch's skipper to radio Cape Town with *Perseverance*'s position. The sailor, a fellow Englishman who was recording the moment on his movie camera, replied that his radio couldn't transmit messages but that he could receive them. He was well aware of not only the BOC race and Richard Broadhead, but also of South African Bertie Reed, who was only 50 miles ahead. Broadhead could barely believe his ears. At least three hard days of sailing remained, and Reed and second place were still within his grasp. He thanked the sailor and made a mental note of the yacht's name, *Aroha*.

"We'll have a beer when you make Cape Town," Broadhead called as an afterthought. Then he trimmed his sails and set out hard on the heels of *Voortrekker*. He could not have known at the time that *Aroha* was an ill omen.

His enthusiasm was short-lived. During the night, a full-fledged gale filled in from the southeast, an occurrence by no means rare off the Cape of Good Hope as spring grudgingly gives way to summer in the southern hemisphere. Broadhead, who had been laying a course just north of Cape Town, could make no headway against the strong 40-knot winds and the northerly set of the Benguela Current. *Perseverance* lost more than 100 miles and at least two days, and was forced to beat back to the finish as the storm gradually and mercifully blew itself out. To add insult to injury, the boat started taking on water—more than 50 gallons a day—on the long bash to windward. Though it would have been no consolation, Broadhead was not the only sailor who would endure a stormy, trying landfall.

As Broadhead pumped the bilge, reefed his sails and clawed his way toward harbor, Reed almost casually sailed into Cape Town in second place, six days after *Credit Agricole* and three days ahead of *Perseverance*. He had completed his roundabout, textbook tour of the South Atlantic by approaching Cape Town from the southwest, and when the barometer fell and the winds and sea rose he laid his course directly for Cape Town's Table Bay and on a single tack sailed home on the gale's crest. The landfall was competent, accurate and without drama. It had Reed's unmistakable signature on it.

Reed arrived at midday on October 21 and was greeted by a modest fleet of local boats led by *Voortrekker II,* the 60-foot yacht aboard which he had set a monohull record for the doublehanded Round Britain race earlier in the year. His wife, Pat, and six-year-old son, Stanley, were aboard, as well as some of the executives of Allied Technology, the boat's sponsor for the race.

"Biltong Bertie"—as he is known in South Africa in reference to the tough, dried meat that is a local staple—put on a sailing clinic for his welcoming committee, reefing the main and changing headsails within two miles of the finish line. A huge assembly of businessmen and secretaries, on noon breaks from their offices, lined the docks as he was towed in. Television crews and newspaper reporters soon clambered aboard *Voortrekker* and sipped champagne as Reed matter-of-factly told of his routine voyage. By his comments, one might have thought he had arrived on a cruising hop from Durban.

Reed, who has carved a career of yacht racing out of his true occupation as warrant officer in the South African Navy, is much admired by Cape Towners. After Jeantot arrived on board, looking somewhat relieved to finally have some company, one photographer had the two pose and then afterwards said, "Look. These are the only two sane men in the fleet." A local yachting writer, in an aside, said, "I'd like to see Bertie, Eric Tabarly, Marc Pajot (a singlehanded offshore racer), Philippe Jeantot—all those Frenchmen—in identical 60-foot monohulls on any longdistance course. My money would be on Reed anytime."

Reed's arrival was irrevocable proof to Cape Towners that there was indeed more than one boat in the race. And after Broadhead arrived several days later, battered but unbowed, a veritable parade of singlehanders began a march into the port city, with eight racers making their landfalls almost in pairs between the 25th of October and the first of November. For each, the land held a different promise. Yet as they approached they each shared an eagerness to get in and a dread of what could happen if their judgment failed them or their fate turned sour.

Desmond Hampton aboard *Gipsy Moth V* and Tony Lush aboard *Lady Pepperell* were the next sailors in. Land stirred in them very different reactions. Partly because of their respective rigs' reluctance to sail to windward and partly because, as Hampton said, "We just thought alike," the two skippers had sailed nearly identical routes from Newport. They, too, followed the gospel according to *Ocean Passages*. Although they were never more than 200 miles apart, and spoke to each other each day over their SSB radios, they were never in sight. They were so close, in fact, that one race plotter observed, "They aren't racing, they're rafted up."

The two sailors, on the advice of Reed, approached Cape Town (which lies at a latitude of 33°S) from the southwest. When they were within 150 miles of the finish line, Lush held a slim five-mile lead after 56 days at sea. Sailing into an easterly breeze, Lush got a good printout from his weatherfax recorder that revealed a high pressure center directly in their paths. It was decision time. As he had for the entire leg, when the machine was working properly, Lush passed the information on to Hampton.

Hampton, the risk taker, the adventurer, decided to chance going north of the high and arrived in Cape Town just after midnight, local time, on the morning of the 25th. Lush, always cerebral, often cautious, took the safer route to the south. He tied up *Lady Pepperell* just after dusk later that day. Their landfalls had brought out their true colors.

After losing to Hampton, Lush remarked, "I think I'll be a little less free with my weatherfax info on the next leg."

The next two sailors to arrive were an odd pair. Their diverse personalities, backgrounds and views on seamanship made their neck-and-neck finish wonderfully ironic. Jacques de Roux's quiet and polite demeanor tempted one to forget he was a skilled and tenacious sailor. His boat, *Skoiern III*, was a tidy, efficient 41-foot cutter. The BOC race was his first foray into competitive offshore singlehanding. Paul Rodgers, originally from New Zealand but now sailing under the Union Jack, had strolled through a gallery of questionable careers, from newspaperman and author to owner of a London hair replacement parlor. His impish grin and dry wit truly came alive in any social gathering. His yacht was the slender, rusting 56-foot schooner, *Spirit of Pentax*, that made the hairs on the neck of many a seasoned skipper bristle. Though *Pentax* was built for long-distance voyaging, its narrow deck and tiny cockpit allowed no concession towards creature comforts. It looked like, and was, an unforgiving vessel. Though Rodgers already had circumnavigated once on the boat, for the race it sorely needed a refit.

When the race began, the two set out in totally different directions. De Roux chose the course of most of the larger, faster boats relying on the conservative advice found in *Ocean Passages*. ("I obeyed his majesty's Queen," de Roux said, "and used the course she said to use.") He spoke little English and was unable to use any of the weather information being traded between boats over the radio. But with his own weatherfax and barometer he worked out his own excellent forecasts. The improvisation he added to the route was a product of his own sharp weather eye.

Rodgers planned on steering a course similar to de Roux, but changed his mind within days of leaving Newport. "I, too, was going to do the geriatric course, more or less, but cutting the corners. But when I was going out I suddenly discovered everyone else was doing that, or so it seemed. I thought, well, you don't really achieve much by following the fleet, although it's usually the wisest course, so I went off on my own."

Going off on his own meant choosing a course more southerly than even Jeantot's. It was easily the most radical route choice, and in the early going it paid high dividends as *Spirit of Pentax* stayed a close second to *Credit Agricole*. Then came the first problem.

"I hit a whale off Bermuda," Rodgers said. "It was in an area quite famous for the singing whales of Bermuda. It was during the night and he struck me amidships. He actually stopped the boat, which is something. It's easily the heaviest blow I've felt since I went onto a reef off New Zealand last year. Quite frightening."

Rodger's problems, unfortunately, were just beginning. Like Jeantot, Rodgers was driving directly across the tracks of the two hurricanes brewing to the east.

"Never has there been an ocean race," Rodgers said, "particularly singlehanded, starting at the peak of the hurricane season. It was easily the most dangerous yacht race that has ever been made, so one had to be careful of it. I think I chose the route down through the hurricanes because I was terrified of it and I thought I should perhaps try to go down there. But it was very foolish."

In Rodger's personal game of Russian roulette, he dodged the tropical-storm bullet. But in terms of strategy and standings, he found the next chamber loaded. As he neared and then crossed the equator, he was met by light and fluky head winds, and literally stopped in his tracks. "My schooner just could not point with those demon sloops, and I did not have the luck of the skipper of the Royal French Navy Barge (Jeantot)," he joked. "He got me on the equator. Everyone got me on the equator."

Rodgers zigged and zagged along the coast of South America. At one point, he came so close to the continent that some race followers believed he'd bagged the whole thing and was heading for Rio. But eventually he picked up the southeast trades and got the boat moving again towards Cape Town.

At noon on October 26th, word came into the Royal Cape Yacht Club (RCYC), the host club for the Cape Town layover, that *Pentax*'s red sails had been spotted and she soon would be approaching the finish line. The wind was from the southeast and building, though the skies were sunny and clear. A group of photographers and a race official boarded a Navy launch to record Rodger's arrival.

When the two boats rendezvoused, *Pentax* had sailed into a windless pocket in the lee of Table Mountain and was bobbing aimlessly in the moderate swell. Rodgers was in good spirits, asking if a girl he'd met in Cape Town on a previous voyage was waiting for him on the docks with tears in her eyes. But most of all, he was hungry, he said, as he'd run out of food three days earlier. Even coming from Rodgers, it was an astonishing piece of news.

"Some people in Newport had put some tins of salami on board," Rodgers said. "I never ate salami before but God I was glad to see it. Otherwise it would have been 10 days without food instead of three." (Rodgers had actually given away food in Newport, believing he had enough stores for the 45 days he believed the passage would take. Jeantot completed the course in 47 days, while Rodgers was in his 58th day when he arrived at Cape Town.)

As Rodgers spoke, a sail appeared on the horizon less than two miles away. It was *Skoiern III,* her sails trimmed tightly, dutifully plodding onward. The two sailors, despite their divergent routes and temperaments, had arrived at the exact same time.

Rodgers jumped onto his afterdeck and began waving his arms wildly. "Go away!" he yelled hopelessly at de Roux.

Before he could return to the helm, *Pentax* was belted with a 45-knot gust of wind. The boat heeled crazily and took off like a runaway stagecoach. The finish line was less than two miles away and directly to windward. For Rodgers and *Pentax,* it was the worst possible direction.

Rodgers tacked once, then again and then once more, making no progress.

Meanwhile, de Roux inched his way forward. He had been at the wheel nearly 48 hours because his self-steering gear had broken and he was unable to repair it. But he now had a target in his sights, *Pentax,* and he continued on.

The wind was blowing a steady 50 with gusts to 60 knots. Rodgers, frustrated and with no options, freed his sails and set a course for nearby Robyn Island to find shelter, regroup and prepare for another assault.

Skoiern III, the tortoise, pressed on and crossed the finish line late in the afternoon to win Class II. But de Roux was by no means home free. A cruising boat from the club, crewed by a merry host of well-lubricated refugees from the men's bar, greeted him and offered him a tow. When they were within yards of the mooring, the towline knot holding *Skoiern* to the cruising yacht parted. De Roux frantically fended *Skoiern* off a berthed freighter, coming dangerously close to slipping under the stern of the big ship and losing his spar. Another towline, from another boat, soon was secured. After a tense struggle in the strong wind, *Skoiern* was tightly moored.

"To go 7,000 miles and then break my mast at the end of my voyage," said an incredulous de Roux, "would not have been good."

Rodgers finished later that day, a tribute to both his perseverance and his grumbling stomach. But even the finish was tainted. When he got to the line it was dark. The race committee missed his finish and made him go across a second time.

"After a long and difficult voyage," Rodgers said, "and very little sleep, and no food for three days, it was just about the limit." But somehow, it seemed a fitting landfall for *Pentax.*

Yukoh Tada about *Koden Okera V* finished one day following de Roux. Francis Stokes aboard *Mooneshine* arrived the following afternoon. The race for Class II had been tight, with many lead changes throughout the course. A mere three days separated the top three boats. All three sailors had sailed admirably close to the Class I boats. Yet, strangely, the fact seemed to elude the three skippers themselves. De Roux was genuinely surprised to find he actually had won the leg, while Tada insisted he was "not competitor." Stokes admitted he was surprised at his third-place finish. "I mean, my boat, well, it *looks* different."

De Roux, who carried a SSB radio, had spoken only to Desmond Hampton and Tony Lush during the first leg, and then mainly for position reports north of the equator. Tada and Stokes, however, became close companions over the airwaves. Tada tried chatting with Hampton at the outset, but the Englishman always seemed terribly busy; what he did say, to Tada's untrained ear, sounded awfully funny. But Stokes was patient and took pains to speak slowly and repeat himself, and Tada arrived in Cape Town with a much better grasp of English then when he left Newport. Not perfect, but better. Whenever his tutor's name was mentioned within earshot, Tada would say, "Francis is my good friend."

The three—de Roux, Tada and Stokes—had been close throughout. But in the final stretch, when it really mattered, de Roux's aggressiveness earned him the victory. Stokes, who used to silently eavesdrop on Lush and Hampton, said, "I don't know, I used to hear Jacques come up and he always seemed to have more wind than the rest of us. I think his anemometer was broken for one thing, but he did move well, especially when he got near Cape Town."

It became apparent as *Skoiern* slowly pulled away near the finish line that the real race would be for second place. Though both Tada and Stokes often would down-play their rivalry, when the going got tough the adrenalin got flowing. Stokes said, "I knew where Yukoh was every day and I thought I could hold my own against him. But he kept gaining on me. Then, one night when we were only a week out, with light air, what do you know, there he was about two miles ahead." A night-long spinnaker duel ensued, won eventually by Tada.

Both Stokes and Tada got hammered by the same southeaster that plagued Rodgers and de Roux. Tada, who stayed further south after opening up the lead over Stokes, was able to use the storm to his advantage and captured the second-place trophy. After docking in Cape Town, a reporter asked Tada about a questionable tactic earlier in the leg. The Japanese sailor had taken to calling his self-steering vane "Mangero," after the 17th century explorer, John Mangero. He considered the query for a moment and replied, "Perhaps I was below blowing my saxophone. I am only the captain. Mangero is the skipper."

When a BOC staffer arrived to escort Tada to a nearby hotel, for a night ashore Tada misunderstood the offer and declined. He said, "My boat is my hotel."

When Stokes arrived the next evening, his production-built cutter was spanking clean from an afternoon scrub down, as was the skipper. Compared to the disheveled appearance of several of his predecessors, Stokes looked like he'd spent an afternoon puttering about the Chesapeake. That he had sailed his 39-foot production cruising boat nearly stride for stride with the sleeker, custom racing yachts in his division—while navigating by sextant alone, unlike the majority of the fleet who carried electronic satellite navigation equipment—was a testament to Stokes' cagey ability.

Tada was one of the first aboard *Mooneshine* with a cold beer for his new friend. The two sailors, who at a glance were so different in their backgrounds and cultures, were in fact kindred souls. And though at the time they couldn't guess it, the neck-and-neck landfalls of *Okera* and *Mooneshine* were a preview of things to come.

Another pair of sailors arrived on October 30th and November 1st. Neville Gosson, aboard the limping *Leda Pier One*, was the first. He was greeted by Rodney Jenkins, the man who, in his capacity as public relations man for both Gosson's sponsor, Pier One, and the Sydney affiliate for BOC, had informed the world that Gosson was lost at sea (a matter still unbeknownst to Gosson). Gosson was handed an Australian brewed Fosters beer, as Jenkins had been thoughtful enough to fly in 25 cases for the occasion. Gosson declined but it didn't matter; there would be plenty of time for promotional shots the next day. Gosson was exhausted and was immediately whisked off to a hotel but he didn't get much sleep that night. The first phone call was from the Sydney *Telegraph,* then came another from the Melbourne *Age,* and then there was an interview with a reporter from the Australian Broadcasting Corporation. It seemed the phone rang all night and Gosson wondered how so many news organizations had gotten his number so quickly.

For Gosson, the landfall was discouraging. He had hoped to do well on the leg and was downcast to learn he was seventh in his class, only ahead of David White who had dropped out, but after repairs in Florida had restarted.

For Jenkins, however, the landfall was an unqualified media success.

Richard Konkolski followed Gosson in and he did not require a press liason to assure a large media turnout. Konkolski had not spoken to the press since his defection was announced after the race start. The world was eager for news about the Czech expatriot. Only Jeantot and Reed enjoyed a similar reception. Konkolski was gracious in front of the press.

"My conscience would never allow me to fight for the Communist system." he said on first arriving. "And I certainly wouldn't like to see my son forced into the position of having to defend an ideology none of us believe in."

It had been a busy time in Cape Town between the arrivals of Reed and Konkolski. Most of the 10 racers who sailed into Table Bay during that period (and those who struggled in in the days after), found conditions vastly different than those encountered during the majority of the leg. While most of the passage had brought moderate to calm conditions —far too calm for some—the approach to Cape Town offered angry winds and seas when they were needed least. Yet all the racers managed in their own separate ways and, aside from some broken gear and a few blown-out sails, no real damage had been done.

Then disaster struck.

On the morning of November 2nd, a farmer tending his land on the coast north of Cape Town spotted something mysterious floating on the sea. He called the police who sent a launch and divers. The police contacted the air force, which sent search planes. The rescue team first found broken pieces of a wooden hull. Divers recovered some photographs of a sailor with the inscription "Rome" on the reverse side and some woman's jewelry. Later they found a dinghy with the name *Aroha* on the transom, and from this they learned the skipper's identity, an Englishman by the name of Rome Ryott.

Ryott was the sailor Richard Broadhead had encountered just before landfall, the same man who had taken movies and spoken so cheerfully of the race and of the beer they would drink together when they all got into Cape Town. His boat *Aroha* had run ashore and broken like an eggshell. Ryott was lost without a trace, along with an Australian woman who was his crew.

Broadhead heard the news at breakfast the next day. It spooked him. "That could so easily have been one of us," he said.

On that calm sunny morning in Cape Town, he and his mates suddenly realized how hard the rocks of a bad landfall could be.

7

Ghosts

ON HIS APPROACH to Cape Town, Dan Byrne was battered by the same storm that sank *Aroha*. Luckily, Byrne was not privy to that morsel of black intelligence. Knowing that two more ghosts had joined the haunts of the Cape of Storms would not have made his final hours at sea any easier.

Like several other racers, Byrne was lulled by gentle winds as he approached Cape Town. He decided to shave off what miles he could by sailing directly for the city, rather than altering course to the south to find more favorable winds. For Byrne, the magnetic pull of land was greater than for the others. His wife, Pat, was waiting for him and he had now set a record for time away from her side.

When the southeast gale filled in, Byrne was blown well north of his intended course. Thus began the longest two days of his life. Beating into the teeth of the storm, his progress was measured in yards rather than miles. Sleeping and eating were impossible. Whenever Byrne climbed on deck, he was doused with the thick spray that flew over the rail as *Fantasy* met the assault of the oncoming wind and seas. He could blink the salt out of his eyes but not out of the white beard that he had grown during the first leg. It soon became crusty and matted. As the hours passed, a weary, numbing fatigue set in.

While the gale raged on, concern grew at race headquarters set up on the grounds of the Royal Cape Yacht Club (RCYC). Francis Stokes, who had spoken to Byrne over ham radio, was worried about a hazardous section of sewage construction at Green Point. Yukoh Tada somehow missed seeing the illuminated obstacle on his approach and had sailed straight through the waterborne building site.

One local sailor said the odds on such a feat were about one in five, and that if Tada were a cat he'd now be down to eight lives.

Stokes' fears were allayed by Cape Towner Bill Rabinowitz, a veteran Cape yachtsman, who served as a race liaison officer for the Cruising Association of South Africa (CASA). Rabinowitz pointed out that Byrne was approaching in the direction opposite from Tada's. But Rabinowitz wanted to lay out a berthing strategy for *Fantasy* should the storm still be howling when Byrne made Cape Town. Stokes listened politely and answered, "Of course it's hard to say what he'll want to do because we're here and he's out there. He understands his situation better. You know, he has a wife here and they desperately want to see each other."

At 1 a.m. on November 2nd, after Byrne had battled the gale for more than 24 hours, Stokes and his wife left their hotel room and returned to the yacht club. They were met by Pat Byrne and a friend and together they boarded *Mooneshine* and raised Byrne on the radio. Pat, who was working with her husband on a film about the race, had hoped to get an estimated time of arrival so she could coordinate a shooting schedule with a cameraman she'd hired. Byrne radioed back that he just didn't know when the hell he'd get there.

Stokes had a pretty good idea of Byrne's location and warned him to stay clear of Dassen Island and it's "scary looking rocks." He was alarmed to hear Byrne say, "I've got a little problem here." Stokes repeated his warning about the island before signing off.

Byrne strayed closer to the rocky shores of the island than he intended. His "little problem" was potentially disastrous. After combing his chart inventory, he realized he had a full supply of charts for the immediate vicinity south of Cape Town, but he had no detailed chart of Table Bay and the area north of the port. Throughout the storm, he had been sailing blind. Around him lay a wreckage of ships from three centuries of seafaring, yet luck was on his side. He could hear the howling of the ghosts in the breakers on the shore, but this time they were not howling for him.

It took Byrne 12 hours to cover the last 30 miles and his actual arrival into the city was difficult but thankfully anticlimatic. Pat never did get the movie photographer straightened out but it did not matter much. After she boarded the boat, she gave Byrne a big kiss and then stepped back to gaze at her man. The lines in his face, which were more deeply etched and seemed to have multiplied since leaving Newport, were packed white with salt crystals. His white hair had gone uncut and jutted from his baseball cap in erratic wisps. His eyes were puffy and red, and he gave the impression that sleep was mere moments away. He had aged terribly during his two months at sea.

"You look wonderful," Pat said and kissed him again.

Only two more sailors made it to Cape Town before the start of the second leg. Guy Bernardin sailed his 38-foot *Ratso II* across the finish line five days after Byrne and immediately called his voyage "a nightmare." He, too, had challenged the South Atlantic high, but fared worse than either Richard Konkolski or Richard Broadhead.

"I have sailed over 50,000 miles singlehanded and once spent four months non-stop at sea alone," he said. "But this has without doubt been the most frustrating voyage of my life." The long, slow passage particularly rankled Bernardin because of the intensity of thought and purpose he brought with him to the sea.

Richard McBride arrived five days later. *City of Dunedin*, his 35,000-pound steel schooner, needed far more wind that what it found on the leg and McBride arrived just three days before the race restart after a voyage of 73 days. He had every right to feel gloomy and depressed, but his attitude was just the opposite.

"Why not?" he said. "I've just come from a lovely ocean cruise."

Despite the country's reputation, it should have come as no surprise that the layover in Cape Town was a success. Although few of the 300 boats berthed at the RCYC ever venture beyond the local waters of Table Bay, the club has become a crossroads for cruising people and a reliable host for such other grueling offshore events as the fully crewed Whitbread Round the World Race. Cape Town earned the nickname "Tavern of the Seas" because of its hospitable treatment of sailors from all nations.

Sailors, provided that they are "seaman in transit," are allowed ashore regardless of creed, color, nationality and politics, providing they leave with their ship. Local residents, as well as the government, are seriously troubled by South Africa's negative image throughout the world and welcome the opportunity to greet oceanbound visitors on the "neutral" turf of the spectacular port city. Politics aside, however, Cape Towners offered their support and friendship because they knew the danger that lay ahead for the BOC racers. In Cape Town, the sailors received free groceries courtesy of Afrox, the local BOC affiliate; the services of a well-stocked, experienced and competent boatyard, which charged only $25 to haul their boats out of the water for bottom scrubs and anti-fouling—an almost unbelievably low price by standards anywhere in the world.

All this was to prepare the skippers for the specter of the ferocious southern ocean, properly called the Indian Ocean. The most practical survival tool for the next leg, however, came from the BOC Group. At a cost of nearly $200,000, BOC decided to purchase the services of System

Argos, a satellite-based position reporting system. With an Argos transmitter mounted on each boat, race organizers would receive daily position reports for each boat. In addition, the individual terminals were fitted with an alarm button that could be activated in case of emergency. And, should a racer be forced to abandon his boat and take to a life raft, the transmitter could be carried along, furnishing rescuers with accurate position fixes. Not only was System Argos a safety measure, it also was good public relations; being able to report each sailor's daily position would give the two coming southern ocean legs the atmosphere of a horse race.

Originally designed as a meteorological tool, the system was first used in yacht racing in the 1980 OSTAR. Overall, it got mixed reviews, mainly because several of the transmitters simply stopped working. But the technology advanced quickly and several subsequent French races had employed the system with nearly flawless results.

One drawback to the transmitter platforms was that their batteries are good for only 180 days. For that reason, and because conditions were expected to be light in the first leg, the BOC Group held off procuring the system until Cape Town. From Cape Town on the batteries would last long enough to cover most of the fleet back to Newport.

Aside from the practical considerations, Tony Lush welcomed the system for a more subtle reason. While Jeantot had followed the rules regarding communications to the letter in the voyage from Newport, officially reporting his position to race headquarters once a week, it still rankled Lush that Jeantot had been able to slip away unnoticed.

"I gather he was reporting in quite regularly to his French sponsors but they didn't give out the information as often as he was putting it in. These next legs, with the Argos, should be a bit more interesting as long as we get the information passed back to us."

The mood shared by the skippers in the final days in Cape Town was jocular apprehension. They all knew the southern ocean was a widow-maker, but with the help of the Cape Towners and the new Argos system they felt well prepared.

One issue, however, broke the calm surface, revealing just how edgy some of the skippers really were. The sailing directions for the second leg stipulated that the route would be Cape Town to Sydney *by any course.* Paul Rodgers, however, felt strongly that the island of Tasmania should be made a mark on the course and left to port, thereby eliminating the "shortcut" between the island's northern coast and the southern shore of Australia, a passage of water known as the Bass Strait.

"There are two reasons," Rodgers said. "The Bass Strait is notorious for its unlit rocks and oil rigs. You take a singlehander who has been at sea, pushing a boat for a long time, and it's easy to make a mistake when there are added obstacles. And a mistake there could easily cost him his boat or his life. Generally speaking, in solo racing, if you lose the boat, you lose your life.

"Secondly, there is the matter of completing a circumnavigation via all five of the great southernmost capes. To go through the Bass Strait, one avoids South Cape on Tasmania, and so completes only a four-cape circumnavigation. It may be a small point, but sailors do not get down this way often."

The one true authority on the Bass Strait, having sailed there several times, was Neville Gosson. When first questioned about it, the day after his arrival in Cape Town, he was ambivalent.

"From a seaman's point of view, it's probably better and safer to go around Tasmania. But it's longer and, as far as getting your Christmas cards on time, I just don't know. The guys are going to get itchy feet and want to take a shortcut through the strait. I'm quite happy to go either way. But if they leave it up to me, I'm going through the strait 'cause it's quicker."

But Rodgers was persuasive. After presenting his argument to Gosson, he found a convert. In the skipper's meeting prior to the restart, Gosson aired his new feelings about the issue. "In my view," he said afterwards, "we should avoid the Bass Strait. First of all, the shipping routes for the south coast of Australia are concentrated there. Also, we have lots of currents there that still are uncharted. The water is shallow and the seas kick up fairly high and we get some stiff breezes there. And, you have to sleep somewhere, sometime, in Bass Strait. To make Tasmania a mark of the course has the advantage of keeping us out of there, and adds the cape for those wishing to complete a five-cape circumnavigation. I have put myself on record with the sailing committee and feel it would be irresponsible of me as an Australian if I didn't register my protest and have it seen on record that I didn't think we should go through Bass Strait."

For its part, the race committee registered the dissent but chose to avoid the issue. There was nothing written into the rules forcing any competitor to navigate through the channel. The decision to negotiate Bass Strait or avoid it was left to the individual skippers themselves. For Rodgers, in particular, the non-decision was a disappointment. Yet he seemed to be clutching at straws, because as the racers prepared to set out for Sydney, the least of their problems, in fact, was the Bass Strait. There was a long, stormy stretch of ocean lying between the southern coasts of Africa and Australia, and of all the racers only Rodgers, Desmond Hampton and Richard Konkolski had ever seen it firsthand, and only Rodgers and Konkolski had sailed there singlehanded. (The Czechoslovakian had transited the Panama Canal, thus avoiding Cape Horn, but he had rounded the Cape of Good Hope and crossed the Indian Ocean.)

But stories of the Roaring Forties are legendary and every sailor had an inkling of the conditions that might be encountered. The region's unsettled weather is caused in part by a continuous series of eastward-moving low pressure centers. They vary in size and strength, and can strike with very little advance warning. Prolonged periods of winds in excess of 35 knots are not unusual, even in midsummer, and such winds can build waves as large as a block of city buildings. When caught in the fury of a southern ocean storm, there is only one strategy: survival.

As if this bleak picture was not intimidating enough, another hazard existed to worry the lone voyagers—icebergs, calved from the great ice shelves of Antarctica. Their size and number are frightening: Bergs of five miles in length are not uncommon, and as many as 4,500 have been reported in a run of 2,000 miles. Their positions fluctuate from year to year, and while it would seem there should be more of them the further south one traveled, there is no guarantee of this.

As the racers pored over their pilot charts and sailing directions to plot their routes, one saving grace was that, unlike the first leg, the southern ocean route had precedents. The first round-the-world race in 1969 had passed this way. All of the BOC skippers studied the routes of these trailbreakers, Robin Knox-Johnston's path in particular. But the skippers were more interested in the routes used by the fully crewed boats in the previous three Whitbread races. Bill Rabinowitz, in his trim moustache and straw boater, provided a wealth of information regarding courses and conditions in past races. Strictly speaking, CASA was not in favor of singlehanded sailing because it violated the COLREGs, (international rules of the road) that a lookout must be posted at all times at sea. However, because such races are a reality, CASA felt obliged to lend its considerable expertise to make the event as safe as possible.

The main difference between the crewed boats and their solo counterparts was in how far south each could sail to find the shortest possible course. The fully crewed boats, which could keep a sharp lookout for ice at all times, would sometimes sail as far as 60°S in their quest to cut miles from the route. The singlehanders, by necessity, would need to be far more conservative, and few planned to venture beyond 50°S.

Knowing the history of past Whitbread races, while helpful, was a double-edged sword. In the first event in 1973, two sailors were lost in the second leg while sailing a fairly conservative course from Cape Town to Sydney. The circumstances surrounding both losses were particularly eerie. North of Kergoulen Island at about the halfway point, the skipper of the French yacht *33 Export* was lost while helping to clear a sail from the foredeck. His safety harness was secured to a lifeline. A large wave knocked the boat and hurled the sailor the length of the yacht. His crew watched helplessly as their skipper's harness clip tore off the tops of the lifeline stanchions like so many dominoes. When he came to the stern rail, the harness broke and the skipper was tossed into the sea forever. On the British yacht *Tauranga,* an army corporal was lost after falling overboard while working on deck. It was the second time he'd gone into the sea, but it was one time too many, and the ghosts of the southern ocean claimed him.

The BOC sailors knew these stories, and others, but rarely spoke of them. In the days before setting out from Cape Town, there was much to be done, and it was not time for counter-productive thinking. Like soldiers on the eve of battle, the fears were based largely on the unknown. Each sailor readied himself in a different way.

On the inside steering console aboard *Credit Agricole,* Jeantot attached a small, bright-red sticker that read simply, "Panic Button!" When asked about it, he grinned and said, "Just in case, that is for the southern ocean." Though Jeantot was smiling, he was only half kidding. His lead was large, but it was fragile. A broken shroud, a failed fitting, a toppled mast and it would all be gone.

Jeantot, like the others, also rechecked his radio equipment and became familiar with the new schedules. "It will be important for the boats to talk together, especially because of the ice," he said. "If someone sees ice, he must tell the others."

Stokes, in his usual thorough manner, was covering all the bases. He said, "I talked to Desmond because he's sailed to Australia from here, and I talked to Bertie Reed, because he knows so much about the area. And I'll read my *Ocean Passages* again. I don't plan on going too far south. I don't hanker after boisterous winds. My boat is small and I can't take advantage of lots of wind, so I've got to play it pretty conservatively."

Gosson looked forward to the heavier conditions. He said, "It'll be more of a test of boat handling than navigation and forecasting. The guys who are out of their bunk, constantly trimming, will do the best. We'll all have wind this time."

The three skippers of two-masted boats all hoped to better their first-leg showings.

Lush had two new carbon fiber spars fitted aboard *Lady Pepperell* for added stiffness and to reduce deflection aloft.

Hampton said, "*Gipsy Moth* should do well. She really needs a good blast up her backside. Twenty-five knots abaft the beam is her kind of weather."

And Rodgers, as usual, put things in an interesting perspective. He said, "Traditionally, in singlehanded events, a two-masted vessel is better than a sloop. I've been amazed to hear the guys in sloops say their time will come. If the sloops are going to be hot again down there then I might as well take the Easter bunnies with me."

But of all the skippers, Tada was the most industrious. His first project was to build a meditating platform. He carefully averaged out his normal angle of heel when under way, and then built a small bench with the "seat" measuring the same 20-degree angle. When placed in a corner of his cabin while at sea, Tada had a flat, stable platform on which to meditate.

Tada hoped he never had cause to test his other Cape Town invention. On the bow of *Koden Okera V,* the Japanese sailor built an eight-foot long fiberglass lance that was anchored to the boat by a steel bobstay. The intended purpose of the ram, in the unhappy circumstance of running into ice floes, was to deflect an iceberg away from the boat and save the hull from a collision. "It is my insurance," Tada said, "in case of accident. But maybe I capsize and sink in southern ocean, anyway. I will go singing my sutra." Tada laughed nervously as he spoke, but the thought, he knew, was not funny.

Several days before leaving Cape Town, Tada held court in a corner of the yacht club bar with several yachtsmen and passersby. He had secured a small cache of imported saki and whenever a new face joined the circle he would rush to get another glass, produce a new bottle and pour another round to the amusement of all.

As the day drew on and the wine kept flowing, Tada's stories, punctuated by much laughter and grand gesturing, became more and more outrageous. A close acquaintance of Tada's began telling a story about the Japanese sailor's deformed hand, which was not noticeable until specifically mentioned. Tada caught on and, trading lines with his friend, continued the tale.

"My village is poor, in snowy country, but is famous for samurai (warriors). The general, Shigeru Fukudome, who makes Pearl Harbor, is from my village. So, when war ends, U.S. air force presents my village with many fire bomb."

A year later, in 1946, 16-year-old Tada attempted to detonate a bomb in the hills outside his village. It exploded in his hands, nearly costing him an eye and burning much of his torso. The point of the grizzly story is made when the friend explains that during the voyage from Newport, Tada broke his left index finger when trying to tame a flailing jib sheet.

"So, Yukoh," said the friend, "now you've got two bad hands."

"Yes," replied Tada, laughing. "But still got three good legs."

By late afternoon the party broke up. Tada, who had been the host and center of attention all day, became melancholy. Over tears, he asked Machai Sakai, a friend and free-lance journalist covering the race for the Japanese yachting magazine *Kazi,* why the other racers got free hotel rooms while he had to stay on his boat. His refusal to take the hotel room offered him upon his arrival, it seemed, was based on economics. Mrs. Sakai explained the misunderstanding to the public relations people handling race affairs, and soon Tada was whisked off to a nearby hotel.

Once in the hotel, an exhausted Tada stretched out on the floor to get some rest. Two companions, who'd escorted him to the room, soon became alarmed at the depth of his slumber. They tried to shake him from his sleep.

Tada, in his dreams, was very alone and very far away. He was in the southern ocean, in a storm. He could feel the violent pitching as his small boat, like a warrior, resisted the sea's endless siege.

One of Tada's escorts feared he might never wake up. He rushed to the bathroom, filled an ice bucket with cold water and poured it in his friend's face.

Tada, still unconscious, could feel the boat breaking up, the water seeping through the hull. He was sinking, and he was not singing a sutra. He awoke screaming in Japanese. He tore at the wall and at the baseboard radiator. He needed to get out of the boat to save himself. Then he realized he was not at sea at all, but in a small room in a high-rise building. Deflated, he slumped against the mauled wall with his face in his hands, weeping.

Tada had taken his first look at the southern ocean.

8

Sailing Through the Wall

IN MARATHON RUNNING and other athletic tests where sheer endurance is a requisite, there exists an unnerving physical and spiritual barrier known as "the wall."

It is a curious phenomenon. Marathoners, in particular, know all about the wall. It invariably greets them at the 20th mile, making the final six miles as difficult as all the preceding.

Physiologists define the wall in scientific terms. It is the point at which all available energy reserves are spent. The body's personal checking account—including all that was left for a rainy day—is withdrawn. The effects can be disastrous. Depression sets in. Winning or losing becomes irrelevant. The event itself loses all meaning. Instead, the wall offers an individual a distinctly inward confrontation that transcends the competition.

To pass through the wall—to go beyond and reap the rewards and benefits that wait like an oasis on its other side—the physical being must be released and bid farewell; the desire to prevail becomes a controlled exercise in willpower. Some athletes, through intangible resiliency, are able to face the wall, pass through it, and draw strength from its conquest. Others, who cannot pass, find ways around it, or even under it. Then there are those who cannot penetrate the wall or trick their way past. These are the losers.

Each of the BOC skippers knew, sooner or later, he would ride over the crest of a monstrous wave and find, waiting in its trough, his own terrible version of the 20th mile. But, like runners, they figured they'd each discover their rampart at different times, under different circumstances. None guessed that the majority of them would face it on the very first night out of Cape Town.

The gale that ripped through the fleet just hours after the start shredded the carefully-knit fabric of community that the racers had worn during the first leg and the layover. It raged for two straight days and scattered the boats like a small boy scatters toys. The storm had no prejudice and played no favorites. It blasted everyone with wholesale abandon. To the sailors who had hoped to dip their toes into the southern ocean and then, like children on a tide-swept beach, scamper away before finally plunging in, that inaugural storm was the wall in all its sobering reality. It was as rigid and awe-inspiring as Table Mountain itself.

The mood throughout the RCYC clubhouse on the morning of the November 12, 1982, starting date for the second leg was hardly eager. Outside, the wind was screeching at 50 knots. Merely unmooring the boats would be a mission of grand proportions. There was some talk of postponing the start for a day until conditions improved.

But as the hours passed the wind gradually receded, and as the 3 p.m. starting time drew near, the breeze pulled a disappearing act altogether. Only 13 sailors assembled for the restart. David White, who had rejoined the race, was just approaching Cape Town and would arrive later that day; South African Greg Coles, who had started the race from Newport 11 days late, was still more than a week out; and Richard Konkolski suffered a back injury earlier in the day that delayed his restart for five days. The light air brought on a feeling of well-being and complacency after the morning's big blow. It did not last long.

At the starting line, Yukoh Tada was in a feisty mood. Most of the skippers had prudently avoided shaking the reefs out of their mainsails or hanking on their big genoas after the earlier, severe winds. In the minutes before the gun sounded, they sat at the helms of their undercanvassed, barely maneuverable yachts, as they drifted lazily in the direction of the starting line and the waters beyond. Only Tada had set his self-steering vane. While he tended to matters on the foredeck and busied himself below, *Koden Okera V* began a pattern of unattended 360° turns. Appropriately, Tada was donning the crash helmet that he and the other sailors were given in Newport, to protect them from ice falling out of the rigging in the extreme southern latitudes.

On the first revolution, *Okera*'s swing came close to the stern of *Perseverance of Medina*. Richard Broadhead yelled to Tada to come on deck and steer his "bloody boat" but his calls went unanswered. On the second pass, *Okera* veered off on a course straight for the self-steering gear on *Perseverance*. Broadhead banged his knee hard on a winch as he ran aft, and then let go with a few choice words for Tada as he hung over the transom and fended *Okera* away. To these Tada did not take kindly, and let Broadhead know by doing a brief imitation of karate star Bruce Lee on his foredeck. It was the high point of the start.

In the first three hours after the starting gun sounded, the fleet made only five miles. Then, at dusk, came the first gentle inkling of a breeze. Within minutes, the whisper grew to a full-fledged, howling gale, directly out of the southeast. The winds seemed familiar to many of the racers; they were the same obstinate winds that had buffeted them during their landfalls. But there was one difference. On the approach to Cape Town, there had existed the option to turn tail and run with the storm. Now, with the winds still coming from the direction they wished to sail, there was nowhere to run or hide. The lee shore was the continent of Africa.

Jacques de Roux, in his halting English, summed up the situation succinctly. He said, "When we left Cape Town, we had no wind at the line of departure. Four hours after, we have received 50 knots, perhaps more. Our course is southeast but it is difficult to do because of the strong wind. Some of the ships are obliged to do a southwest course and go toward Argentina in South America. Only four ships go in the right direction— *Voortrekker, Credit Agricole, Gipsy Moth,* and *Perseverance.* All the other ships go to the south or the southwest. After the first day, the four ships have a big advance because they manage to sail past the southeast coast. I was not one of those ships."

Through luck and skill, and the considerable advantage of sailing the larger boats in the fleet, Bertie Reed, Philippe Jeantot, Desmond Hampton and Richard Broadhead all escaped the full wrath of the first storm. Their early days were, on the whole, miserable and uncomfortable—but tolerable. Their ability to get in the groove with little drama paid high dividends over the length of the course. But they were by no means home free. Their appointments with the wall were postponed, but not canceled.

Others did not fare so well. Aboard *Skoiern,* a sail not reefed in time was blown out. On *Spirit of Pentax,* a combination of halyard and winch problems forced Rodgers back into port before the day was out. And by midnight, a radio message from Dan Byrne relayed a laundry list of serious problems with *Fantasy* and the disheartening news that, he too, was turning around and heading back to port. Byrne and Rodgers ran headlong into the wall and both careened backwards. They would, however, be back for a second try.

Those still at sea were coping as best they could. For Francis Stokes aboard *Mooneshine,* the storm was a demonic teacher who did not overlook subtle details. It taught the 56-year-old sailor lessons he thought he'd learned long ago. In his log for the second leg, Stokes made the following observations for the entry that covered the first two days out of Cape Town:

"There had to be a Rude Awakening and it was quick. The race start was a disappointment. Patches of 35 knot winds outside the breakwater gave way to nothing further out. Choosing the right sails was a no-win proposition. I used the 70 percent Yankee and double-reefed main taking out the reefs right after the start . . . Philippe had his Mylar 150 genoa up but it didn't do any good. I took pictures showing *Mooneshine* ahead, just for the record.

"Wind came to us outer boats first as it was getting dark. Great. I watched *Credit* heeling over and felt smug with my conservative sail choice. Soon I had to reef and then got the staysail down. I could see *Credit*'s mast light moving off to leeward as Philippe changed sails . . . I remember keeping *C.A.*'s light in sight for some time but the wind increased and I had to take down the main. The small Yankee was still too much sail. I ran off to take this down and we seemed to be going six knots under bare poles. For reasons unknown now I did not get the storm jib on. It was indecision and the fact that the storm jib was all tidy and inaccessible in its turtle instead of ready to go. So, I lay ahull, and so much for my aggressive racing image . . .

"You lose track of time. I lay on the starboard settee, boots and foul weather gear on, from time to time looking out for ships or other boats. I don't know if I was asleep but there was a trememdous crash and I felt the boat roll and I was showered with books, canned goods and water which could only have come from the bilge. The G-forces are considerable as the boat is struck by a breaking wave and lands with a jolt in the trough. I have no idea whether the mast went in the water. We're such creatures of gravity—all you know is something is really wrong when it's black and things are falling on you from God knows where . . .

"All was secure (on deck) except the new hatch dodger was in shreds. I had already begun to like it, too. From the deck, the waves did not look that big, but the wind was certainly hard and there was no thought of putting on sail . . .

"My race preparations included the expectation of being dumped just like this—but not yet. In the back of my mind I knew that the books and canned foods stowage was not really secure . . . Books belong in cartons not on shelves . . . The radios by good luck were just out of line of fire . . .

"What a night. I saw lights of three ships coming at me. With no sail, I felt rather vulnerable and put out calls on the VHF radio, getting no response. In the cockpit, the seas did not seem terribly threatening as I watched the ships but I didn't need any prompting to use the safety harness . . .

"Weather was no better in the morning and I knew I was doing very badly race-wise . . . I went into the (second) night with just the storm jib and things looked secure enough. The waves surely did not look dangerous and I slept in the aft cabin with the board in place. At some time in the night—I have no idea when—there was that same awful crash. My head hit the door jamb and I was on the floor, really shaken. There was the same mess in the cabin except for the cans of food I had put in cartons. Two volumes of Gibbons' *Decline and Fall (of the Roman Empire)* again flew from port to starboard . . . Dirty pots from the sink were on the chart table. This time we didn't go so far over but if anything it was more violent—like being in an auto accident. I was and am very sore on the left side.

"*Koden* and *Spirit of Pentax* were also knocked down by waves. There is something unusual in those waters off the cape, at least when the southeaster is blowing.

"Besides my ribs, I was most concerned by the radio. It wasn't right when I called Alastair on the morning net and then quit altogether. I found water had found its way into the fuse holder . . . Then I couldn't find a spare and had to cut the fuse holder out of the power leads. It's now okay though I know it received water on its innards about which I am ignorant and helpless. This is my only communication link and I will cover it with plastic and padding in bad weather henceforth. My DR (direction finding) radio also blew and is broken but I think I can glue it together.

"So much for the first two days of this race."

Stokes was dazed but not defeated. When the weather began to moderate soon after, he slowly and cautiously began adding sail and making his way both south, towards 40°S, and east, towards Sydney. His sore ribs, which were painfully bruised in his second knockdown, would continue to plague him for the better part of his journey. But Stokes was careful to think out his movements before attempting them, and was soon back in the middle of the Class II pack.

Of all the skippers, only Tada found the wall more intimidating, and hence, more challenging. His 44-foot boat, *Okera,* was at six tons extremely light for her size due to her fiberglass and carbon fiber construction. Lightness equates to speed in yacht design, but *Okera* was conceived as a downwind boat. The heavy pounding she took as she inched her way into the teeth of the gale quickly took its toll.

The boat's one saving grace was its incredible strength. Tada had dropped all his sail but steering was impossible. *Okera* bounced and rolled like a raft shooting the rapids. Tada was knocked down to 120 degrees twice, dunking his mast in the water each time. Several times the boat was thrown literally on its side, and remained flat and motionless for endless moments until the weight of the keel slowly righted the craft and readied it, like a bowling pin, for the next breaking sea. Tada gave up counting his crash landings. Later, recalling the ceaseless bucking of his first days at sea, he said, "My boat like rodeo."

Okera suffered her worst damage on the first night. Tada had rigged a sail to the outer point of his "bergsprit," and left it unattended when conditions turned for the worst. The combined pressure of the wind on the sail and the confused, lumpy seas proved to be too much of a strain on the spear, and within hours of the start it snapped off like a wishbone. Tada was able to repair the four small holes left in the hull ("My construction very bad," he said), but his problems were just beginning. Next to go were the slides on the mainsail track that secured the sail to the mast when it was raised or lowered. These popped off like buttons on an old shirt and left Tada with a huge flapping sail to corral and a lengthy sewing job when the weather cooperated. Another gear failure occurred on the second night, when his spinnaker pole, which was attached to a small storm sail hanked onto his forestay, snapped like kindling after taking the brunt of an especially vigorous gust. The total effect of the breakage was not crippling or irreparable—but it took its toll in terms of the boat's seaworthiness and Tada's peace of mind.

If the storm's carnage had confined itself to wreaking havoc on *Okera*, Tada probably would have emerged with his understated confidence well intact. But after battling the storm for two straight days, by the third night Tada's stamina ran out. He collapsed in his bunk while the gale surged on. He awoke under a pile of rubble. "It was first time I sleep in oilskins and helmet," he said. "I feel too tired, so I was deep sleeping. Then *Okera* is knocked down. I wake up at that moment and cover my face in blanket. I feel heavy weight on my body. My sewing machine and my saxophone. My sewing machine likes me very much."

Lying under his pile of possessions, Tada chose an interesting next step. He tugged on his construction hard hat, reached over his bunk to adjust the videotape camera that had been installed in his cabin by a Japanese television network (another was mounted on the boat's stern), switched the device on, and in calm and steady tones described exactly why he was wearing a plastic headgear in bed with a jazz instrument and groceries in his lap. It was an absurd reaction, but a therapeutic one. When Tada did arrive in Sydney weeks later, and showed the tape to several friends over a small portable screen in *Okera*'s saloon, he gave the impression that, under the circumstances, there wasn't much else to do.

However, his ordeal was far from over. Several days later, just when *Okera* was once again a going concern, Tada took a nasty spill that, like Stokes', would also take weeks to heal. While working below, *Okera* was jolted hard by a breaking broadside sea. Tada, who was not holding onto anything, took off as though a rug had been pulled out from under him. Airborne, he flew across the boat, stopping only when his ribs rendezvoused sharply with the corner of the chart table. Tada went down in a heap. The awful hurt in his side was at first accompanied by a strange tingling in his legs, but soon the sensation matured into a dull ache. He slithered across the cabin sole and managed to rise just enough to slump into the refuge of his bunk.

"This condition lasted five days, maybe one week," he said. "I did not know if my boat moved south or east, I did not know. Next day I try hard pressure on ribs, Chinese finger pressure. Then I make vinegar and potato poultice. It got better. One week later maybe, I get my heading. But I walk like ant on deck. Small moving."

Tada and Stokes both endured close encounters with the wall in those first awful days of their journey to Sydney. But once they had passed the threshold and learned their vessels could withstand just about anything if they could, they realized the worse was behind them.

Three of their fellow skippers did not fare as well. Paul Rodgers was the first to be stopped by the wall. Equipment problems had forced him back to harbor within hours of the start. Moreover, Cape Town had been a difficult port for Rodgers to leave in the first place. He had stopped and made friends there before, when his quest to sail alone around the world twice without stopping was halted by damage to *Pentax*. When Rodgers sailed away that time, he left behind a girlfriend and fond memories. Upon his return in the BOC race, he learned the disturbing news that his old heart-throb was engaged to another man. Rodgers exhibited poise in the light of feigned tragedy and ran signal flags aloft aboard *Pentax* spelling the name "Julie" in honor of his lost love. At the top of the tribute, he added a homemade banner—a ragged scrap of cloth emblazoned with an arrow-pierced heart.

A reconciliation with Julie during the layover did nothing to boost the intrepid side of Rodger's nature, but with resignation he was determined to sail on and complete the race. His strained pocketbook and limited financial resources also hampered his effort. But he was able to unjam his halyards and have his winch serviced within hours of returning to port. He set out from Cape Town a second time on Sunday the 14th, a day behind the fleet.

Trouble soon descended on Rodgers again. Running before a large sea soon after setting out, *Pentax* flipped over and began surfing upside-down —more like an overturned kayak than a 55-foot steel sailboat—for what Rodgers estimated to be more than 125 yards before righting. The jolt loosened the boat's large centerboard. Later, in 45-knot winds, the self-steering gear was wiped off the boat's stern. *Pentax,* difficult to control in the best conditions, was coming apart a piece at a time. The final nail in the coffin was losing the use of the main compass when it mysteriously ceased to function properly. Rodgers, low on money and not keenly ambitious for the masochistic and daunting voyage in front of him, considered the options and decided that a summer in Cape Town with pleasant company far surpassed risking his neck at sea in a broken boat. It was not one of the tougher decisions Rodgers ever had to make and he soon was berthed at the RCYC. Little did he know, he was soon to have company.

For David White, the BOC race had become a long series of lofty expectations and shattered dreams; the chance for greatness had landed in the palm of his hand, but had slipped away before he could clench his fist. In Newport, several local yachtsmen and observers questioned White's commitment to the race from early on. Organizing a race of such magnitude is one thing, they said. Actually sailing it is quite another. When word got back to town soon after the race began that White had taken a hard right and was heading towards Florida, there was more than one "I told you so" making the rounds of the waterfront grapevine.

But while White had discovered that the dual roles of race administrator and sailor/boatbuilder was one task too many, his sheer desire to compete and win should never have been questioned. If winning had been a matter of raw courage—if, for instance, the victor was chosen by demonstrating his ability to step off a high building or drive a sportscar at 150 miles an hour—then White most certainly would have won. But as Philippe Jeantot and Jacques de Roux had learned and were proving, courage was important, but finesse and sound judgment were the qualities that win races.

When White hit the wall the first time, six days after leaving Newport, he thought his race was over. After radioing his intention to retire, White stashed his charts of the Atlantic Ocean and dug out the ones of the Caribbean Sea and the coast of Florida. He was certain the whole thing was finished. He only wanted to make it to Sarasota where he could put the race and his ignominious failure behind him. He was down and he thought he was out.

But once he got to Florida, he ran into some old sailing buddies who helped him change his mind. After inspecting the damage to *Gladiator* and offering their time and skills to make the necessary repairs, his friends convinced him to make repairs and set sail once again. The first leg was a write-off, they reasoned, but there were still three legs to go and if he made exceptionally good time, he might even make the Cape Town restart. It was early in the race, and White himself had said that in a 27,000-mile voyage anything could happen. Even if he couldn't win the whole thing there was still the possibility of taking first in one of the legs, and after the effort it took to make the race a reality, he at least owed himself that.

White had quit the race on September 5. On September 21, he started out again for South Africa, this time from Fort Lauderdale.

His Florida departure was a particularly poor place from which to sail through the doldrums, which cost him more time. But once into the

South Atlantic, he began averaging better than 180 miles a day with many days more than 200 miles. *Gladiator* was fast, but she was still fragile. Off the coast of Brazil, White once again noticed telltale signs of stress on the forward bulkhead, and relayed the information to race headquarters. In Newport and in Cape Town, many still speculated whether White would be able to continue the race after the first leg. Still, it was heartening for all concerned, with the exception of Jeantot, to see there was a boat with the capability of going stride for stride with *Credit Agricole*.

White arrived on the afternoon of the restart, and could make out some of the sails of his departing mates as he made his way into Table Bay. It was the last he'd see of them as a competitor. Unwittingly, he sailed smack into a Catch-22 situation. A last-minute rule change before the Newport start dealt with time limits. The rule stated that for each class, no competitor would be allowed to start after 30 days had elapsed from the time of the first finisher. Jeantot had arrived on October 13. White's arrival date was November 13. He was one day late. But because of the extenuating circumstances involving the damages, the race committee ignored the rule.

Four days later, White began his pursuit of the fleet. Before he got far, an unsympathetic system of low pressure overtook *Gladiator;* it did not pass by until it had blown a large portion of the boat's self-steering gear into the sea. His backup system, an electronic autopilot, packed up soon after. With no self-steering, and 7,000 miles of the world's stormiest waters ahead, there was no alternative but to return to Cape Town.

White immediately ordered a new part for the electronic unit from its English manufacturer. The company responded by immediately putting the wrong part on a plane for South Africa. It was the final straw. When the piece arrived, White checked the Argos positions of the fleet, now more than 1,000 miles away, and waved them goodbye. This time, he meant it. He could have gotten the correct part eventually and he probably even could have made the next start in Sydney. But the three or four-day layovers he figured to get in each port were barely enough to get caught up on rest, and should repairs be necessary at some point in the race there simply would not be enough time.

There was now no possible way to make a race of it. With nothing to win, there was little incentive to sail on. White had built his own wall brick by brick and then proceeded to run right into it.

One other skipper could not make it past the Cape Town barrier. At 26, Greg Coles, a native of New Zealand who had taken up residence in South Africa, was the youngest and least experienced sailor in the fleet. From the outset, the cards had been stacked against him. Coles' boat, *Datsun Skyline*, was from the design board of South African Richard Glanville. The lightweight carbon-fiber hull, with an unconventional wing mast, catboat rig and hydraulic keel—experimental features all—was eas-ily the most radical yacht in the fleet. Coles had helped build the boat but was actually the third choice for skipper, and had been unceremoniously offered the helm when the first two candidates backed away. There had been trouble getting *Skyline* to the States, and when Coles finally sailed into Newport the rest of the boats had been gone well over a week. The sail from North Carolina, where the boat had been off-loaded from a freighter, to Rhode Island had served as Coles' qualifying sail for the race. It was the first time he had singlehanded a sailboat.

By necessity, Coles was anxious to get under way, so his turn-around time in Newport was brief. There had been a problem with the mast on the delivery trip but there was little time for proper repairs. His strategy for the first leg seemed to include a generous allowance for crossing his fingers until the boat got to South Africa, where there would be ample time and resources to put the boat right. On the morning of the day Coles started—trailing the fleet by 11 days—the scene aboard *Datsun Skyline* was one of high confusion. Richard Glanville's father sat at the base of the mast patiently cutting empty Budweiser beer cans into tiny strips, which he jammed into a gap between the mast and the deck, as one might do with a matchbook under the wobbling leg of a table. It was not a reassuring sight. Meanwhile, Coles was busy trying to accomplish several tasks at once so he could get started with a favorable northerly breeze. The smartest thing he did during those last days was to call Rob Koziomkowski in Portsmouth, who came down and said hello to Coles and informed him of the radio schedule he was monitoring.

Coles' voyage seemed cursed. On his first night out he hit something hard—he suspected a whale. In the light of day, his worst fears were founded. On the base of the mast, a small but visible crack had opened. In addition, the movable mast was locked into a position that made *Sky-line*'s one huge mainsail set in a peculiar position. Because of the crack, Coles feared sailing the boat on starboard tack. Thus hampered, he had to sail into head winds rather than reaching off for the steady trades that the rest of the fleet had sought after. For support, Coles chatted on the radio with Koziomkowski. Often.

It was fortuitous that he did, for in Koziomkowski he found a helpful and willing ally. Two weeks into the journey, he sailed into a collision course with Hurricane Debbie, which was bearing down from the east. He called Koziomkowski and told him he was turning around, but Kozi-omkowski would hear none of it. He told Coles in no uncertain terms to hold his course, advice that was grudgingly taken. Within 48 hours, the storm veered off to the north. Had Coles turned back, he would have sailed directly into its path.

The voyage of *Datsun Skyline* was long and slow. But while approaching

Cape Town, Coles was treated to a startling revelation. During an especially frustrating day with little wind or progress, Coles unreefed his mainsail and even hanked on a small headsail. Unexpectedly, the wind kicked up abruptly, sending the boat over on its ear. When she popped back up, Coles could barely believe his eyes. Not only was the mast still standing, but the boat had come alive and was sailing . . . very, very fast. In the week before pulling into Cape Town, *Skyline* made consistently fine times and even managed 230 miles during one 24-hour period—an amazing speed for a 44-foot yacht.

The fleet had a two-week head start by the time Coles arrived on November 27, but Richard Glanville already had assembled a work crew and had new mast parts machined so that *Datsun Skyline* would be ready as soon as possible. Upon inspecting the wounded mast, he discovered a sorry piece of news. The crack in its base was merely in the cosmetic plaster that was added to keep the tincan shims in place. Structurally, the rig was as sound as the day it left the shop.

As the time neared for Coles to once again set out, there were loud whispers around the RCYC, of which Glanville was a member, that *Datsun Skyline* should not be allowed to continue the race. Like White, Coles had finished more than 30 days beyond the winning time of Jacques de Roux —but because the rule had been changed for White, it was waived for Coles as well. Still there had simply been too much trouble with the boat, and Coles just didn't have the miles under his keel to withstand the arduous journey that waited ahead. Coles himself was not overly thrilled with what lay ahead in the southern ocean, nor was his girlfriend. But he felt a strong allegiance to the Glanvilles, who had put their faith and trust in him; and the Glanvilles, in turn, felt committed to the boat's sponsor, Datsun automobiles, which had helped bankroll the project. In the end, Coles made up his mind to continue and prepared to give chase to the other racers, not one of whom he had ever met.

If there was one incident that characterized the *Datsun Skyline* campaign, it was epitomized by a strange occurrence that happened the night before Coles was to leave. The Glanvilles and Coles spent a long day at the boatyard and were returning home late in the evening to pick up the remaining gear that had to be brought aboard for the trip. When they turned up their street, they saw their home, or rather, the place where their home once stood, was a pile of smoldering embers. The house had burned to the ground, consuming not only all their possessions but also all of the food, navigation charts and logs, sails and rope that Coles needed for his voyage.

Tempting fate, new goods were rapidly bought, including a set of secondhand sails for another boat that were somewhat sloppy but seemed adequate. Uncertain at best, Coles set out on December 7. But on the second day out, while chatting over the radio to Cape Town, he learned his Argos system was not sending a signal to the South African recording station. Then, with the disturbing news fresh in his mind that there would be no automatic Mayday button to push, Coles' radio ceased operating. Later, Glanville was informed that the Argos signal was coming through clearly in the States, but through oversight had not yet been programmed to Cape Town. But by then, it was impossible to pass the word on to Coles.

With the Argos system, race followers were able to plot a steady course as *Skyline* bore away from the coast. Then, they watched the track make an abrupt about-face, and begin returning to Cape Town. A small crowd was waiting when Coles returned to the RCYC, expecting that perhaps the boat was damaged. But *Skyline* was unmarred and Coles in good spirits as he pulled alongside the dock for good. When first the Argos and then the radio failed him, he recalled Koziomkowski's advice regarding the hurricane, and how his ham pal also had boosted Coles' confidence by saying he could make it if he had good communications. But once the communications went, so did Coles' resolve. Returning beaten but whole, Coles' final decision as skipper of *Skyline* was seamanlike and responsible. For him, the wall had won convincingly, but if the opportunity rose again, he would be around to give it another shot.

While Coles' exodus from Cape Town proved to be ill-fated, that of his fellow countryman, Bertie Reed, appeared at the outset to be blessed. Armed with vast amounts of local knowledge and well rested after his time at home, Reed took off from the cape city like a scalded cat. For the first three days of the voyage he held the lead, and even after surrendering the top spot due to the unalterable fact that he sailed a slower boat, he continued a fine pace. Reed didn't know it, but lying just over the horizon was a blind date with the wall.

His first problem, and one that was plaguing several other sailors—Jacques de Roux and Richard Broadhead in particular—concerned his self-steering gear. After a fast first week, Reed's wind vane system became ornery, then stubborn, then nearly intolerable. Every day it seemed a new problem arose, and it compounded the previous day's trouble. Reed said, "Self-steering is a real hassle. There's just no self-steering that's been designed to drive a light boat that accelerates as fast off the wind as *Voortrekker*. If it's not working properly, you can lose 20 to 30 miles a day, which adds up on a leg that's over 30 days long."

But although the self-steering unit proved to be an annoyance of the highest degree, it was something that could be overcome, even if it meant long and boring hours at the helm. But during his second week at sea, a dilemma presented itself that could not be rectified simply by applying strong willpower. It was just the sort of predicament that could cost a man his life.

Reed said, "About two days into the race I had a diesel leak. When I was trying to fix it I broke the fuel pipe on the side and it sprayed all over my arm. It was really stupid because I know about diesel; it's bad news. Anyway, the diesel sort of got in my pores and the next thing I know my arm is going lame. So as well as a messed-up steering system I had a lame arm. It was difficult changing sails but I had to keep going. Eventually I got ahold of Alistair over the radio and asked for a kitchen remedy. I knew there had to be something. He suggested sugar compresses so I dumped it into this open wound that was sort of a lump the size of an egg. After the sugar, it kept discharging like soggy macaroni just pouring out of this lump on my wrist. For four or five days the arm was going all red, and the glands were swelling under the armpits. I thought of trying to get to Amsterdam Island. Then it started to go blue and I thought if it kept up I'd eventually have to get rid of my arm."

Reed's grisly tale had a shadowy parallel in the history of singlehanded sailing. In 1942, a famous Argentinian solo-circumnavigator, Vito Dumas, began a journey from South America to Africa. From the very beginning of the sail, Dumas was living a nightmare. Later he would write, "I knew before I started it would not be a joyride, but imagination always falls short of the truth."

An early, violent storm left his boat, *Legh II,* with a serious gash in her wooden hull. While trying to stem the flow of water into the boat, Dumas cut his right hand. In the morning, it was infected and useless. He gave himself an injection to combat a rising temperature and went to bed. The next day brought no relief, and a steady temperature of 104°F. While attempting to administer another shot, Dumas dropped the needle in the bilge. It was hours before he could locate it, disinfect it and take the medicine.

By the third day, with no improvement, he realized there was only one alternative. "My arm was dying and dragging me along with it," he wrote. "It was septicemia. I could not give in without playing my last card. With an axe or my seaman's knife, at the elbow, at the shoulder, I knew not where or how, somehow I would have to amputate . . .

"On that unforgettable night was born a fervent prayer—my only hope. I commended myself to little St. Theresa of Lisieux; I asked her help; and I lost consciousness.

"I do not know how long it was but (later) I awoke . . . As I moved, my arm felt lighter. Thank God! There was a gaping hole about three inches wide in my forearm; pus was flowing from it."

Reed's recovery, similar to Dumas', came swiftly and unexpectedly. It

Bold and brash, race founder David White in **Gladiator** (*top*) promised to lead his 16 rivals around the world. Before the start, he slapped a pair of boat shoes on the dock (*bottom left*) to ensure his victorious return. But behind the façade hid an uncertain and ill-fated man. Others prepared differently. Yukoh Tada (*at left in bottom right photo*) imported a Zen Buddhist monk from Japan to bless himself and the fleet. (Photos, clockwise from top, by Herb McCormick, Bernadette Brennan and Dale Nouse.)

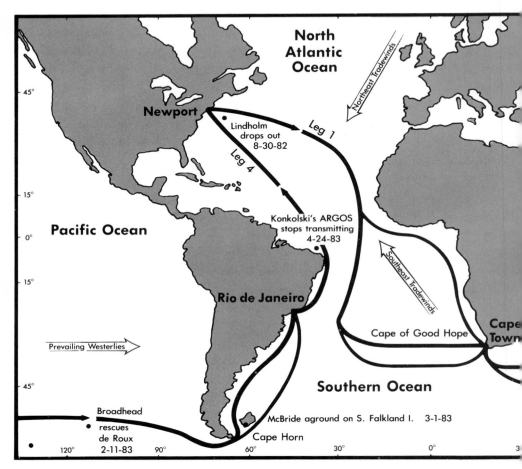

45°

North
Atlantic
Ocean

Northeast Tradewinds

Newport

Lindholm
drops out
8-30-82

Leg 1

Leg 4

15°

Pacific Ocean

Konkolski's ARGOS
stops transmitting
4-24-83

0°

Southeast Tradewinds

15°

Rio de Janeiro

Cape of Good Hope

Cape
Town

Prevailing Westerlies

45°

Southern Ocean

Broadhead
rescues
de Roux
2-11-83

McBride aground on S. Falkland I.   3-1-83

Cape Horn

120°   90°   60°   30°   0°   3

Four Legs Around The World

Those who raced around the world race visited the farthest reaches of the earth. They were tested by storms and calms, by strong currents and icebergs. Only 10 of the original 17 completed the 27,500-mile course and it took them eight months to do it.

Starting in Newport, Rhode Island, on August 28, 1982, they sailed first to Cape Town, South Africa, along three tricky routes, depending on each skipper's racing strategy. Leg II carried the sailors into the storm-swept Southern Ocean, where American Tony Lush nearly lost his life. After stopping in Sydney, Australia, the fleet set off for Cape Horn and the last stop in Rio de Janeiro, Brazil. Along the way, Frenchman Jacques de Roux lost his boat. Cape Horn proved the crowning test of the arduous race. The final leg, Leg IV, carried the sailors home, to Newport, where they became the newest members of the elite corps of solo circumnavigators. (See Appendix I for more information on routes and weather.)

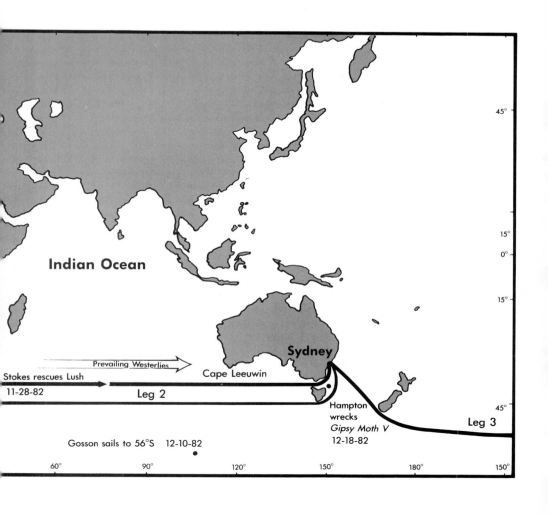

Indian Ocean

45°

15°

0°

15°

Sydney

Prevailing Westerlies

Cape Leeuwin

Stokes rescues Lush
11-28-82

Leg 2

45°

Hampton
wrecks
Gipsy Moth V
12-18-82

Leg 3

Gosson sails to 56°S   12-10-82

60°   90°   120°   150°   180°   150°

The August 28, 1982 start was dramatically won by Nike II, *whose skipper, Richard Konkolski, had announced his defection from Czechoslovakia that morning. Just six weeks earlier, Konkolski and his family (bottom right) left their homeland forever. Californian Tom Lindholm (bottom left) became the race's first casualty* (Photos by Bernadette Brennan.)

Screaming through the southeast tradewinds, the 56-foot French cutter Credit Agricole *(left) built a hefty early lead. Skipper Philippe Jeantot (right) nearly ran out of water and arrived in Cape Town with a strong thirst. New Jersey grandfather Francis Stokes worked wonders with his production boat. (Photos, clockwise from left, by Philippe Jeantot, John Rubython and Bernadette Brennan.)*

Tenacious Bertie Reed (top) got the most out of his 49-foot Altech Voortrekker (center). French racers (bottom) Guy Bernardin, Jacques de Roux and Philippe Jeantot had the most to prove. (Photos, from top to bottom, by Roger Kennedy, John Rubython and Patrick Riviere.)

Englishman Richard Broadhead (left) was shy but not timid. One of the youngest in the fleet at 29, he had previously worked as a cowboy in Australia and a plantation manager in Brazil. His boat, the 52-foot Perseverance of Medina, was designed for crewed ocean racing, not solo adventures. But she was a magnificent sight reaching past Cape Town's Table Mountain. Broadhead's voyage was the most arduous of all who finished. (Photos by Barbara Lloyd, top, and John Rubython, bottom.)

Of the 17 starters, Californian Dan Byrne seemed one of the odds-on favorites not to finish. His yacht **Fantasy** (above) was hull number one of the popular Valiant 40 line, and also one of the smallest boats in the fleet. Byrne himself was an ex- L.A. Times *newspaperman with limited singlehanded sailing experience. Off Cape Town, his worst fears were almost realized when his boat began to fall apart beneath him. But after a shoreside reunion with wife Pat (right), his luck changed.* (Photos by Chris Cunningham, top, and Roger Kennedy, bottom.)

A wealthy Australian businessman, Neville Gosson (top) shocked both friends and business associates when he boarded his 53-foot aluminum **Leda Pier One** (bottom) in the midst of a major real estate project and set out for America and the race around the world. It was his first attempt at crossing an ocean alone. (Photos by Patrick Riviere, top, and Chris Cunningham, bottom.)

Paul Rodgers' (inset) wild Spirit of Pentax *(above) did not make it past Cape Town. Dick McBride (bottom left) grounded* City of Dunedin *in the Falkland Islands, yet he finished the race. Greg Coles started late and then dropped out. (Photos, clockwise from inset, by John Rubython, Bernadette Brennan, Chris Cunningham and Stewart Colman.)*

On November 11, 1982, Tony Lush's 54-foot Lady Pepperell *(top)* suffered mortal damage under a Southern Ocean wave. Lush radioed for help. Twenty-four hours later Francis Stokes arrived and saved his life. The two sailed together to Sydney *(below)*. (Photos by Bernadette Brennan, top, and Patrick Riviere, bottom.)

Racing for Leg II line honors, Desmond Hampton (inset) struck disaster. On December 18, 1982, he overslept and sailed Gipsy Moth V *onto Australia's Gabo Island. Making no excuse, Hampton blamed the wreck on "human error." He salvaged what he could from his boat and then flew by helicopter to a Christmas reunion with his wife Kitty and their children.* (Inset and top photo by Ace Marine; photo at right by Patrick Riviere.)

The greatest sea rescue of all time: On January 9, 1983, Jacques de Roux's sloop Skoiern III *(bottom) was rolled and dismasted. In mortal danger a thousand miles from land, de Roux set off his emergency signal. His only hope lay with Richard Broadhead on* **Perseverance of Medina**, *350 miles away. Broadhead (top, foreground) altered course and 59 hours later found de Roux, his boat awash beneath him. Four hours later,* Skoiern III *sank. Broadhead saved de Roux's life, but he couldn't have done it without the help of the world-wide ham radio network, which coordinated the rescue effort by communicating each boat's position. (Photos by Herb McCormick, top, and Chris Cunningham, bottom.)*

In Sydney, the fleet moored at Pier One (above), where Yukoh Tada (below left) played his sax and put on an art show. At the start of Leg III, Richard Broadhead tangled with a starting buoy (inset). Francis Stokes' self-portrait while rounding Cape Horn shows the strain of the journey. (Photos, clockwise, from inset, by Herb McCormick, James Latter, Francis Stokes and Herb McCormick.)

Light winds and lazy days led up to the start of Leg IV in Rio. The closest contest was between Francis Stokes on Mooneshine and Yukoh Tada on Koden Okera V (top); their rivalry was not resolved until the finish. Frenchman Guy Bernardin's 38-foot Ratso II (below) was the fleet's smallest boat. (Photos by Herb McCormick, top, and Lise Torok, bottom.)

On May 9, 1983, Philippe Jeantot sailed Credit Agricole *across the finish line in Newport to win the race and to break the round-the-world, singlehanded record. Although lionized by the press, Jeantot said,* "It was the friendships that made this race special to me." (Photo by Dan Spurr.)

was only partly a case of Divine Intervention, and partly a result of the sugar compresses, antibiotics and massive doses of vitamins with which he treated himself. But his brief and perilous experience of teetering at the top of the wall, not knowing which way he would fall, left a lasting impression. During the remainder of the voyage to Sydney, Reed often came up on the radio. But rarely did he speak of the trouble with the self-steering equipment hung over his stern; the thought of coming so close to losing a far more important appendage did not leave him. No longer did the long hours with the hand locked to the tiller seem so bad.

At the start of the race, Richard Konkolski had plenty of reason to believe that his defection was surely his most difficult hurdle. But he never figured on the long, windless days on the first leg. Then, on the eve of the second leg, with a fresh start and another chance beckoning, the curtain went up on the second act of Konkolski's luckless play.

In Cape Town after his long trip, Koskolski had had little time to sort out his affairs before the restart. The boat did not require much work, but there were genuine personal distractions regarding his family, who had remained in Newport.

On the day before the start, Konkolski slipped a disk in his lower back while lifting a sheet of plywood. The pain, sharp and intense, told Konkolski with unquestioned authority that he would not be sailing anywhere in the next 24 hours. Konkolski consulted local doctors, whose advice was contradictory. One wanted him admitted directly into a hospital. Another advised against continuing the race. Eventually, Konkolski reached a compromise with the physicians after convincing them of his need to sail on. He promised to wear a corset at sea. After five days of rest, and with large doses of painkillers, the husky Czech wriggled into his supportive underwear and got underway.

In retrospect, Konkolski's late departure was a blessing in disguise. It was also the first justice he had received since the day he sailed into West Germany and told his son they had just become free men. Sailing behind the fleet, he was spared the devastation of the first storm, so he rapidly got *Nike II* settled into true racing rhythm. Finally, things were beginning to fall into place.

"It was a very great feeling," Konkolski said. "Every day I am catching somebody." Within 10 days Richard no longer needed to take his pain pills (though he still wore the corset), and in that time he had, incredibly, sailed past the entire Class II fleet with the exception of Jacques de Roux. He was in second place by a mere 60 miles.

"It was something that really picked me up," he said. "But maybe it pushed me to risk much more. Maybe I carry too much sail."

Just when Konkolski was beginning to make a real boat race in Class II, his luck once more ran out. A mere half day behind *Skoiern III*,

Konkolski opened a book recounting other round-the-world races and decided that a memorial service was in order.

"I passed near the place where the first man died in the first Whitbread race. So, I drew a picture of a flower and put it in the water. It was a tribute, like flowers on a grave. Also, I did not want it to happen to me. Then, four hours later, when I am below, I hear a loud noise in the rigging. It sounded like a shot."

Always fearing a reprisal from the Soviet Navy for his defection, Konkolski had cause to believe he'd heard live ammunition. During the first leg, his position was a secret known only to the inner circle of the race organization. There had been strange, anonymous phone calls requesting his position, so it was not posted on the board with the routes of the other sailors. In the second leg, Argos routes passed along to the press falsified *Nike II*'s true position. Konkolski sailed with the thought that retribution at sea—perhaps a perfect elimination—was a distinct possibility.

But when Konkolski ran on deck, the horizon was empty. He looked up the mast hesitantly, afraid he would see the rigging dangling from above. But the mast and its supporting wires were standing true. Then he looked down on deck and there, just forward of the mast, lay an albatross. It was dead.

"It looked big," Richard said. "But he was very light. Maybe he tried to fly close to the sails. But he hit my forestay instead. He had broken wings and he be very dead. I feel very sorry for him. I was going to take some feathers for my son but I said no. I threw him into the ocean. Then I felt something bad would happen. It was bad luck, like an old sailor's story. Albatross have souls of dead sailors."

Later that night, Konkolski's premonition came true.

A combination of a building westerly wind rushing against the resisting force of an overabundant amount of sail area pushed *Nike* over on her side while her skipper was below. By the time he was able to undo the bolted hatches, scramble topsides and lasso the sails on the yawing, pitching boat, his main and foresail were severely ripped. And the forestay, a "wire rope" that helps support the mast, was flailing about like a wire bullwhip. Worst of all, his engine had been running to charge the batteries. Richard shut it down. The next day, it went out for good.

Of all the boats in the fleet, only *Nike II* relied exclusively on electrical power to run his self-steering. Without a way to change batteries, the system was worthless and catching Jacques de Roux was no more than a sweet dream.

And there was no radio, so he could tell no one of his plight.

Konkolski could not even flick a switch and have light. He knew then, that he would do no better on the second leg than he had on the first. He needed to repair *Nike* and the only place he could safely reach for repairs was Fremantle in Western Australia.

Konkolski had cleared a small fence, only to find the wall waiting for him on the other side.

9

The Second Happy Life
of Dan Byrne's Fantasy

THAT FIRST LOOK at the southern ocean at the start of Leg II was chilling. For Dan Byrne aboard *Fantasy*, the gale that struck just off Cape Town made real all the fears he brought to the race and to the southern ocean in particular. Byrne hit the wall and it transformed him into a humbled, quivering man, forced by his adventurous longings to stare his own mortality squarely in the face. It was an encounter that would make or break the adventure of sailing alone around the world.

By midnight the first day out the wind had built from a dead calm to 50 knots. The rigging screamed and the confused swells grew larger and more erratic by the hour. The night promised to be long, wet and cold. Byrne reefed the main and then went forward to drop the working jib, which he left on the headstay but tied to the stanchions before hoisting the storm jib.

"During the course of the night the wind rose to 60 knots. It caught the folds of the secured sail, lifted it and then shredded the top three panels. I was getting pretty well pounded. The boat was getting hit by waves and below it sounded like sledgehammers hitting oil drums."

During the night *Fantasy* broached to 75 degrees, very nearly putting the mast in the water. On *Fantasy*'s stern, were two large solar panels for charging his batteries, mounted on aluminum frames attached to the stern stanchions. The wave that knocked *Fantasy* down bent one of the panels in half like a piece of soft bread.

Losing his solar panel was just the beginning of the carnage that made that night the most memorable of his voyage around the world. On deck he lost the jib and the mainsail halyard. The boat was crippled. Down below, the furniture began to break loose. *Fantasy* resembled a house hit by an earthquake. The large water tank under the port settee berth in the main saloon came adrift and shifted into the middle of the boat, bringing the settee with it. The canned goods stored behind the berth were scattered throughout the cabin interior. Byrne was concerned that he had holed the water tank. But after inspecting it closely, he found only a broken water pipe, which was not a critical piece of damage. Nevertheless, he lost all the water from the tank into the bilge, leaving him with only half his water ration after only 24 hours.

"Okay, all well and good," he said, "but all of that was not really enough for me to go back to Cape Town. Then an odd thing happened. The starter switch was shorting out on the engine causing it to start spontaneously. I got very concerned, so I decided to start the engine deliberately. I heated the glow plug on the diesel and fired it up. Then I heard this god-awful noise. The starter switch was shorting out and the starter motor was engaging while the engine was running. I said, 'Oh my god, I'm going to rip up the Bendix gear (on the starter motor). What the hell can happen next?' Well, I turned off the engine and tried to stop it and then the ignition switch burst into flames. By that time I was really rattled. It didn't dawn on me to switch off the battery, which was driving the starter, so I just pulled the wires out of the back of the ignition switch to stop it.

"So, there I was without an ignition switch and about 100 miles south and west of Cape Town, the wrong direction. Most of the boats were being blown down that way, too. I took a look around at the damage. The cabin was a mess, the engine was lost and the mast partners were leaking. So, I decided to go back to Cape Town to get repaired."

Byrne put the helm over and headed back, his tail very much between his legs. He was able to raise Cape Town on the radio and managed to reach his wife, Patricia, before she departed for the United States.

"Hold on, I'm coming back," Byrne radioed. So Pat Byrne held on while her husband spent the next 24 hours retreating from the maw of the southern ocean.

Of all the men who made it to the starting line in Newport at the start of the race, Byrne was the least likely to finish. A large, rugged man of 53 with a weathered face, he looked like an outdoor entrepeneur—a rancher or the operator of a ski resort. Byrne looked his best when squinting purposefully at the horizon and one might have expected him to be arrogant and full of bravado. But that was not Dan Byrne. A career reporter, writer and editor for a number of different news organizations

—a career that ended when he retired at the age of 51 as editor of the Los Angeles Times Syndicate—Byrne had a disarmingly genuine and frank manner. He was very human and very vulnerable. But while vulnerability might be an asset for a writer or editor, it had no place in the Roaring Forties.

If temperament was not on Byrne's side, neither was his boat. He was sailing one of the three production cruising boats in the fleet. *Fantasy* was hull number one of the Valiant 40 line. She was a husky double-ender with a long keel and a cutter rig, but as a production boat, she had not been designed for singlehanding nor to round Cape Horn. To make *Fantasy* more seaworthy, he added two large cockpit drains, bolted angle irons to his water and fuel tanks (the braces proved insufficient), replaced the standard ⁵⁄₁₆-inch rigging wire with ⅜-inch wire, rigged running backstays for the staysail and replaced his steering cables with heavier wire. Still, there was nothing Byrne could do to transform her into either a new or single-purpose boat.

For three years, *Fantasy* was his escape from the frantic, air conditioned, fluorescent-lighted hubbub of the *Los Angeles Times*. In her, he had gone off to seek solitude, first in the 1979, 300-mile Marina del Rey singlehanded race and later in the 1980 singlehanded Transpacific Race from San Francisco to Hawaii and the 1981 Guadaloupe Island (Mexico) Singlehanded Race. Even so, he was relatively inexperienced. In all, before the round the world race, he had sailed only 6,500 miles and of those only 3,500 were sailed alone. He was hardly in the same league with Francis Stokes, despite the similarity of the two men and their boats. Only Richard McBride in the funky steel schooner *City of Dunedin* knew less about offshore singlehanded sailing.

The open sea to the south of Cape Town is a long way from Santa Monica, California, or Marina del Rey or the newsroom at the *L.A. Times*. As a newsman, Byrne by profession was an expert at summarizing events quickly and lucidly, a master at giving names to circumstances most people find unnameable. What he had to name after the first night out of Cape Town was his own raw fear.

One can speculate on the range of headlines that could have run through his head as he slowly worked his way back to port. "California Solo-Sailor Lost Without A Trace." Or, "Monster Waves Disable Former *L.A. Times* Editor." Or, "Storm Foils Byrne's Fantasy To Circumnavigate." The headline most accurate at the time might have read, "Byrne Retires, A Beaten And Frightened Man."

An exhausted and discouraged Byrne approached Cape Town. It was time to quit.

"As I was coming in I kept rehearsing stories I was going to tell Pat that would explain why I had turned back. I thought I could say I had hurt my back and couldn't go on. But it was a lie and she would know right away. Then, I toyed with the idea of telling her that the boat wasn't seaworthy. The interior was broken apart, a mess and the rig was a shambles. But I knew it wasn't true. In the end, I really didn't have a story palatable enough to peddle either to Pat or to friends in California."

When Byrne arrived in Cape Town, his wife, a big, ebullient blonde brimming over with enthusiasm, met her husband on the dock. She was ready to do what was necessary to repair *Fantasy* and get Byrne underway again. But Byrne was unenthusiastic. He felt beaten and in Cape Town he found the gale had beaten a few others as well. Paul Rodgers had returned after the first day, and restarted. But after getting clobbered again south of Cape Town, Rodgers returned to retire once and for all. David White, who had arrived in Cape Town three hours after the fleet had started the second leg, got underway three days later only to lose his self-steering in a knockdown. He, too, sailed back to the safety of Table Bay and to the bar at the Royal Cape Yacht Club. Greg Coles was out with a disabled boat and a lagging time on the first leg. And, two months earlier, fellow Californian Tom Lindholm had retired, when he suffered sail and engine damage just after the start of the first leg.

Byrne could have slipped into this pattern of failure. Nothing could force him back into the cold and wet and wind of the southern ocean if he did not wish to go. The race was his to sail or not. The lies he had conjured during his slow trip back into port had not washed with Byrne. He had not pawned them off on his wife or anyone else. "But I still wasn't sure I could go on," he said. "I still toyed with the idea of telling Pat that I was physically incapable of going on."

But he never did. Once back into Cape Town, he had *Fantasy* hauled at the shipyard where the BOC fleet had been serviced during the layover and he and the yard mechanics got to work. He never let on just how close he was to abandoning his dream.

Fueled by his wife's optimism and energy, Byrne persisted. The sail was repaired and the halyard retrieved. Belowdecks, the water tank was bolted back into place under the port settee berth and then the berth above it was repaired. A mechanic sorted out the wiring to the ignition and found the short that had caused the problem. Byrne's attitude was changing as the boat was repaired.

"I was continually surprised by the support I got, and it made me remember how strong my obligation was to continue the race."

In the year prior to the start, Byrne had committed himself entirely to the race. He was not only going to sail alone around the world, but he planned to make a movie and write a book about the adventure. His actor friend, Hal Holbrook, already had consented to voice-over the narrative for the movie. In order to drum up support for *Fantasy*'s entrance in the race, Byrne wrote and printed a sophisticated brochure, called *A Personal Odyssey Alone Around The World,* which he circulated to the Oceanic Society, members of the Pacific Singlehanded Sailing Association of Marine del Ray, 500 companies and 100 book publishers.

In it he wrote, "The purpose of this adventure is to fulfill the dream of navigating a sailboat alone around the world.

"There is, however, a subordinate purpose—to produce in print and on film a detailed, personal record of one man's fulfillment of a dream so that other men and women who dream of high mountains, vast seas and unknown shores will be emboldened to dream on, then to plan and, perhaps, to do."

Quitting in Cape Town would make a lousy ending to a book or movie about fulfilling lofty dreams. Byrne had built around himself a trick box. There was only one way in, Newport, and only one way out again, Newport. Along the way were many apparent exits and many obstacles to overcome. But he had made so many promises to so many people, had signed a book contract and secured the support of his old friend Holbrook—also a singlehanded sailor—and had committed himself so totally to the "idea" of the race, that he simply could not quit. Continuing the race came down to a matter of pride.

The work on *Fantasy* was completed in six days. Byrne now had to face sailing back out into the southern ocean. He procrastinated and complained about the weather. Pat Byrne urged him on. He was reluctant. She said, "Finally, I told everyone that he was leaving at three in the afternoon and then when the time came, I untied the lines and cast him off."

Byrne marched backwards back out to do battle and did so with fear and trembling. "I was timid. I was waiting for the ocean to really live up to its reputation. I kept kind of sticking my toe into the lower latitudes testing the water temperature."

Nevertheless, he was under way again. Despite having a hard time getting himself psyched to sail south into the Roaring Forties to find the wind, he was still fulfilling his dream, still meeting his obligations and, most importantly, still honoring his promises to himself. It was a difficult threshold to overcome. By coincidence, the sea did not choose further to torment him.

"Finally, I got down to 40°S," he said, "and things started to go nicely, other than a five-day period when I ran into easterly winds. The starboard tack got me furthest east, and that was good, but it also was carrying me north out of the Forties. So I got up to about 38 degrees latitude. Finally I said, 'Screw it, if I have to go due south or even southwest, I'm going to get back down there.' And then I really started to go. I had one day's run of 192 miles and there were a lot of days when I had the fastest day's run in the whole fleet between Argos fixes. This encouraged me immensely."

Byrne was getting better speeds out of his 40-foot production boat than everyone in his class except de Roux in *Skoiern III* and Konkolski on *Nike II*. He was overtaking everyone. But, most important to him, he was catching Stokes aboard *Mooneshine*. Stokes was Byrne's hero, a true seaman and offshore sailor, the kind of sailor and man Byrne himself wished to be. And if Stokes exhibited one quality that Byrne admired most, it was his intelligent calm in the face of terrifying winds and seas.

"I felt a lot of anxiety after I left Cape Town," he said. "I kept saying to myself, 'What the hell am I doing this for?' After all, it's one thing to read about heavy weather in books, but when you spend day after day out there, you're always wondering what's going to happen next, always asking yourself when will one of those big graybeards come crashing down on my stern? Ha, the answer was, they were crashing down on Francis' stern and didn't come close to me."

Stokes suffered bad weather to the south where the low pressure systems were moving persistently eastward in the Forties. Byrne, meanwhile, had fair weather and winds of 25 to 30 knots. It was the advantage he needed and he recovered many lost miles. At one point, *Mooneshine* was 1,100 miles in front of *Fantasy*. But by the time Byrne got to the east coast of Australia on his way to Sydney he had clipped nearly 700 miles off Stokes' lead. Byrne had one good sailing week after another, often making 1,100 miles in seven days and averaging approximately 157 daily miles through the water. Once Byrne got into the groove, the voyage almost seemed charmed. The sky stayed clear and the wind blew steadily from the west. *Fantasy* suffered no more breakdowns. And, when Byrne reached the Bass Strait, the narrow passage between Tasmania and Australia—the shortest route to Sydney—he had winds on his tail and clear visibility.

In the Bass Strait, *Fantasy*'s charmed run really paid off. Byrne cleared the major islands within Bass Strait, and next had to sail through an area littered with offshore oil rigs before he would gain clear water. It was dark but the lighthouses on the islands and the lights on the oil rigs gave him good piloting information. Then a very scary thing happened.

"I was piloting through the rigs visually," Byrne said. "I was taking care and knew exactly where I was. There was one last rig to pass and it was lit up like a Christmas tree. I had been taking 30-minute naps with the kitchen timer to wake me and I had plenty of time before I got to the last rig to grab another 30 minutes. My course led right at the rig, so I thought after my nap I'd see how we stood and decide whether to take the rig to port or starboard. I went down below, set the timer for 30 minutes, lay down and slept for four hours.

"When I woke up I realized I had overslept. I ran up on deck and the rig wasn't even in sight. I had obviously passed it, or sunk it, or something."

But he didn't hit it.

The sea does not care about the men who sail over it. Only sometimes is it benign. Byrne's luck in finding good weather and in missing the oil rig brought him into Sydney with the second fastest elapsed time in Class II. De Roux led the way, yet even to be breathing down de Roux's neck was a triumph for Byrne. He had sailed out to face the southern ocean, failed and retreated. He had sailed out again to make a remarkable passage. The man who sailed into Sydney was not the Dan Byrne the other racers and those following the race had known in Newport and Cape Town. He had grown calmer and more self-assured.

In his promotional flier he tried to put into perspective what it means to undertake a sailing voyage around the world. "In a circumnavigation in the high latitudes of the southernmost Pacific, the Roaring Forties, the modern sailor stands watch with Magellan's mate and Drake's helmsman. Four centuries separate them in time, but they are one in place and circumstance."

Byrne had to struggle to attain that place and circumstance. But in the end he had legitimately made them his own.

10

Sinking Is not Logical

WHEN TONY LUSH's voice crackled faintly through the ham radio receiver, Alistair Campbell knew at once that trouble was brewing. Alistair, a sugar farmer sitting before his ham radio set in the basement of his farmhouse in landlocked Uzumbe, South Africa, had heard a sailor's urgent call before. And he knew how it could end. Just a year earlier, a young American professor on the yacht *Drambuie* was caught in appalling weather off the Cape of Storms. He needed help at once. But help was a day away. Campbell was the last person to hear the sailor's voice. *Drambuie* was lost without a trace.

Although the American sailor was a stranger, Campbell had come to know many of the singlehanders in the BOC race. He had maintained radio contact with several of them on their approach to Cape Town in the first leg, passing along weather reports and position updates. When the second leg began, just 17 days earlier, he continued his regular daily schedule. This schedule, however, did not include Lush, who carried a single-sideband radio, not a ham unit, aboard his 54-foot *Lady Pepperell*. So the fact that he'd come up was puzzling.

Lush's cryptic message did little to clarify the situation. "I have structural damage but am in no immediate danger," the static-filled voice said. Then the airwaves went silent.

Lush's problems first had appeared in the dead of night nearly 12 hours before his conversation with Campbell. The weather and seas had been heavy throughout the evening but not alarmingly so. Certainly they were not as severe as the gale that tore through the fleet the first night

93

out of Cape Town, blowing *Lady Pepperell* far to the west of her intended course and leaving Lush with a bad case of the blues. It had taken him the better part of two weeks to fall into his seagoing routine and get his boat moving reasonably well.

Throughout that time, it had not been the high winds that wreaked havoc with *Lady Pepperell* and the nerves of every skipper so much as the confused seas. While everyone generally assumed they would encounter big waves, they also expected the waves would come in long rollers from astern, allowing boats to run with them, rather than bash against them. But the waves rolled from two and sometimes three directions—against the wind, with it, alongside it, without rhyme or reason. The seas had been close and steep—"short squat suckers" is what Lush called them. The resulting ride was miserable. Other than curse, there was little to do. On the night before calling Campbell, after a long day of being pitched about in his light boat, Lush hove-to. He had a bit to eat, doused all sail, set the electronic autopilot and went to sleep.

The roar of the ocean boiling under *Lady Pepperell* awoke him. Lying in his bunk he felt the 54-footer do something very odd—it was like he'd just slipped over Niagara Falls in a barrel. First there was the weightlessness, then a strange sense of vertigo as in a dream about falling. Despite the rude awakening, Lush escaped without injury.

Lady Pepperell did not fare so well. As goes the old paratrooper joke, it wasn't the fall that hurt so much, but the sudden stop. Half asleep at the time, Lush had no idea what his flight dynamics had been. But once day broke, the severity of the knockdown was apparent. His two masts were standing, but the instruments and lights at the top of the mast were broken off. The entire rig had been submerged.

Belowdecks was a shambles of books, food and everything else that was not tied down. The most annoying item was the jar of raspberry jam that had been stashed in the sink. There was jam on the chart table, in the bunk and smeared on the deckhead—though not a shard of glass was to be found.

Piecing the evidence together, Lush figured *Lady Pepperell* was lifted by a huge wave and then thrown forward into the trough while at the same time being rolled more than 90 degrees—"a swan dive with a twist," Lush said. But although it had been a nasty incident, Lush reckoned he'd dodged the bullet. The spars were standing; the mess could be cleaned up.

Then he noticed that his floorboards were floating.

At first, it looked like the bilge pump had somehow come loose and malfunctioned, but that didn't make much sense. On closer inspection, he discovered the terrible truth: The keel—the backbone of his boat—had loosened with the jolting crash. He didn't seem to be taking on water at the time, so he calmly took a pencil and made marks in the bilge to record the outer movements of the swaying keel.

It was then he realized that *Lady Pepperell* was not going to make it around the world.

Still, Lush had a sizeable investment at stake, especially in the time he'd spent working on the boat and the commitment he'd made getting her ready to race. Though his keel was moving, he felt he could save the boat. Even as he spoke with Alistair Campbell, he was formulating a plan to get his yacht to a port where it could be repaired. He had two choices. He could return to Cape Town or head towards Durban, South Africa, which was about 500 miles closer. However, distance was not really a consideration. To make Cape Town, Lush would have to sail directly into the teeth of the prevailing winds, *Lady Pepperell*'s least favorite point of sail. Also, the resistance and strain on the disabled keel would be immense. The boat would surely break up beneath him.

Durban was the more logical goal and Lush is nothing if not a logical man. With a little luck, he reasoned, he could sail a roundabout course to safety by taking advantage of favorable reaching winds, thereby easing the pressure on the keel. He studied his charts and penciled in an ideal course. First, he would head due north, then gradually bear off to the northeast. Finally, when he was well above the Roaring Forties, he would get the easterly breeze that would push him gently back to South Africa. All he needed was a little cooperation from Aeolus, the god of the wind, and a little luck.

With the decision made, Campbell alerted and the wind directly from the north, Lush breathed a little easier for the first time in many hours and settled back to wait for the southerly to fill in.

The path that led Lush into his formidable predicament—bobbing about in a time bomb of a boat thousands of miles from his home—was a winding one, indeed. He was born in England 33 years before, the second of 11 children fathered by a NASA space engineer. Lush was not born into a nautical family. In fact, he spent most of his childhood in the Mojave Desert, where his family moved when he was young. In his early 20s, when most world-class sailors are well into their second decade of sailing, the extent of his yachting experience consisted of about a dozen daysails in rented dinghies.

After attending college in California, Lush gathered his belongings and headed inland. In 1974, while pursuing a masters' degree at landlocked Michigan State University in East Lansing, he was struck by an idea that soon consumed him. Though he'd never done any woodworking other than a dining room table, and had never been offshore in any kind of boat, Lush decided he would construct his own sailing vessel, sail it alone across the Atlantic via the Great Lakes and the St. Lawrence Seaway, and then race it home in the '76 OSTAR (the *Observer* Singlehanded Transatlantic Race).

By necessity, Lush became a boatbuilder before he became a sailor. He named his simple creation *One Hand Clapping*. It was a 28-foot plywood Viktor Harasty design, intended for weekend trips along coastal waters. To rig the boat, Lush sent to England for a copy of Jock McLeod's book *Design Your Own Junk Rig*. When the book arrived, he went about doing just that.

His first voyage, across the North Atlantic to Plymouth, England, for the race start, was a memorable one. "I had gales all the way across," he recalled. "But of course I didn't know it." Lush was the last finisher in the 1976 OSTAR, the 75th sailor to cross the finish line after a voyage of 61 days. It was an admirable accomplishment; 51 other competitors quit the race, including two who vanished at sea. Lush never considered not finishing. His motivation ran deeper. "I wanted to see if I really liked sailing."

After the courtship came the serious romance. Lush went to work in Gainesville, Florida, as chief engineer for Hunter Marine, a builder of fiberglass sailboats. He bought himself another boat, overhauled it completely and sailed in the 1980 OSTAR, finishing in 39 days.

When Lush first heard about the singlehanded round the world race being organized in Newport, Rhode Island, he immediately began planning to compete. While Lush was still a college student, Joshua Slocum's *Sailing Alone Around The World* had captured his imagination. To chart his own course through those same oceans now seemed the appropriate thing to do. Methodically, Lush began setting his priorities for the race and how to achieve them.

First and foremost, he needed an appropriate boat. As a boatbuilder, that was a problem easily solved. Lush persuaded his boss, Warren Luhrs, an accomplished solo racer himself, to sell him the materials and lend him the facilities to build a modified Hunter 54, the company's top of the line boat. The deal was contingent upon Tony finding a sponsor. Lush planned to make a few changes to the standard production version. He wanted to lengthen the boat's keel to make her more sea-kindly and to position the rudder off the stern (rather than on a skeg below the waterline) to improve control and maneuverability.

His choice of rig, however, was the kicker.

Upon hearing his plans, many seasoned sailors shook their heads in disbelief. Instead of the sloop rig that is standard on the production model, Lush opted for twin, unstayed spars, the "cat-ketch" arrangement becoming popular among cruising sailors. To Lush, it made perfect sense.

First of all, the simple rig would permit all sail handling from the cockpit, something that pleased Lush immensely. Unlike many of his fellow sailors, Lush brought a very relaxed attitude to the business of racing across oceans. For instance, among his more perplexing problems in preparing for the race was deciding which books to take; he'd set himself a self-imposed limit of 10 per leg, feeling that any more reading would be a little too self-indulgent. Lush's voracious appetite for books was matched by his affection for good food; he often joked that he usually returned from a voyage weighing more than when he left.

Second, the cat-ketch rig was relatively inexpensive. This, too, was an important port of Lush's sponsor-hunting scheme. Two carbon fiber spars, in the long run, cost less than one conventional spar and the elaborate rigging and hardware needed to support it. By cutting corners where practical and feasible, Lush knew his project would be more appealing to the potential corporate sponsor who would be greatly interested in the bottom line.

The rig, however, did have its drawbacks. The boat would not sail as well into the wind as a sloop or cutter, the boats that would predominate his class. But, given Lush's attitude about racing, it was easy for him to concede the first and last legs, where most likely he would find upwind conditions. He figured he'd fare better with the strong tail winds of the middle two legs and, ultimately, it didn't matter all that much to Lush who won. Being at sea and making a safe and respectable passage, as far as he was concerned, was much more to the point.

Unlike the other Americans entered in the race, Lush had little trouble persuading a company to sponsor his effort. He originally approached Georgia's West Point Pepperell Company, whose main product line is bedding and linens, to obtain a free supply of Coremat™ a felt-like product that is sandwiched between layers of fiberglass to stiffen and strengthen boat hulls.

To cover all the bases, Lush, with the support of a professional public relations firm, drafted two separate proposals and budgets for his money-raising campaign. At the time, he didn't see any one company swinging for the entire cost of the adventure. In addition to the Coremat from West Point Pepperell, he also hoped to gather separate sponsors for sails, deck hardware, cordage and so on. But when Lush arrived in West Point, Georgia, in the fall of 1981, something unexpectedly clicked.

Don Downes, the firm's director of public relations, recalled the session. "Tony came in with a well-organized plan and a well-prepared presentation. The chairman of the company was there as well as many department heads, and he was as impressed as the rest of us. Tony had made an A and a B budget, the latter being things he would skimp on to get a sponsor. We went for all of it. Not one thing came along that he needed we didn't go for. We never made any pretense about being yachting experts. We left it all up to Tony." In December, 1981, with a firm financial commitment, work began in earnest on the boat. Lush hired about 15 Hunter employees during the Christmas vacation break at the plant, and in less than three weeks the hull was completed.

The relationship between Lush and his sponsor—by design a business transaction—soon took on decidedly personal overtones. To West Point Pepperell, Lush was an adopted son, and its role as proud parents was to happily spoil the lad. Making and selling sheets is not exactly a dream-fulfilling occupation. But executive and production workers alike saw in Lush the same qualities they liked to nurture in themselves. He was cut from the same unpretentious blue-collar cloth as their friends and neighbors. It was easy to live vicariously through his preparation and anticipation. He was living their dream.

In the days before the start in Newport, *Lady Pepperell* was abuzz with activity. While many of the racers provisioned and made final repairs alone or with their family, Lush's decks usually hosted a small army of helpers, partyers and well-wishers. On the day of the start, West Point Pepperell hired a double-decked tour boat, loaded it with food, drink and employees, and shadowed their proxy dreammaker as he patiently tacked back and forth behind the starting line. When the gun sounded, Lush raised his arm in a final salute to his benefactors. A new Rolex watch, a gift from the company's chairman of the board, gleamed on his wrist.

Lush's passage to Cape Town was largely uneventful. Lush lived and ate well. Until the final five days of the 57-day voyage, he slept under the stars in his cockpit each evening, happily snuggled in an oversized bean-bag chair.

In Cape Town, Lush replaced his fiberglass spars with new carbon fiber models, which escaped South African duty fees because they had been labeled "secondhand flagpoles." The idea behind the new masts was to reduce the swaying and deflection aloft in the strong following winds of the southern ocean legs. To oversee the installation, West Point Pepperell flew in Rick Viggiano, an engineer at Tillotson Pearson, the spars' manufacturer. He was joined by Warren Luhrs of Hunter, who immediately dove into the bowels of the boat and, with almost surgical precision, began removing every cushion and item that he considered superfluous in hopes of further lightening the 16,000-pound yacht and increasing its speed.

"Tony's been a little too comfortable," seemed to be Luhrs' sentiment. "After all, this is a yacht race."

Luhrs also was aware that, although *Lady Pepperell* was a far cry from the boat he built, his company's name and Lush's efforts, good or bad, were inexorably linked. From a businessman's point of view, it was important that the boat fare well.

Still, even with the strong financial support and technical expertise, several other racers looked at *Lady Pepperell* as the black sheep of the family. Sitting on the dock one day, Philippe Jeantot gave the boat a quick but disdainful glance. "Maybe it is unfair of me to say, but I would not take that boat, with those masts, into the southern ocean."

But Lush remained even tempered. Before the second leg start, he thought about the many friends and supporters who'd made his entry in the race possible. He likened the group effort to a line from an old Jefferson Airplane song.

"No man is an island," he said. "He is a peninsula."

As Lush waited for just the right winds to nudge him toward Durban the day after "the acrobatics," he had no idea how far that peninsula extended. Fatefully, the breeze he needed never blew and he and *Lady Pepperell* spent the day and all the following night making no real progress in any direction save for rising and falling with the rolling sea.

The following morning, the skies were overcast but not threatening. Lush waited patiently beside his radio at 8:30 for Campbell's "morning rounds." The first to come up was Francis Stokes. By the clear, resonant tones of his voice it was immediately apparent to Tony that, relatively speaking, the two sailors were in the same neighborhood.

The previous day's erratic transmission had clued Campbell and Stokes to the fact that Lush probably would attempt to make contact on the regular morning schedule. So they were alert when he did in fact come up. Lush first spoke to Stokes, asking, "How are *you*, Francis? Is everything okay with you?" Though perfectly in character, it struck Stokes as funny. "Under the circumstances, it seemed like a strange start to the conversation," he said.

Lush described his crash and the resulting damage in detail, and also told of his scheme to save the boat, which he was gradually beginning to doubt. The two sailors exchanged rough positions, and determined that *Lady Pepperell* was approximately 50 miles due north of *Mooneshine*. Campbell passed along the weather report, which was not good; two low pressure systems were bearing down on the racers, promising high winds and seas to match.

Stokes, a man of good judgment, considered the options and issued Lush an ultimatum: Stokes said he would heave-to for an hour, effectively stopping *Mooneshine* in her tracks, to let Lush decide his next step. If, at that time, he wanted to abandon his boat, Stokes would be ready to lend assistance. If not, Lush was on his own.

The next hour was the longest of Lush's life. He removed the floorboards that masked his boat's open wound. Then, like a Buddha, he curved his large frame around his considerable middle ("Baby Pepperell" was what one dockside wag in Newport had nicknamed Lush's stomach) and sat cross-legged on his haunches to study the keel.

He immediately realized that, even in the light conditions, the damage had worsened. What, he asked himself, would happen if he began sailing and did lose the keel? His life raft was mounted in a canister on his afterdeck. If and when the keel fell off, the result would be like a dam bursting. The boat would immediately list and he would have to crawl out of his skewed companionway onto a deck half underwater, then scramble to a near-vertical afterdeck before he could even begin inflating the raft. It would be a mean obstacle course for an Olympic decathlon champion; for Lush, it would be impossible.

Lush thought about the people who had worked hard hours and spent plenty of good money to get him to sea. His death, though he was somewhat indifferent to the subject in personal terms, was not going to help his friends or sponsors or the race organizers. He figured he had a responsibility greater than himself.

Self-doubt wracked him, but only for a moment. *Maybe I should have had some sail up,* he thought. *Why didn't I use more fiberglass when I was reinforcing the keel.* But such thoughts had little to do with the matter at hand. It was not a time for self-defeat through analysis.

In more practical terms, it was not lost on Lush that it was a stroke of particularly fortuitous fate that Stokes was the closest sailor. He'd first met him in the 1976 OSTAR, and had admired him as a person and a seaman ever since. Lush realized that if he let Stokes sail on and then needed assistance later, his "choice" of rescuer might not be so copacetic.

At the end of the hour, Lush got back on the radio and passed along the message that Stokes knew was coming: "I'm going to get off . . ."

The two sailors swapped positions as best they could—Stokes was having trouble getting good sun sights with his sextant and Lush's SatNav had malfunctioned—and then planned their rendezvous. Lush was upwind, and thus could steer a direct course to *Mooneshine*'s estimated position without tacking. So Lush set his foresail and set off for his last sail on *Lady Pepperell*. Stokes, in turn, waited and attempted to get an exact position fix.

Lush had covered about half the distance to Stokes when it all caught up with him. He leaned over the rail and lost his lunch. It wasn't the fear of losing the boat so much as his deep, dark apprehension of being in the water. Incredibly Lush had never learned to swim. In the great age of sail, this was a common, even admirable trait. A sailor who couldn't swim would drown quickly and relatively painlessly if his boat went down. But Lush was a survivor.

By late afternoon, Stokes spotted *Lady Pepperell's* lone sail and white hull slowly bobbing in and out of sight beyond the deceptively gentle six-foot swells. Though the low light made judging distances difficult, Stokes guessed the two boats were about a quarter of a mile apart. That the two boats were even that close after Lush's eight-hour sail was not only an excellent piece of navigation but good luck, as well. Stokes fired a para-chute flare, and Lush soon after tried a few hand-held flares until he got one to work. By then, each had the other in view. But as the yachts closed the gap between them, what had seemed like calm conditions in the open ocean now took on a new and violent nature. When the boats drew alongside, the pitching *Lady Pepperell* nicked *Mooneshine's* stern, coming dangerously close to smashing the self-steering gear. *Lady Pepperell's* masts, slashing the air like sabers, were another source of danger. If they became entangled with *Mooneshine's* spar or rigging, neither yacht would ever make safe harbor.

The two yachts would have to stay well apart. On the second try, Stokes managed to get a line to Lush. The umbilical cord was made fast. Lush had gathered together some items and stashed them in a seabag and this was transferred to *Mooneshine* by another line. By now, Stokes was impatient. It was nearly dark, the wind was rising and storms were coming. He hollered at Lush to pick it up. Lush was dressed in full foul weather gear and a safety harness. He took the line between the boats, tied it firmly around his waist and plunged into the cold southern ocean, abandoning the boat and his dream.

The other boats that had dropped out had done so while safely tied to a pier. Everyone connected with the race believed a boat would be lost at sea at some point. But the general feeling among competitors was, "Yes, that can happen, but not to me." Now that it had happened, the odds on it happening again were even greater. The southern ocean repre-sented a game of Russian roulette: Too many variables were beyond the control of a single sailor, no matter how well prepared. Lush was not the first racer to quit, but he was the first not given the luxury of choice.

Once in the water, Lush pulled himself hand over hand the 40-odd feet to *Mooneshine.* When he reached the boat, Stokes rigged the swim-ming ladder and Lush clambered aboard. On *Mooneshine,* the reunion was strange but not forced. Lush changed his wet clothes on deck so he wouldn't mess up the cabin below. Stokes went forward and set a small headsail and *Mooneshine* was once again on her way to Sydney. *Lady Pepperell,* her navigation lights burning, drifted into darkness.

Once below, Lush dug deep into his seabag and from the small inventory of his remaining possessions produced a full bottle of Scotch. The two sailors drank deeply and together sailed on in the night.

11

A Measure of National Pride

THE MORNING OF November 30, Tony Lush woke up with a hangover unlike any he had known. It wasn't so much the Scotch he and Francis had consumed to celebrate the rendezvous and Lush's safety, and to mourn the passing of *Lady Pepperell,* but the shock of being out of the race once and for all. Twenty-four hours before, he had been a skipper with his destiny in his own hands. Now, the adventure was over, but Lush was still on the sidelines and watching the game with interest.

The sailor he and Stokes watched most carefully was Lush's closest rival during the first leg through the Atlantic, Desmond Hampton on *Gipsy Moth V,* who was well ahead and east of *Mooneshine* and running at the head of the fleet with Jeantot in *Credit Agricole* and Reed in *Voortrekker.* Lush felt a bit wistful, listening to the daily positions reports, because in slightly different circumstances he would have been trying to catch Hampton and *Gipsy Moth V.* Yet, they had brought very different boats and sailing habits to the theater of the Southern Ocean. As Stokes wrote in his journal on November 21: "I overheard Desmond and Tony on the radio this morning. Desmond said his tendency is to carry all the sail he can until something breaks; Tony said he holds back because he's afraid something will break. That pretty well sums it up."

It is possible to speculate that Lush lost *Lady Pepperell* because he was not carrying enough sail and therefore not keeping the boat moving ahead at the same speed as the large breaking waves. That is idle guess-

103

work. Even Lush can't say for certain and he was there. What is certain, is that Hampton was getting miles out of the old wood ketch *Gipsy Moth V* that no one—especially Jeantot and Reed—thought possible.

Up at the front of the fleet that now numbered 13, Jeantot, Reed and Hampton were having the first real boat race of the voyage. They were racing in weather that would make any veteran of the southern ocean squirm. The day after Lush lost *Lady Pepperell*, 18 days into the second leg, the three leaders ran into an easterly gale that played havoc with the west-running sea. Jeantot was leading by about 60 miles over Hampton and had sailed slightly farther south, toward Kerguelen Island, in an attempt to sail the great circle route from Cape Town to Sydney—a course that curves toward the pole and is the shortest possible route. With a large lead from the first leg, Jeantot was not pushing to the limit. But he wanted to win the second leg, too, so he couldn't ease up much.

Hampton was right on his transom, although a bit north, and Reed was not far behind. For Reed, the sailing was drudgery. In the three weeks since leaving Cape Town, he had lost the use of both his Aries wind vane self-steering devices. Losing both wind vanes would have been enough to send most of the rest of the fleet looking for cover, either at Kerguelen or to the north in the calmer regions of the Indian Ocean. That is not Reed's way of doing things, nor the manner for which he earned his nickname, "Biltong" Bertie. He said, "We eventually got down to the region where *Ocean Passages* says the westerlies start coming through, 40 degrees south or so. You'd find that the sea was at times like mountains and you'd just be surfing down the faces at incredible speeds, 15 and 20 knots and more, sometimes."

Hand-steering for long hours and then relying on his small Combi Autohelm electronic autopilot to steer the boat while he slept, Reed managed to keep *Voortrekker* vaulting ahead at speeds she had never before attained. He was keeping the pressure on both Jeantot and Hampton, who were jockeying day by day for the lead of the race.

Hampton was making remarkable progress (which kept Stokes and Lush cheering from 600 miles astern) and was getting daily runs from *Gipsy Moth V* that would have amazed Francis Chichester. The wood-hulled staysail ketch had been designed for these conditions by Robert Clark, who had the benefit of Chichester's vast singlehanded experience as well as the old gent's unbridled opinions on every subject, whether it be seafaring or not. The boat originally had a length of 57 feet and had been designed as a singlehander's machine. Her keel made her easy to drive under a press of sail, and easy for the self-steering unit to steer in just about any conditions. While Jeantot and Reed wrestled with their Aries self-steering units, Hampton sailed on, while his Gunning (a British device very similar to an Aries) operated flawlessly.

Hampton said, "I used to feel so sorry for Bertie, who was having such a frightful problem with his self-steering gear. He'd say, 'Aw, the boat's yawing around all over the place, what are you doing?' And I'd say I was running straight as an arrow with the wind on the quarter. Honestly, I think *Gipsy Moth V* would run downwind without any gear on her at all."

But as good as *Gipsy Moth V* was for racing through the conditions of the southern ocean, it was Hampton who drove her to reach her potential. At 41, Hampton had owned a boat of his own for only 10 years before setting off on the chartered *Gipsy Moth V*. He had begun sailing—cruising primarily—in 1958 with friends who showed him Brittany, the west coast of Ireland and the coast of Spain. He and his wife, Kitty, bought a 32-foot Westerly Centaur in 1972 and cruised in her for several years. He eventually ended up with the 35-foot sloop *Wild Rival*. In *Wild Rival* he and Kitty sailed in the 1978 two-handed Round Britain Race and in 1980 he sailed in the OSTAR. The Hamptons were a sailing team and they included their two daughters, Vanessa, 11, and Emma, 9, when delivering *Wild Rival* between races. Kitty, also, had sailed in the 1981 Two-Star (Doublehanded Transatlantic Race).

At the beginning of the race, Hampton said, "A man might have in his lifetime only one chance like this race. For me, it happened right when I was due a reasonable sabbatical. I am lucky to have Kitty behind me in this. I don't think she entirely approves because it is such a long race. But at least she understands."

Hampton was used to sailing alone offshore. But perhaps more importantly, this was not his first trip through the southern Indian Ocean on *Gipsy Moth V*. In 1979, he had joined Giles Chichester, Francis Chichester's son, for the Cape Town to Perth, Australia leg of the Parmelia Race that ran in two legs from Plymouth, England to Perth. Sailing with a full complement of crew, *Gipsy Moth V* had shown a good turn of speed and a comfortable motion in the tumultuous seas. There is no doubt, the lessons on route planning and sail handling Hampton learned during the Parmelia Race served him well while he forged along toward Sydney.

In a very real sense, Hampton carried with him the torch of British singlehanded ocean racing, following in the footsteps of Chichester and Robin Knox-Johnston. It was a torch Chichester had lit in England during his singlehanded voyage around the world in 1966, a voyage in *Gipsy Moth IV* made from Plymouth, England, with one stop at Sydney, and leaving Cape Horn to port. Chichester's route was very nearly the route sailed by the BOC racers. There can be little doubt that, while sailing the old man's last boat, Hampton was bound to feel at times the skipper's cold eye staring over his shoulder, while at other moments he would feel a kinship with Chichester fostered by the same challenges in the same seas.

One twist of fortune they did share in this same stretch of ocean north of Kerguelen Island and along the great circle route to Sydney was the appearance of easterly winds. Chichester wrote in *Gipsy Moth Circles The World:* "I sweated up the main to get it setting better, and felt most unfairly treated, because according to the U.S. Pilot Charts a southeast wind should have been pretty rare in that area of sea. I wrote in the log: 'What an indignity to have to cope with an easterly wind in the Roaring Forties.' "

Seventeen years later, Hampton said: "Coming up to Kerguelen, Bertie and I had three days of easterlies, pure easterlies. They drove me from 45 degrees south to 48 degrees and I had intended to go no lower than 47. I entered in my log at the time that if I had wanted to spend my time beating into head winds, I'd have gone around the other way."

Characteristically, the British were the first to institutionalize single-handed racing. In 1956, Colonel H. G. "Blondie" Hasler, a retired military officer, tried to launch a yacht race across the Atlantic from England to the United States that would measure a singlehanded skipper and his boat in every conceivable way. But Hasler, who invented the wind-driven self-steering devices, descendants of which were used by all but one of the BOC fleet, was ahead of his time. His race, first called the STR and then the STAR and finally, after *The Sunday Observer* newspaper became a sponsor, the OSTAR, did not get off the ground until 1960, when four other adventurers took up Hasler's challenge. It was a come-as-you-are event without a lot of flag waving, band playing or commercialism. It was a race of five ordinary men setting out to test themselves in an age-old arena. Francis Chichester, then 58 and only just recovered from a bout with lung cancer, won the inaugural race in his 39-foot sloop *Gipsy Moth III.*

Already a prominent figure for his records and feats in long-distance singlehanded air travel, Chichester's name at the head of the finishers' list gave the OSTAR a degree of credibility it might have lacked otherwise. As well as being a canny flier and sailor, Chichester was also an able public relations man, who knew there was mileage and perhaps money to be made promoting and writing about his adventures at sea. In 1961, he wrote *Alone Against The Atlantic,* followed by *Atlantic Adventure* in 1962, his autobiography *The Lonely Sea And The Sky* in 1964 and *Along The Clipper Way* (an anthology) in 1966. The sea tales established him as the laureate of sea adventure in England and the Commonwealth and, importantly, the books sparked the imaginations of young sailors around the world. Hasler dreamed up the race, but Chichester popularized it.

In 1964, Chichester entered the second OSTAR and finished second to the young French sailing star, Eric Tabarly. Tabarly had built a boat especially for the race and brought a tough professionalism to the game that gradually would alter its amateur appeal. It was a quality Chichester appreciated, because he enjoyed winning. Yet, the old loner had his sights fixed on a larger target, the ultimate target for sailors, Cape Horn. Instead of preparing for the 1968 OSTAR, Chichester built a new 54-foot yawl in which he set off on August 27, 1966, from Plymouth, England, on a 28,000-mile solo adventure around the world. When he returned to Plymouth nine months later, on May 28, 1967, he was greeted by an enormous crowd on the Plymouth Hoe. The voyage earned him a knighthood and transformed the popular adventurer into a modern-day Lord Nelson.

Many followed Chichester. There was Alec Rose, the green-grocer who sailed his 36-foot yawl *Lively Lady* around the world the next year and arrived home to find that the public imagination was still stirring and that he too was a national hero. For his voyage, Rose also earned a knighthood. And then, like the transatlantic race eight years before, the idea of voyaging around the world alone was institutionalized in the 1968 Golden Globe non-stop, singlehanded around the world race. In his winning effort, Robin Knox-Johnston became the third British singlehanded sailor in three years to complete a circumnavigation and for his efforts received, not a knighthood, surprisingly, but a Commander of the British Empire. Nonetheless, Knox-Johnston joined the elite club, presided over by the crusty Sir Francis Chichester himself.

After the three great circumnavigations, singlehanded racing in Britain and Europe came of age. In the OSTAR, the 1960 race had had five entrants, the 1964 race had 14 and the 1968 race had 35 (although only 19 finished). In 1972, the first race after the Golden Globe, the number of inquiries for the OSTAR jumped enormously and at the starting line 55 boats sailed out into the North Atlantic. Of those, there were 15 British, 11 French, five Americans and the rest hailed from ports around the world. England was humming with this new sport and was ready to crown new heroes one after the other. Among those who had stepped up into the limelight with Chichester and Knox-Johnston, were Chay Blyth, Geoff Williams and the late Rob James, all of whom have made remarkable voyages and won their share of races.

In the 1972 OSTAR, offshore singlehanding graduated from a marginal sport of interest only to sailors and adventurers into a thriving international sport, attracting audiences of millions of non-sailors via television and newspapers. Something was lost and something gained in the transition. The early OSTAR and the Golden Globe had been adventures carried out by rugged individualists who had the ability to put together a boat for such an ordeal, and then the skill, nerve and endurance to carry the race off with no outside help or hindrance. Those early racers were men who sailed to be alone with their own competence, for better or worse. Despite his penchant for public relations, Francis Chichester epitomized that essentially personal desire to carry one's destiny in one's own hands. That he was able to do so in the face of great challenges is what made him worthy of his lofty perch.

He entered the 1972 OSTAR in a new boat he had built for the race, the 57-foot staysail ketch *Gipsy Moth V*. Although 70 years old and suffering from a debilitating blood ailment that gradually was destroying his bone marrow, he sailed across the starting line and valiantly set off one more time into the North Atlantic. But, 11 days after the start, a passing merchant ship sighted *Gipsy Moth V* limping back toward England. Several days later on June 29, Chichester by radio asked his son Giles to meet him in Brest, France, closing the transmission with the words, "cold and weak."

In a debacle of poor seamanship, the French weather ship *France II* tried to lend him a hand but managed only to collide with the wood ketch and damage the mizzen before being waved away by the frail skipper, wearing his billed yachting cap, who sat almost motionless in the cockpit. That night, while standing by, the *France II* ran down an American cruising yacht that was on a mission of mercy to Chichester, causing the death of seven cruising sailors. The morning after the tragedy, Giles Chichester and a friend were put aboard *Gipsy Moth V* and they sailed her back to Plymouth, arriving on July 3 to end Sir Francis' last voyage. He died seven weeks later on August 25, 1972, at the Naval Hospital in Plymouth. All England mourned.

Deep in the southern ocean, during the third week out from Cape Town, Desmond was pushing the boat and himself to new limits of performance. He had the others shaking their heads in wonder and surprise. Francis Stokes understood perhaps as well as anyone what was going on aboard *Gipsy Moth V*. From his vantage point 600 miles astern, Francis wrote in his log on Tuesday, November 23: "*Gipsy Moth* and *Credit Agricole* are making a real race of it. Both are about 10 degrees east of here. I'm sure Desmond is putting a measure of national pride into his effort."

12

They All Fall Down

THE FIRST THIRD of the leg to Sydney had been a maelstrom. The fleet was hammered by six gales in 17 days. The last one had tossed *Lady Pepperell* head-over-heels, breaking her keel beyond repair. By the time the fleet reached Kerguelen Island, the midpoint between the continents of Africa and Australia, the skippers were tired and their boats showed the wear and tear of battling the enormous seas and high winds. Three boats—*City of Dunedin, Perseverance of Medina* and *Nike II*—lost their main engines, hence their main electrical generators. Several others suffered gear and rigging problems. Self-steering equipment was giving everyone fits, even those sailing ahead at record speeds. The horrendous conditions that had faced the racers from the first night out of Cape Town had not measurably improved in the intervening weeks.

Now, at midpassage, the fleet was finding the sea no more favorable. The front runners—*Credit Agricole, Gipsy Moth V* and *Altech Voortrekker*—sailed into an easterly gale the night after Tony Lush abandoned *Lady Pepperell*. The fierce head winds forced Philippe Jeantot to sail further south than he had planned in search of the great circle course to Sydney. Jeantot was leading the fleet and making remarkable daily runs. After struggling with his large double headsail, which he flew on twin-spinnaker poles, Jeantot discovered his light cutter sailed better and faster under the medium-sized twin "booster" sails. With these flying, he charged on ahead of the rest toward Sydney. But he made a tactical error at this point of the race and sailed too close to the remote, windswept Kerguelen islands. The prevailing westerly wind had been light during the day and he had dropped the twin sails in favor of the large spinnaker, which was difficult to fly by himself but gave him an extra knot of speed. With the spinnaker and not the twin headsails flying, Jeantot was hit by the easterly gale just as he sailed over the shallow water of the Kerguelen shelf.

The combination of circumstances was almost devastating. The deep sea swells ran up on the 60-fathom shelf, producing a wild collection of breaking waves. The seas became massive and broke in wild and unpredictable patterns.

And then a wave bigger than the rest, a rogue wave that rolled strangely contrary to the breakers, caught the 56-foot *Credit Agricole* and threw it down on its side like a toy in the hands of a bored child. The spinnaker, which should have been doused hours before, filled with water and acted like a hugh counterbalance, preventing the boat from righting itself. Moving quickly, sensing that another such wave could dismast his boat, Jeantot set free all the sheets, and the halyard on the large headsail, losing it in the process but saving *Credit Agricole*. "It has never been so dangerous," he said. "I was quite afraid."

Jeantot was bruised but not broken. Yet, he had witnessed again the awesome force of southern ocean waves. It was a sight (and a sound) that would haunt Jeantot and his fellow skippers until they left the open sea and exchanged those dangers for the confines of the Bass Strait.

Like Jeantot, Jacques de Roux continued a French sweep by once again leading Class II. De Roux and *Skoiern III* were setting a rapid pace against nearly overwhelming odds. During the gale the first night out of Cape Town, his engine quit for good. His solar panels became his sole source of electricity to run his sailing instruments, navigational equipment and shipboard lights.

Then, in a knockdown two days before *Lady Pepperell*'s demise, he lost the use of his self-steering gear, his running lights and the antennas for his VHF (very high frequency) radio and his satellite navigator. With limited electricity, communications were difficult, so he kept radio chats to an occasional contact with Guy Bernardin.

De Roux discovered that by flying the same double headsails that Jeantot used aboard *Credit Agricole* and lashing his wheel with line, he could get *Skoiern* to steer herself for hours at a time. Still, he figured such an arrangement was temporary at best, and planned on stopping at tiny Amsterdam island to make repairs. He told Bernardin of his plan during a rare radio contact. Bernardin informed him of his lead, and told de Roux he would surely be overtaken if he stopped for even a short time. De Roux continued on.

He also changed his strategy, staying north of the majority of the fleet, and sailing at 42° and 43° South instead of heading into the higher latitude of 47° and 48° South, which would have carried him closer to the more direct great circle course. *Skoiern III* handled the steep seas well and made excellent daily runs in the prevailing 25 and 30-knot winds he found in the more northern (and less stormy) reaches of the Roaring Forties.

"All this leg I have problems with my autopilots and electrics, so I stay north. If I have a problem then, it is less difficult for me to go quickly to a part of the sea where it is not so rough."

Despite staying above the main procession of low pressure systems, de Roux still had his share of heavy seas. As he sailed off the western end of Australia, a huge breaker blind-sided *Skoiern III* while de Roux lay in his bunk.

"This time I was rolled to 160 degrees, not quite upside down. But my mast was pointing to the sea. I wasn't hurt. Luckily, I was in my berth. The boat lay over for a moment and then slowly came up again and the cabin began to fill with water. After the first time, I knew we were not sinking. The water was running down from the mast that had filled. And then I smelled diesel fuel. The fuel tank had ruptured and there was diesel over everything on the top of the seawater. This was difficult, yes, most difficult."

But for all de Roux's problems, he kept his boat moving towards Sydney at a remarkable pace. Though he had little idea of where he stood with regards to the competition, he continued to drive himself—and *Skoiern*—to the limit.

From the midpoint of the passage, de Roux's nearest competitor was Neville Gosson on the Class I *Leda Pier One*. While de Roux stayed north due to equipment trouble, Gosson found himself the farthest boat south, due, once again, to a rigging failure. Gosson was the only boat to sail south of Kerguelen Island. He had not planned to dip so far south, but the easterly gales that hit Jeantot, Bertie Reed and Desmond Hampton just north of Kerguelen, drove *Leda* southward. Gosson had planned, after rounding the islands to head north again, to avoid the cold and possible floating ice. Weather reports from a ham radio operator, Arthur Oliver, in Perth, Australia, put the limit of the floating ice at approximately 55° South. Gosson, however, didn't want to take unnecessary chances. Before Gosson could make miles north out of the fog and freezing temperature of the Fifties, his headstay broke as it had during the first leg at the top casting and fell onto the deck. The rig failure coincided with a second easterly gale. Without a headstay, Gosson was unable to sail upwind, so he slacked his mainsheet and ran off south farther into the frozen murk as he tried to make repairs.

The first order of business was to find a way to fly his headsails without the stay. Flying them free proved impossible. The force of the wind was too much for the Dacron sailcloth and even the heavy Dacron patches. First the top and then the bottom of his working jib ripped away. Cold and frustrated, he finally hit upon the idea of adding a wire to the sail's leading edge that would bear the weight and force of the wind. Using a sailmaker's leather palm and a needle and thread, he sewed a spare wire halyard into the luff of the sail. It was not an easy job, but he got the sail flying again and found it was a workable solution to his otherwise dire problem. The wire allowed Gosson to haul the sail up quite tight, improving *Leda*'s windward sailing ability.

But it was not a total success. After several days of jogging slowly north toward the less frozen regions, another problem cropped up.

"Then," Gosson said, "the halyards began to break. I think I went through four of them. By the time I sailed into Sydney, I was flying the headsail on two spinnaker sheets knotted together."

At 53°S, he had to climb *Leda*'s mast to retrieve the last of the jib halyards that had escaped to the masthead. It was a daunting task. *Leda* is 53 feet long and her mast stands approximately 70 feet above the water. The height was one problem, although he had been to the masthead often enough to repair his broken headstay. A more serious problem was the cold. The temperature hovered at freezing and the water temperature was not much higher. No ice glazed *Leda*'s deck, but the heavy fog condensed on her rigging and hardware—winches, hatches, the mast and boom—forming thin sheets of ice. The mast was as slippery as a greased fire pole.

To scale his mast, Gosson constructed a makeshift ladder of spare rigging wire that was joined together by rope rungs. To go aloft, he hoisted the top of the ladder to the masthead with a free halyard, securing the bottom to a cleat on deck. As he ascended, he tied the entire ladder off first at the lower spreaders, and then again at the upper spreaders. The wind was blowing 25 knots and the sea was rough. As he climbed, Gosson and his ladder swung out over the cold, icy sea in a wide arc. Only after securing the ladder to the mast was the contraption stable.

Somehow Gosson made it to the top of the mast, freed the halyard and started down once again. He stopped at the top set of the two sets of spreaders on *Leda*'s mast to untie his restraining line and to clap some blood into his fingers before continuing down. But as he worked on the line, his foot slipped from the rung on his ladder and he hurtled down toward the deck. Somehow, he managed to catch himself on the next set of spreaders, 20 feet below, where he hung on for dear life.

"I was mighty lucky," he said. "I only dented my ego, but it didn't help my backside much, either."

Had he fallen 50 feet to the deck, he might have broken his back and been unable to crawl to the radio. No doubt, sitting on the second spreader, catching his breath before climbing the rest of the way down, Gosson had second thoughts about what he was doing alone at the edge of the world. Perhaps, for this semi-retired businessman who at 56 had won many battles at work and at play, this race was madness? He didn't think so.

"To sail around the world is one thing, to race is quite another. So few people have done this. I just want to show myself I can keep up the pressure and tenacity to push a boat of this size 27,000 miles. So it's pressure, pressure, all the time."

Richard Konkolski's detour to Fremantle, Western Australia, to effect repairs was a voyage without pleasure. Steering with swollen hands for 18 hours a day, and dropping the sails for eating, sleeping and navigation, he slogged northeastwards out of the Roaring Forties. The weather soon grew sunny and hot and he had to protect himself with scarves and a hat while he sat for hours on end whether at the wheel or at the emergency tiller, alternating between the two to relieve the boredom and break up the routine.

Konkolski's fate during the first two legs of the race was adversity. He found no relief from it in Fremantle, where he was greeted enthusiastically by old acquaintances whom he had met during his first singlehanded circumnavigation in 1973. He arrived over the Christmas weekend and found every store, mechanic's shop, sailmaker and rigger closed for four days. Exhausted from his steering marathon, Konkolski collapsed on his bunk and slept until Fremantle revived from the Christmas holiday. Then he set to work repairing the damaged headstay and torn genoa. Next he installed a new generator on top of the port quarter berth of *Nike II*. He worked at a fever pitch to complete the repairs. The race that he had hoped to win, to show his adopted country what he was worth, now was rapidly slipping through his fingers.

On New Year's Eve, he finally got *Nike II* ready once more for the sea and, forgoing a New Year's party thrown by his Fremantle friends, Konkolski hauled up his sails and started on his way to Sydney. But his start was ill-fated. The new generator had been installed next to the compass for the automatic pilot. The magnetically sensitive compass had not been compensated (adjusted) for its new steel neighbor. Before sailing a mile, Konkolski dropped his sails and anchored behind a small island in Fremantle Harbor, where he spent the rest of the night swinging and compensating his autopilot. It was a tedious task made even more difficult by the sounds of the New Year's party wafting across the still harbor.

In the morning, he weighed anchor and set off for Sydney as fast as *Nike II* could carry him. By now his goal was not to win Leg II, but simply to reach Sydney before the rest of the boats departed again for the long leg around Cape Horn to Rio de Janeiro. Throughout his ordeal, Konkolski challenged the same high seas and gales that tired the rest of the fleet. Yet during the second leg, as in the first, he seemed to be sailing under his own particular set of crossed stars.

While *Nike II* languished in Fremantle for repairs, the rest of the fleet sailed on beneath the Australian continent toward the Bass Strait. In Class II, four boats jockeyed for second place behind de Roux in *Skoiern III*. One of the four was a stunning surprise. Dick McBride aboard *City of Dunedin* had finished well behind the rest of the boats in Leg I, but in the southern ocean he was able to make his black steel schooner fly. For much of the second leg he ran second to de Roux, with Bernardin, Stokes and Tada not far behind. Originally, McBride planned to sail to 50°S looking both for wind and the great circle course. But when he got down to 45°S, three weeks out of Cape Town, he found good winds and a strong southwesterly swell that forced him to run northeastwards with a stiff westerly breeze on his stern quarter. The southern ocean proved to be just the place for the sturdy *City of Dunedin* and she chewed up miles at the rate of 170 per day.

But the going was rough. On the 27th day out of Cape Town, McBride was hit by a wave that sent the 42-foot schooner flying into a deep trough. He wrote in his log that day: "Knocked down past horizontal. Green water was visible through the main cabin skylight and everything inside was jumbled up. Tins, books, God what a mess. I was sitting on the windward berth with my feet braced on the leeward berth and I was holding onto the pole amidships when the thing hit. No injury, not much water shipped and no apparent damage."

And then he added: "Found pair of scissors sticking into the coach roof above the galley. Had flown from the workbench on the other side of the boat."

That day was to be one of adventure for McBride. He was leading Stokes by 50 miles and had even more of a lead on Tada and Bernardin. Yet he was suffering from serious migrane headaches that incapacitated him for hours at a time. Both the high seas and the odd-shaped waves that developed in the contrary conditions—"steep pyramidal seas, leaping up and breaking"—made him feel cautious. Perhaps more than the others, McBride was willing to confront the uncertainty of his fate alone on the raging seas. He had written earlier: "With what lies ahead (the southern ocean and Bass Strait), must always beware not to let down after a tough day." It was the human factor that worried McBride, a point worthy of thought. He knew, as did the others, that it was not the sea that would kill them, but their own inability to cope with what the sea had to offer.

Hours after *City of Dunedin* was knocked down, McBride was steering the boat in the cockpit. A huge wave broke on the quarter, filled the cockpit and washed over the deck. He wrote in his log: "Took an enormous wave in the cockpit from both sides. It tried to wash me overboard. I was completely soaked but saved by the harness and lifeline."

A thin thread of a line had saved his life. Five days later, after a period of slow sailing because he felt "gun shy" from the knockdown and the breaking wave, he was hit again. The wind had increased quickly and the waves grew enormous. He was washed out of the cockpit again and in the process he hit a winch hard, bruising his ribs. He was soaking wet and cold. The self-steering was broken. McBride entered a terse log note: "In retrospect, not a pleasant day. Learned a few lessons and survived."

As the fleet sailed eastward, every boat was knocked down, and rolled or jolted by breaking seas. Disaster was evident almost every hour of the day, in the wind, in gear failures, in human error—yet they survived and that in itself was one of the main points of sailing alone around the world —to look your own mortality in the eye and not waver. For some, this idea held a stronger sway than for others, and because of its almost morbid undercurrents, the more practical and down to earth of the skippers would shrug off the notion. Yet for romantics, Bernardin, McBride, and Konkolski, it was real enough.

Bernardin, the Frenchman whom even the other French sailors called "that stubborn Frenchman," endowed the confrontation with nearly mystical properties. Thirty-three days into the passage to Sydney, Bernardin was hit by a full gale. The winds rose to 50 knots, spawning high and confused seas. Bernardin did not feel in particular danger, despite having broken the autopilot coupling to his main steering wheel, because the storm seemed to be abating. He had changed into dry clothes and was sitting in the cockpit watching the storm dissipate when the roar of a breaking wave cascaded down on him. Darkness obscured the ocean beyond the cockpit's rim. But he knew what was coming. He reached out— sensing everything now in slow motion time—and wrapped his arm around a winch as he had numerous times before. He wore no harness. The wave descended on *Ratso* like a torrent from a broken dam, filling the cockpit rapidly and then tossing the little 38-foot sloop on her side.

"As this was happening," Guy said, "I suddenly realized that my feet were leaving the cockpit, slowly, nicely."

The force of the wave lifted him free of the cockpit. He felt his arm slipping from the winch. The cold rush of water and the dark liquidy colors of the wave collapsing in spray and foam upon itself enveloped him. The water tore him from the boat, forcing him overboard. Yet, in the time-lapse images he later recalled, he felt no fear, no panic, no horror.

He said, "I did not realize at the time that the boat was turning over. I felt well. It was like floating free in space. For a short time, I felt very nice."

For a second, or perhaps a fraction of a second, Bernardin had left the boat and merged with the great, rolling force of the sea. He had gone like Jonah into the belly of the whale, uncomplaining, glad that his long wrestling match with the sea finally was over. Perhaps, he thought, that is how it is when the end comes. Once over the side, we go gladly.

Then, after the moment, after the face-to-face look at something few men ever see, Bernardin realized he had better grab something. He reached out into the dark water all around him and found a line. He grabbed it and held on until *Ratso* completed her full sideways roll and surfaced again on the backside of the huge wave. Bernardin found himself hanging onto a running backstay quite high in the rigging, so he slid back down into the cockpit of his still floating, still sailing boat.

Looking back on the capsize and on the eerie sensation of floating away from *Ratso* in the torrent of the wave, Bernardin said with a smile, "The moment was the best souvenir of the voyage."

He survived. And he had a momento that can be acquired no where else. With his self-steering systems—both wind vanes and the autopilot—seriously disabled, he pressed on as fast as he could toward Bass Strait, trying to catch Stokes and McBride.

Stokes, meanwhile, was sailing toward Sydney with as much dispatch as possible without straining himself or his boat. With Lush aboard, the voyage changed completely for Stokes by depriving him of the solitude that he seeks in singlehanding. It is notable that three days after rescuing Lush, he ceased making journal entries. In a letter to the race committee following the second leg, reassuring them that Lush had not assisted in the sailing of *Mooneshine,* he also mentioned the detractions of carrying a passenger.

He wrote:

To The Race Committee:
   This is to explain further on the roles of Tony Lush and myself aboard *Mooneshine* regarding conduct of the race.
   I continued to do 100 percent of the sail handing, navigation, maintenance and watchkeeping as required. We shared the household tasks. Tony prepared dinner while I often made breakfast and lunch and did the baking. Cleanup was shared.
   Having someone on board with you changed the character of your race in that there is someone there with you to share the anxieties and frustrations. You gain in companionship but lose the pleasure of solitude. I believe the net result is to detract slightly from the racing effort.

I would be happy to meet with the committee to discuss this, if it is appropriate.

Francis Stokes
Mooneshine

No doubt Stokes would have preferred to sail the Indian Ocean alone, as would any of the skippers. He would have preferred to face the gray-beards and the high-pitched wind without the complicating addition of someone with whom to talk about it. But unlike Bernardin or Gosson, Stokes came away with a more practical observation.

He said, "Down here, I think there is a potential to be capsized at any time. I had heard stories about the southern ocean swells being long. But the seas were close together and the big ones seem to come in threes. There is no real pattern. Basically, I feel boats of this size are too small to be sailing way down there."

Perhaps he was right. Every one of the boats took a beating on the 7,000-mile slog to the Bass Strait.

13

A Death in the Royal Family

AT THE END of the second week of December, 30 days into the passage to Sydney, the leaders were 500 miles from the Australian coast and closing at nearly record speeds. They had sailed through the tough southern ocean course and had graduated with honors. But Bass Strait, the 50-mile-wide narrows between Tasmania and Australia, lay ahead and that was to be their final exam.

Philippe Jeantot was at the head of the fleet. *Credit Agricole* was in a groove, clocking off daily runs that regularly exceeded 200 miles—distances that would have been the envy of many crewed racing boats. Jeantot was rewriting the record books. In the second week of December, he ticked off a seven-day run of 1,244 nautical miles—an average speed of 7.3 knots. That was fast sailing, but it did not compare to what he achieved in the first week of December. With the wind blowing sharply from the west and the sky a busy white scud, he drove his yacht 1,437 nautical miles over the seven-day period, averaging 8.6 knots. It was the fastest weekly run for a singlehanded monohull (multihulls have their own record) and beat by 27.5 miles the previous record of 1,409.5 nautical miles, set in 1971. It was ironic that the man who had set the speed record 11 years earlier was Sir Francis Chichester, during a transatlantic run from Africa to the Caribbean. The boat he was sailing, then, was none other than *Gipsy Moth V*.

Desmond Hampton was only 85 miles behind Jeantot as they closed

Australia, and sailing *Gipsy Moth V* as if he had the devil or perhaps Chichester himself sitting on the transom. He was averaging 190 miles a day in the stiff, 30-knot northwesterly winds that prevailed south of Australia. It was vicious going. The sky had frozen in a blank overcast, preventing him from taking sights, so Hampton spent hours each day working up his estimated position with as much accuracy as possible. He was working his way northward. *Gipsy Moth* took the running swells on the beam. She rolled hard as she thundered ahead, her sharp bow slicing showers of spray from the waves. This was *Gipsy Moth*'s weather and it was her ocean. She had been here before. But she was a dinosaur compared to *Credit Agricole* and no one, not Hampton, not Jeantot, not one of them, had expected she would be able to run stride for stride with the newer boat. Hampton said, "Quite frankly, I was surprised to be so close to Philippe. It was exciting sailing."

Hampton was enjoying the time of his life. Nothing made him happier than to drive a big powerful boat at high speed through a solid breeze and a riding sea. At 41, Hampton had set aside his profitable real estate concerns in England for a year's sabbatical. His ebullience over the race and over the wonderful speeds *Gipsy Moth* delivered in the southern ocean made the race for first place a pleasant contest between comrades in adventure.

As Tony Lush said, "As old and slow as *Gipsy Moth* was, Desmond got exceptional performance from her. He was Mister Navigator and was busy giving the fleet positions throughout the race. In fact, he was probably the best navigator in the fleet. He's pretty good for a real estate agent."

Two hundred miles behind the two front runners, Bertie Reed on *Altech Voortrekker* was giving chase and, if either one had faltered, he was there to quickly take advantage. Hampered by persistent trouble with his self-steering devices, Reed steered by hand 12 hours a day. In the second week in December a fast-moving gale swept down over Australia, clobbering him with 50-knot winds and steep seas. One blast of wind knocked *Voortrekker* down on her beam ends, holding her there for seconds that seemed hours. Slowly, the mast rose up from the water and Reed sailed on, his hand still on the tiller. The oldest boat in the fleet, *Voortrekker*—like *Gipsy Moth*—was built of wood and had not been designed with the benefit of the modern single-handers' experience. Yet, she was making 190-mile days regularly and now and then was ticking off 200. Reed was getting speeds out of the 17-year-old *Voortrekker* he didn't know were possible.

"I've spent more time with *Altech Voortrekker* than I've spent with my wife, and that's a fact, so you'd expect I know how she sails. I've sailed her in a lot of offshore races in the South Atlantic, the race from Cape

Town to Uruguay, and so forth, and to get a 200-mile day was unreal. But on this leg, we were getting 200-plus. And it wasn't just one or two days, but a number of them."

By December 15, Jeantot was closing the Bass Strait. Several times during the night, as he approached King Island at the entrance to the strait, he thought he could see the flash of the King Island lighthouse. But each time, the sparkle at the wave top was nothing more than a flash of phosphorescence in the dark. The next evening, he had King Island in sight dead ahead and was sailing toward it in a light breeze. As he approached the first land he had seen in 31 days, he hoisted his light, reaching spinnaker to gain a boost in the dying breeze, and then he went below to plot his route around the island's off-lying rocks.

Suddenly, the wind picked up, knocking *Credit Agricole* over on her side. Jeantot scrambled on deck and tried to free the big sail's sheets before it ripped. But he did not move quickly enough and it tore from head to foot. He struggled to grab the torn halves and pull them to the deck, but the top of the sail wrapped around the roller furling headstay and stuck there, making it impossible to fly another headsail in its place.

Skirting the south coast of King Island, Jeantot faced the unpleasant prospect of having to climb the mast in the dark. For five hours, he wrestled at the top of the mast and on deck with the torn sail and the headstay and finally, shortly before dawn, he managed to clear the mess away. He hoisted a working jib and, exhausted, collapsed into his berth for a much-deserved sleep.

After sailing the last 200 miles through the strait, he cleared Redondo Island at the eastern end and turned the corner at last for Sydney. The only obstacles ahead were the oil and gas drilling platforms off the coast of Victoria and then the coast of Australia itself. Jeantot sighted the first oil rig just after dawn the first day out of Bass Strait and then sailed by the second just after noon. The sun was out and it was a clear hot day. After the gray weeks in the high latitudes, he made the most of it by sunbathing in the buff on the afterdeck.

He was relaxing, in fact, for the first time in the voyage. No doubt he deserved a little rest after his successful passage through the strait. But he knew he could not let up. Hampton was 120 miles behind and charging through the strait on a fresh breeze. *Gipsy Moth V* would be yapping at his heels if he didn't keep on a press of sail.

Jeantot said, "During the first leg when I was leading by a thousand miles, sometimes when I was tired or when the wind came up I didn't rush up and put up a different sail. But this leg I knew *Gipsy Moth* was right behind me and *Voortrekker* was close, too. I had to work harder to win more miles. It was very exciting. With this competition between boats, it obliges you to sail better, to make the boat work better, to try to find better solutions. I think it was very good."

Hampton agreed. The close competition had driven him to get the best out of his old ketch and he plotted *Gipsy Moth*'s and *Credit Agricole*'s daily positions carefully after his regular chats with Reed, who was playing radio intermediary between the two. Reed assumed this role since he carried both ham and single sideband radios while Hampton carried only single sideband and Jeantot only ham. Every day Hampton could see whether he had gained or lost miles and it spurred him on.

"The fact that Philippe was right up there did encourage me to carry more sail and drive a bit more."

Hampton entered Bass Strait about 15 hours after Jeantot and passed King Island in daylight. He sailed on through the strait in darkness and then had to negotiate the knotty chain of small islands, Redondo and several others, and then the oil fields, before sailing again into clear water on the morning of Saturday, December 19. The last remaining obstacle was Cape Howe in the eastern corner of the state of Victoria. It was well marked by a lighthouse on Gabo Island that stood just off the coast. The wind blew a steady 25 knots all day under a clear sky. *Gipsy Moth* charged ahead at eight knots under twin headsails strapped down hard on spinnaker poles. Hampton was exhausted after the arduous passage through the strait—not to mention the long hard days reaching toward Australia in the steep cross seas—but he was catching Jeantot and did not want to sleep until he had *Gipsy Moth* around Cape Howe and on the homeward course.

The day passed slowly. He cleaned up the boat as he always did before arriving in port and he catnapped from time to time. He felt pleased with himself because the voyage had been a success. He had sailed a nearly perfect great circle course from Cape Town to Bass Strait, had kept the boat moving well and then had negotiated the most difficult hazard on the entire race around the world without incident or worry. Ahead in Sydney lay a long awaited reunion with his wife, Kitty, and their two children, Vanessa and Emma. The family would spend Christmas together. It would be an especially happy holiday after Hampton's four-month absence.

Late in the afternoon, as the sun descended over the high country of Victoria, Hampton closed Cape Howe. With the wind still behind him and the running rig pulling him along at a good speed, he planned to stay 15 to 20 miles offshore and, after passing the cape, alter course for Sydney. At 4:30 p.m., he sighted Gabo Island. He took bearings and estimated he was 16 miles off the island and in a good position. He knew where he was and knew that he had at least 10 miles—a bit more than an hour of fast sailing—to go before he could head north. So, he climbed down the companionway ladder and lay down on his bunk for a one-hour nap, as he had done so many times during the past 35 days at sea. It was a routine that had become such a reliable habit that he did not even bother to set the alarm clock that sat on the shelf.

But the habit failed him.

Two hours later, he awoke to "the most amazing sort of crash." He thought, at first, the mainmast had come down. But when he scrambled up through the companionway, he realized at once what had happened. He had overslept by an hour. The wind had shifted, and the wind vane self-steering device had maintained its relative bearing to the wind as designed. As a result he had not sailed past Gabo Island with 15 miles to spare, but had sailed directly onto the bare rocks that rimmed the little windswept island.

"She went in doing about eight and a half knots," he said. "It put a great hole in her nose."

He leapt to the halyards and quickly got all sail down onto the deck. It was not an easy job because his headsails, main staysail and mizzen were strapped out with preventers and vangs. But it was done in a flash. Next, he started the main engine after opening the seal that had been put on by the race committee prior to the start of the leg to guard against cheating. But the feathering propeller would not open in reverse. It needed to be run in forward, but with *Gipsy Moth*'s position against the rocks, that was an impossible task. The engine revved, but nothing happened. He was embayed.

The waves rolled hard under *Gipsy Moth*'s stern. Each one shoved her slightly sideways, until, after a few minutes, she pivoted on her keel and swung stern-first into a crevice deep in the rocks. The rudder and propeller broke off as she slid backwards. At that very moment, Hampton resigned himself to the sad fact that the famous and able old staysail ketch was lost. But he did not stop trying to do whatever he could to save her and her gear.

"What it comes down to is that I had no ability to maneuver," he said. "There was no chance of me getting the boat off the rocks myself and I was in a position to get ashore and get some help."

It was all happening very fast. Even though his only sleep in three days had been the two-hour nap that afternoon, Hampton carried on. He set off his Argos emergency signal—attached to the Argos transmitter on deck—and his emergency radio beacon (EPIRB) for a local rescue effort. Then he sent a Mayday call on the international distress frequency (2182) over his single sideband radio.

Ironically, help was a stone's throw away. Hampton scrambled ashore over the broken stern and onto the rocks. He climbed toward the top of the nearest boulder and from there he saw the Gabo Island lighthouse standing above him. Moreover, a man was running toward him. Ted James, the lighthouse keeper, had received Hampton's distress call and was flabbergasted to have a castaway land virtually on his doorstep. The 58-year-old lighthouse keeper said, "I was amazed to receive the call, but I have to tell you it was a shock when I saw what boat it was. It was heartbreaking to see Chichester's beautiful *Gipsy Moth* smashed on the rocks like that."

With the help of James and five other men who came from a cruising yacht anchored on the other side of the island, Hampton began to dismantle *Gipsy Moth*. He took a chain saw to her decks and coamings to remove the winches and hatches. With his rigging knife, he cut the electronics free from their installations. He worked through the night, trying to salvage whatever he could from the boat. His error was not his to bear alone. The boat was on charter from the Chichester family, so he felt a deep need to save as much of their property as possible. Besides, anything he could return would be a down payment on the replacement cost of the boat.

There can be no doubt that something else drove Hampton on that night, as he hacked *Gipsy Moth* to pieces. She was a legend entrusted to him for the duration of the race. As her custodian, he had performed wonderfully and then ultimately failed. Nothing could replace the error, nothing could put the split timbers back again and nothing could resurrect the legend. But knowing that did not keep Hampton from trying.

By morning, the bulk of the boat's movable gear and stores lay heaped on the rocks above the wreck. Four hundred yards to the east, the point of Gabo Island jutted into the Tasman Sea. Had the wind shifted only a few degrees less, or had *Gipsy Moth* got a favorable set from a shore current, Hampton would have awoken to find himself on the last sprint to Sydney. Instead, the game was over. After working all night, he sat down on a rock 20 feet above the battered hull and gave a heavy sigh. He had grown his hair since leaving Newport so that the jaunty forelock now hung wildly over his eyes. He had let his beard grow, too, but it grew unevenly on his chin and cheeks, leaving him looking motheaten. The hair was a kind of emblem of his sabbatical. He had put the natty, polished and clipped businessman into the closet for a year or so and had let out an energetic, fun-loving bohemian. While it lasted, it had been wonderful. But sitting there on the black basalt, he wore the look of a tired and beaten man. He had deep circles under his eyes. His mouth hung slack and his shoulders hunched. While *Gipsy Moth* was dashed by waves in the crevice below, Hampton sat holding a wood-handled deck mop, unable to do anything more for her. It was a desolate scene.

Out to sea to the south and east, the outlying reefs boiled with the surf breaking over jagged rocks. Hampton also had been lucky. At eight knots, the reefs would have torn the keel out of *Gipsy Moth* and left the boat wrecked and her skipper far from the dry rocks and the helping hands. But such a thought offered little comfort. All of Gabo Island, the black volcanic coastline worn smooth by waves and wind, the higher contours covered with scrub growth stunted by Tasman gales, was a reef to Hampton, a reef he was eager to leave.

The public relations firm in Sydney working for BOC—Hall & Jenkins —sent a helicopter to the island to take pictures and offer whatever assistance Hampton might need. He wanted a lift out. Leaving the two masts of *Gipsy Moth* jutting crazily from the crevice and all the gear and stores piled on the rocks, Hampton climbed into the helicopter and flew to Sydney. He returned two days later with an insurance adjuster to perform the post-mortem. But, at the moment, he wanted only to run to his wife, and daughters, who had arrived in Sydney that morning from England.

None of them had slept in days. Hampton had struggled with the wreck and Kitty and the girls had suffered the slow torture of the 24-hour flight halfway around the world. They were staying with friends outside Sydney and it was there the public relations people drove Hampton from the airport.

Kitty ran out to meet her husband and kissed him. An energetic, attractive blonde with level and determined eyes, Kitty managed in the instant of their greeting to transform Hampton from his bohemian persona to his old, established self. Under the gaze of the public relations men and the press with their cameras, the Hamptons were excited and emotional, but more than anything else, they were polite to each other and everyone around them. There were no public tears, no arguments or recriminations. Alone on the rocks of Gabo Island, Hampton had been a lost soul. Together with Kitty and his daughters, the starch returned to his upper lip. In the driveway of their friends' house, Hampton's sabbatical ended once and for all.

Hampton's tragedy was a hot news item and the world apparently was waiting for some analysis of what had happened at the far corner of the Antipodes. The family had to pose for photographs on the front lawn. They looked awkward and nervous under the banana plants. Vanessa and Emma, 9 and 11 respectively, did not want to sit still. When they did, they looked tense and unhappy. But Hampton handled the media onslaught with aplomb. He said, "I was possibly more tired than I thought I was and that was the reason I overslept. But I do not think that is an excuse. I forgot to wind up my alarm clock and that would have done the trick. I should have taken more trouble. I think pride comes before a fall. In this case, it came before a very big fall.

"One might say that I made a small mistake by oversleeping and that I didn't deserve the degree of retribution I got. But the sea isn't like that. It tends to extract a fairly severe penalty from any mistake you make. So you can't afford to go and make mistakes. That's what makes this race and singlehanding so worthwhile."

While Hampton struggled, Jeantot sailed through Sydney Heads to win the 7,000-mile second leg in just over 35 days. The young Frenchman had proved that his modern vessel was more than a match for the old ideas built into *Gipsy Moth*. He had shown for the second time that he was leading the way into a new era of long-distance sailing. But none of that mattered to Jeantot when he arrived at Hampton's house to console his comrade and competitor. They had not been friends, especially, but they greeted each other warmly, with great affection, like men from an army platoon who once had gone through a bloody battle together.

That night, Jeantot and Hampton went down to Sydney Harbor to greet Reed as he sailed in to a second-place finish. They rode out on a police launch to record Reed's time and when *Voortrekker* sailed in out of the darkness and crossed the finish line, Hampton was visibly moved.

Standing next to Jeantot, Hampton said, to no one in particular, "I've always wanted to sail alone into Sydney, too."

14

Walkabout

SOMETIME IN THE life of nearly every Australian aboriginal male there comes a season for a walkabout. The trip is looked upon with both trepidation and longing because it is a reaffirmation and reevaluation of our most human traits. A walkabout is to the nomadic aborigines of the sprawling Central Australian outback, what crossing the wall is to athletes and adventurers—and what sailing to Cape Horn is, in particular, to men of the sea. It is a solo journey into the bush. It is a time away from work, away from people, to be alone in the wilderness and commune with it in its most intimate terms.

A walkabout is taken alone because only by relying on the self for every need and every pleasure is community truly appreciated upon return. This is important because people by nature are a dependent lot. If a man must change, if he must stop and think and then look at himself and life in a new way, he must do that by himself.

At 56, Neville Gosson was a highly successful businessman who made his home overlooking the harbor of cosmopolitan Sydney, Australia. Although Gosson was far removed from the heart of his continent, many of his features were those that Australians like to nurture in themselves. He was athletic, independent and self-made. At a time of life when most men cut from his cloth were looking for new ways to multiply their assets, or settling down to reap the rewards of their long toil, Gosson did something that many of his friends, associates and acquaintances would never understand.

He went for a walkabout.

The seed that grew to be Gosson's discontent was, ironically, planted in the very work that made him a wealthy man. Rising through the ranks of the automobile business, Gosson found himself at the top of the heap when he became the country's primary importer of a popular Japanese line of cars, the Dhiatsu. His company duties called for lots of old-fashioned hard work, but the benefits were handsome. Always a sportsman—he played professional rugby as a young man—Gosson's greatest passion was the outdoors. He was a man for all seasons. In the winter, when time allowed, he would take off for his ski resort in southern Australia. But it was summer that Gosson enjoyed most because that was the time for ocean racing. Nothing made him feel more alive than taking the helm of his yacht in stiff competition and putting her through her paces while a highly skilled crew of eight sailors leaped at his command.

In 1974, Gosson traded in his 45-foot steel boat and bought *Leda*, a custom 53-foot aluminum yacht that, at the time, was one of the hottest racers in the land. He kept it berthed at the Cruising Yacht Club of Australia (CYC), the nation's mecca for serious sailboat racing. He campaigned her in all the biggest regattas and races, including the Sydney to Hobart, the Sydney to Brisbane and the Admiral's Cup trials. In short, *Leda* sailed in the big leagues, requiring generous commitments of desire and money. Gosson had both.

Between 1975 and 1978, Gosson continued to race often. But the high-pressure thrills began to fade due to the sheer complexity of organizing a crew for long-distance events. In 1979, Gosson sold *Leda* and replaced her with *Thalia*, a lovely steel cruising boat. It was a sign of changing attitudes and a nod toward simplicity. To go sailing no longer required a small platoon of trained yachtsmen. Gosson's time on the water was spent chasing contentment, not rival yachts.

Not surprisingly, Gosson's career outlook changed during those years as well. He already had sold his share in the car business at a healthy profit. By no means idle, he now spent his energy and dollars developing Sydney real estate. But somehow, the quest to make money in a business climate that seemed less favorable all the time, just for the sake of it, also was troubling. He felt caught up in a system out of his control.

Gosson's changing values were seen by some, especially his old racing cronies at the CYC and elsewhere, as a matter of indignity or aloofness. One seasoned Sydney yachtsman said, "Neville was very highly respected in the local yacht club circles. He had a big boat and he sailed her well. Oh, bigger boats came along and sailed better, I guess, but that was okay. Neville was still quite a success story, a man looked up to and respected. But business soon lost its flavor for him. I really don't know what happened after that."

By 1981, Gosson felt an overwhelming need to do something different.

In October of that year, while thumbing through an issue of an American sailing magazine, he was struck by a small news item announcing the singlehanded round the world race. Gosson's only singlehanded racing had been on a whim several years earlier when he entered a quick 40-mile jaunt to Pittwater Bay and back in beautiful weather. But he pulled the page out of the magazine, just in case. On December 14, he decided to give himself an early Christmas present and made out a check for the $400 entry fee. He had second thoughts, and hesitated mailing the check. But on December 24 he gave in and put the check in the mail, addressed to David White at race headquarters in Newport. He had no suitable boat for such a venture and was in the midst of wrapping up an important construction project that would undoubtedly demand his undivided attention for many months. Little did Gosson realize how radically his life was about to change.

Methodically, but surreptitiously, he began forming plans to make the August 28 starting line in Newport. When the BOC corporation became the race sponsors early in the year, Pier One, a former ferry terminal renovated into a restaurant and shopping mall, was chosen as the site for the Sydney layover. Gosson wrangled $50,000 from Pier One in sponsorship funds. It was only a fraction of what the project eventually would cost, but it would help defray expenses and Gosson knew that if he sacrificed a year from his work that he would need the money. Next, he began to make inquiries about *Leda*. It was barely suitable for singlehanded sailing, but he knew the boat and trusted it, and correctly reasoned that with the right sort of offer the boat would be for sale.

Gosson rebought his old boat on May 2nd and renamed her *Leda Pier One* after her partial benefactor. On May 23, he set out for America. In the interval, he gave power of attorney to his accountant over his newly-built property—an eight-unit waterfront condominium, only two of which had been sold. For the first time in his life, Gosson was turning his back on his business. It left him uneasy.

"The sky was just starting to fall in business-wise," he said. "The other units weren't selling and it was fairly obvious that we were going to go down a spell but there was no way of knowing how far down. The news in real estate at the time was bad, but I don't listen too much to other people because they never have the same outlook as you do yourself. So there was gloom and doom talk when I left, but no one knew it was going to fall in."

On the day Gosson left Sydney, a group of sailors gathered at the CYC to bid him farewell. One of them said, "A bunch of us got on a boat and watched *Leda* sail through the heads. It was kind of sad. We reckoned that might be the last time we'd see old Neville." Gosson's friends were not alone in that opinion. The Australians love to bet and, upon Gosson's departure, odds against him making Rhode Island in time to start the race were 6 to 4. It looked like easy money and, as the Sydney bookies would say, the gamblers were "going for the hip."

From the very beginning of his long journey, Gosson's strength and will were sorely tested. "I had as much drama as I've ever had off the coast of New Zealand," he said. "It was 4°C in a Force 9 and the boat was just pounding . . . bang, bang, bang! It was the first time in my life that I've ever been on my hands and knees belowdeck on a yacht. Then I heard this tremendous noise and somehow managed to get on deck. The boom had sheared off at the gooseneck fitting and was flying around like a 300-pound battering ram. It was bad news, it was."

The swinging boom smashed the surrounding stanchions and pounded against the shrouds before Gosson could secure it to the mast. Then his SatNav stopped working, leaving him with no way of knowing his exact position in the foggy, tricky and hazardous waters off New Zealand. At that point, within days of leaving Sydney, Gosson knew he would have to stop in New Zealand to repair his electronic navigation instrument. But that was not the only reason for pulling in.

"On my exit from Australia, I was so frantic I forgot my clothes. When I got to New Zealand, I was walking around in a pair of shorts in the middle of winter and a pair of yachting shoes. Everybody must have thought I was bonkers, and I probably would've thought the same, but I was so cold and miserable that I couldn't get into the store quick enough to buy myself a pair of slacks and some jerseys."

By the time Gosson crossed the Pacific Ocean and neared the Panama Canal, he was well aware the start was drawing near, and that if he ran into any problem transiting the canal, he would surely arrive in Newport after the fleet had left. His lady friend back in Australia, Annie Wilson, knew that as well, and telephoned Nigel Rowe of the BOC Group in London who in turn contacted the people at Airco, the company's American affiliate.

"I arrived at the canal on a Friday and there were all sorts of yachts waiting to get through," Gosson said. "Then I met Karl Knacken, the South American representative for Airco, who had just flown in. He spoke Spanish and had the paperwork all lined up. Later that day, I got measured and cleared customs and quarantine. At half past six the next morning, the pilot and rope handlers showed up. On Sunday I went through, while all the guys who had been there when I got there were still waiting. I don't know who he paid or what he said, but he sure must have thrown a few bob around."

Gosson arrived in Newport on August 19. He had sailed nearly halfway around the world in 79 days, an average of 142 miles a day over the 11,233-mile voyage. The race was only nine days away and there was much work to be done to *Leda*. But Gosson figured he'd had a pretty good practice run. If the BOC race had been a school reunion, he would have won the prize for having come the farthest.

On the day he arrived, Gosson received a telegram from the prime minister of Australia. "Great stuff," it read. "All Australia is proud of you for carrying its banner."

The next day Gosson received a telex from his accountant. "Come back, right now," it read. "Don't bother tying up the boat. If you don't everything is gone."

"It was a bit frustrating," Gosson said. But he was determined to see it through. "I had to go on the race. I simply had too much to lose by not starting. You can't take a sponsor's money, have everyone wish you off, set sail for the race start, and then not go when it's so close at hand. It is just not possible, irrespective of the financial cost."

Gosson had set up an emergency restructuring plan for his company before leaving to assure that standby finances would be available if needed during his time at sea. The plan never came off and, when the critical moment arrived and the company's future relied on his presence to rearrange loans and tap a few long-standing debts, Gosson was temporarily unavailable. He got on the phone and was told by his accountant to come to his senses, to be responsible and return to Sydney and take control. Gosson suggested politely that he might try stalling the creditors. If the company were going down the tubes, then so be it. He would be back soon enough and there would be time to dispose of the company's assets in an orderly fashion when he returned around the new year. Then he hung up and went back to mending sails and taking on provisions, truly pressing matters.

The round-about return voyage to Australia was frustrating, as Gosson's competitive spirit remained healthy while his business acumen faded. He did not help his cause by removing 3,400 pounds of lead from *Leda*'s keel before the start of the race.

"I crucified myself," he said. "But based on my studies I felt that mostly we'd either have light winds or winds abaft the beam, and I wanted to improve the boat's performance in those conditions. In actuality, I had winds forward of the beam 65 percent of the time. It made me a knot and a half slower, which adds up to more than 30 miles a day. Also, it was a rougher ride and the boat was tender." Gosson arrived 10th overall into Cape Town after the initial leg, partly because of the rigging problem that reoccurred in Leg II.

He kept the vow he made in Cape Town and sailed below Tasmania, thus avoiding Bass Strait. When Gosson turned north towards Sydney, he discovered he was in a close duel with Jacques de Roux for third place overall. De Roux and *Skoiern* had persevered through a miserable voyage, and continued to lead Class II convincingly. As the two skippers sailed along the east coast of Australia, they were first teased by light air and then hammered by strong head winds and a contrary current. De Roux held a slight lead over Gosson in the Bass Strait, but the margin was slowly chipped away. *Leda* took the lead for good in her home waters. On December 26, as Gosson sailed north, the 128-boot fleet in the annual Sydney to Hobart classic sailed south out of the city towards Tasmania. The irony and symbolism of the large crewed fleet bearing down on lonely *Leda* was not lost on Gosson. For in Sydney, a tidy group of local businessmen were keeping a curious and steady eye on *Leda*'s daily position.

On the evening of December 29, under a full moon accompanied by gentle summery breezes, Gosson again sailed into Sydney Harbor to be greeted by the spectacular skyline—shimmering and aglow. It was a fitting night for a triumphant return. One year and five days had passed since Gosson sheepishly posted his entry for the Around Alone race. Now, as he sailed back home, he was completing a record solo circumnavigation of 187 days, 14 hours and 43 minutes. But the return was bittersweet.

When Gosson first heard of the singlehanded race, he knew it was exactly the sort of challenge he needed, though he did not understand precisely why. Upon his return, it was obvious to all that he was enjoying the time of his life. Bearded and fit, he not only looked, but felt, different. His fulfillment stemmed in part from the fact that daily at sea he had to take chances and then stick to them. That his life was often at stake was one of the accepted consequences. The stimulation and satisfaction Gosson found while sailing alone was not unlike the gratification he had once received from making hard business decisions. But in Sydney, he knew there was the matter of his failed business to resolve.

Gosson didn't have much time to dwell on these thoughts upon his arrival at the main dock of Pier One. Blaring television lights erased the soft moonlight. A girl in a koala bear suit adorned with a natty "Pier One" sailor's outfit climbed aboard *Leda* and hugged Gosson for the cameras. A ragtime band played "Waltzing Matilda"; and once he stepped onto the dock he was immediately seated behind a candlelit table where he was served a sizzling steak from a nearby restaurant. The TV news cameras recorded the awkward moment. A puzzled Gosson wolfed his dinner and answered reporters' questions.

It was his first human contact in 53 days.

The dockside celebration had not been spontaneous. Instead, it was attributable to none other than Rodney Jenkins who, in addition to his role as public relations adviser to BOC affiliate Commonwealth Industrial Gas, was also the PR man for Pier One. This was the same Jenkins who had helped inform all Australia to Gosson's "mysterious disappearance" during his temporary communications problems in Leg I. Gosson may have been a solitary sailor but his exploits had become a matter of public record in the preceding weeks largely through Jenkin's inroads with the local media. His adventures had been shared with everybody who read the front page and, briefly, Gosson unwittingly became a bit player in the game of corporate communications.

In the course of the layover in Sydney, Gosson's fame and his personal business crisis forced him to stay at center stage: First, to defend the sport of singlehanding and, second, to defend his personal right to go on a walkabout. Despite all the lights and celebration, his homecoming was destined to be bittersweet.

Jenkins, though brazen and forthright, was doing his job well. He generated heaps of publicity for BOC and its hosts. But in doing so, he missed the point of the race. In fact, in Cape Town, Jenkins made the bizarre remark that his job would be much easier if one of the boats sank. He meant, of course, that such a disastrous event would be scooped up immediately by the media and the public, thus promoting the race in a way he never could. It was an easy sort of comment to take out of context, which some racers did.

The amount of press the race received and the way in which it was embraced by the populace was puzzling, however, because singlehanding yacht racing was "unofficially" banned by the nation's premier yachting authority, the Australian Yachting Federation (AYF). Jenkin's skewed publicity, in the eyes of sailors, did nothing to help its cause. The AYF sanctions were placed not because of the BOC race but after a fatality in a singlehanded race from New Zealand to Australia four years before. The main reason behind the ban was that in singlehanded sailing, because the skipper must sleep, a proper lookout can not be kept for 24 hours each day, thus ignoring a tenet in the COLREGS, the international rules of the road.

Originally, when David White laid out the projected course for the race, the layover for the second leg had been a yacht club in Hobart, where local yachtsmen felt little pressure from the AYF's headquarters in Sydney. When the BOC Group entered the picture, one stipulation to its sponsorship agreement was to change the second leg venue to Sydney, headquarters of its Australian affiliate. When the city's several prestigious yacht clubs were approached regarding berthing for the fleet, they replied negatively. For that reason, Pier One became the berth for the BOC boats. This arrangement was a far cry from the professional reception given in Cape Town, and the problem was compounded by the fact that nearly everyone with the slightest connection to Sydney's marine industry sailed off to Hobart as the singlehanders arrived. Not only were there no facilities for getting work done, but when space could be found there was no one to do the work. This, along with the general carnival atmosphere of Pier One, led to frayed nerves for several racers.

Tony Mooney, the director of the AYF, felt that the accommodations were compatible and appropriate considering the goals of the sponsor. He said, "A sponsored yacht race is a product to sell. And remember that we're talking about racing and not cruising, and a situation where there is always pressure to push the boat harder. I question whether a sponsor would have gotten as much exposure at a yacht club as at Pier One."

Mooney's contention was that race sponsors treated such ventures as strict business transactions, with an eye on the bottom line. Sponsors of individual boats were mainly interested in results and placings. In both cases, the safety and welfare of the skippers were relegated to a back seat by economic necessity. When Richard Broadhead arrived in Sydney aboard *Perseverance of Medina,* he looked as battered as a sailor could be. He personified all the worst nightmares Tony Mooney or anyone else could have about singlehanded sailing. Broadhead's second leg made his first trying voyage from Newport to Cape Town seem like a canoe ride on a lake. At one point, he was nearly pitchpoled when his bow burrowed deeply into the crest of a passing wave. He was thrown against his bow pulpit while making a headsail change, breaking the pulpit but saving himself by clinging to the sail. His three self-steering gears all broke. He almost hit a whale during a storm. His mast step slipped and his rigging went slack. He ripped both his mainsails and damaged his genoa. He had to steer with little rest for the last week of his voyage and did not sleep at all the final two days. Worst of all, his alternator broke down within two weeks of departing Cape Town, leaving him with no power and no radio communications at all for 47 days.

Broadhead arrived, dead tired, on the morning of January 3, crossing the finish line just as the first long rays of daybreak began to crawl over Sydney Harbor. A lone powerboat from the Volunteer Coastal Patrol, with a sleepy staffer from Jenkin's firm aboard, was his reception committee.

"Who was first?" Broadhead asked.

"Credit."

"Second?"

"Voortrekker. Pier One's also . . ."

"What about *Gipsy Moth*?"

"On the rocks at Gabo Island."

Broadhead threw his arms into the air. "Oh my God," he said. "I didn't know. How is Desmond? What about the others?"

Desmond's okay but *Lady Pepperell* pitchpoled and sank."

"You're kidding. I nearly pitchpoled too."

Broadhead's voice was barely audible by the time he was safely tied up at the docks. He quietly answered the questions of a few journalists and then was led to a car for a drive to a hotel. Broadhead fit Mooney's description of a beleaguered sponsored sailor to a "T". But there was one hitch. Broadhead had no sponsor. He was sailing the most difficult boat in the race—("It was not jokingly called *Perspiration* in its old racing days for nothing," Hampton had said)—but he owed nothing to anyone but himself. When Broadhead was whisked away that morning, no one expected to see him again for a good 24 hours. He was back on his boat, tidying up and assessing his damage, later that afternoon.

But there was a side to sponsorship that Mooney would never know about. It transcended money matters and went straight to the heart of camaraderie and caring, which Gosson and the others had slowly nurtured among each other as the difficult race evolved. It was characterized when Tony Lush arrived in Sydney.

The doublehanded portion of *Mooneshine*'s second leg—with Francis Stokes serving as skipper, navigator and baker of bread and Tony Lush mastering his duties as "first-class passenger," dinner chef and chief bottle washer—had been annoying only because of a lack of wind. The shipboard routine was pleasant. "We ate rather well," Stokes said. "I'd really had a shopping spree in Newport and we probably both gained weight."

"I never did finish *The Rise and Fall of the Roman Empire*," Lush said.

The pair arrived two days after *Perseverance,* on January 5. *Mooneshine* sailed through Sydney Heads near sundown, the first of the fleet to arrive in daylight. Stokes trimmed the sails and worked the boat while Lush popped his head out through the companionway and photographed the many photographers. After crossing the finish line, Stokes eased the halyards and dropped the sails and, for the first time in many weeks, Lush went about his first sailing-related task and helped furl the main. Soon a police launch came alongside to tow *Mooneshine* to a dockside rendezvous with an international press corps and several hundred curious onlookers. The first people to step aboard the boat were Don Downes and Charlie Kurtz, two executives of the West Point Pepperell company —Lush's sponsors—who had just arrived from Georgia.

From the AYF's point of view—that sponsors cared only about standings and results—the company might have been expected to ignore the ill-fated captain of their failed ship, whose publicity was certainly not all positive. (It was, however, substantial, lending support to Jenkins' Cape Town remark that a sinking would draw media attention that mere public relations never could.) But that was not the style of the southern gentlemen. "To have just let this thing be," said Kurtz, "for a lot of reasons, would be the wrong thing to do. We're here to get some feedback from Tony. There were lots of good things that came from this project and some things that were not so good. But West Point Pepperell is a better company for having been in this race."

The sponsors and the sailor left Sydney together two days later. Before they went, the businessmen bought Stokes a new Sestrel compass for *Mooneshine* as a way of saying thanks for bringing their boy home.

If there was one highlight for Gosson during the Sydney layover it came on January 11, when he was asked to serve as keynote speaker for a luncheon at the Cruising Yacht Club of Australia in honor of the BOC Challengers. That the singlehanders were being recognized at all in such hallowed surroundings was certainly setting a precedent. Gosson took full advantage of the occasion, and before a packed room he made his position known on several pertinent matters.

"In Australia here we have a terrible lot to learn as far as singlehanded racing is concerned. I think it will take us quite a long time to catch up. There's no doubt about France; they're just so far in front of us at the moment that I just do hope that the yachting federation sees its way free to accept singlehanded and shorthanded racing. I really think that yachting in Australia at the moment is taking the form of specializing—either you're a helmsman or you're working point or you're working somewhere on a coffee grinder somewhere. But we are becoming a race of specialists in yachting as we are in commercial life. I think singlehanded racing is a chance to let a man who is prepared to be a general all-rounder show his wares. So I hope in Australia here in the future that we will accept this racing. Let's learn from some of these other countries and give the chappie who's prepared to be an all-rounder the chance to stand up and sail around the world."

Gosson spoke passionately about singlehanded sailing that day and on several other occasions. Usually one to avoid interviews, Gosson would talk long and hard when the questions posed related to the politics of the sport, or the pleasures of it.

"So many people here want to know about it," he said. "I've sort of got the foot in the door. Now we've got to get the door opened.

"Singlehanding can and should be the decathlon of yachting and the Grand Prix of ocean racing rolled into one. I really believe the AYF is out of touch with reality. Can everyone else be wrong, not only the other countries who run these races but the prime minister and the man in the street? It is becoming evident to me that the thinking of the people in Australia is not necessarily in keeping with that of the AYF. I think with local interest and club pressure mounting in the future, the next running of the event will be difficult for the AYF to ignore."

Almost imperceptibly, between his preparation for the race and participation in it, Gosson became a rebel with a cause. In Cape Town he had been tentative in answering whether he would continue to race after Sydney. But as the days neared for the beginning of Leg III and the long passage to Rio, Gosson tackled the remaining work on *Leda* with renewed vigor. Only one hitch remained.

Gosson believed that if he'd abandoned the race before starting he could have saved his company. That was no longer an option. On the eve of the start, however, his firm's creditors were none too pleased with the notion of Gosson sailing off with one of their assets—*Leda* was registered in the company's name. There was even some talk of chaining the boat to the pier if an equitable arrangement did not crop up.

"If you owe people money, the best thing to do is to talk to them," Gosson said. "If you ignore people, that's when the real trouble begins. I thought I was going to have to talk long and hard to get out of Sydney, and I did. I said there'd be better resale value from *Leda* in the States, especially if she finished the race. It took three meetings for the final approval to come through. And even then, one man came down the day before I left to make sure the insurance on the boat was paid up. They weren't taking any chances.

"I realized later that the most logical thing I could've done when I left Sydney the second time for Leg III was to never go back. I could go chartering in the Bahamas and have a jolly bloody time for the rest of my life. But I love my country. That's where my friends are."

On the morning of the start of the third leg, one of those friends arose at 5 a.m. with a special mission. She went into the clear morning and gathered armfuls of fresh frangipani, a delicate wildflower indigenous to the gentle South Pacific climate. Following tradition, she wove the flowers into a lustrous lei, and this she presented to Gosson before he boarded *Leda*. Gosson wore the flowered necklace all that morning, during the start and out through Sydney Heads. Then, as sailors from that part of the world have done for uncounted years, he took the fragrant jewelry and tossed it into the sea. When it washed up ashore, it would guarantee his return home.

Gosson's walkabout was only half over.

15

Hard Training from the East

IF THERE WAS one reason for the BOC Challenge, it lay two thirds of the way through Leg III, from Sydney to Rio de Janeiro, Brazil. Rounding Cape Horn at the southern tip of the South American continent over the centuries had become the ultimate measure of seamen. But to achieve Cape Horn, an apprenticeship had to be served.

In January and February, 1983, the 11 skippers still in the race were to find that a string of easterly gales—unusually uncommon in the prevailing westerlies—would test their abilities, their resolve and their wills to survive. Not all were destined to reach Cape Horn.

The afternoon of the start, Pier One and Sydney buzzed with activity. The city was in the midst of the Festival of Sydney, a month-long celebration, and the day's activities included the annual ferry-boat "race", the BOC start and a buoy race among the local fleet of Australia's exciting unlimited 18-foot class. The harbor was abuzz with boats of every size and description and the shore was lined with spectators on blankets, eating picnic lunches. A festive blend of merriment and confusion was in the air.

Among the 10 skippers ready to start for Rio (Richard Konkolski was just approaching Sydney from Fremantle and would start seven days later), the mood was appropriately frantic, but less so than it had been in either Cape Town or Newport. The numbers had been pared, but those still racing were confident after successfully negotiating their first south-

137

ern ocean stint. The sky was bright and clear, the wind blew steadily but moderately from the east. It was a good day to go to sea.

Along the dock, last-minute details kept everyone busy. A feisty group of more than 20 New Zealanders ("Sydney is our country's second largest city," one said in reference to the large number of local Kiwi's), all decked out in *City of Dunedin* T-shirts, stood ready with cameras and beers to wish Richard McBride a fair journey. Tom Lindholm, the American sailor who retired from the race in its first days, had flown in from California to serve as "support crew" for Dan Byrne and *Fantasy*. Along with Pat Byrne, Lindholm busied himself about the boat's deck until it was time for Byrne to leave. Philippe Jeantot, with a miniature stuffed koala bear pinned to his collar, stood at the bow of his immaculately prepared *Credit Agricole*, posed for snapshots and signed several autographs. Bertie Reed did a final interview with an Australian newspaperman and then, apparently bored with it all, went for a last, quick beer. Robin Knox-Johnston shook hands with each of the sailors. And Richard Broadhead and Jacques de Roux, in many ways the most disparate of those still sailing, huddled together for a few moments on the foredeck of *Skoiern III* discussing radio frequencies. Their chat was prophetic.

The docks were off limits to everyone except families and photographers. But one level up, on the main concourse of Pier One, the railing was lined four and five-deep with curious spectators. As the boats were towed away from the pier, one by one, a public address system announcer described each skipper and his boat. These announcements were followed by tremendous cheers. It was like the introductions of the starting lineups at a championship basketball game. Then the boats were gone.

Only one sailor was left at the docks. The steering system aboard Guy Bernardin's *Ratso II* had stopped working. Guy had repaired the system earlier in the week, but when his turn for towing came up the wheel was inoperable. The towboat passed *Ratso* and Bernardin dove into the lazarette to again tackle the cable and quadrant linkage. In his haste, he led the cable backwards so the boat's wheel steered right when it was turned left and left when turned right. But Bernardin was not overly worried and relaxed with his wife, Mitzi, in the cockpit with a cup of coffee while the others made for the starting area. The applause and craziness of the start held little appeal for Bernardin. He sat back and enjoyed the spectacle. When the crowd thinned, he returned to the lazarette, took the assembly apart, straightened out the cables and bolted the system together. It worked fine and Bernardin crossed the starting line alone several hours later.

Nearly a thousand pleasure boats crowded the starting area, including several large ferries laden with paying spectators. Volunteers from the Royal Sydney Lifesaving Squadron did their best, and were mostly successful at keeping the starting area clear. The sailors waved to the crowd and to each other as they milled around the starting line, mostly under mainsail alone.

The merriment was contagious, and so was the drama. These men were once again off, with their destiny in their own hands, into the deep reaches of the Pacific Ocean. Those in the spectator boats watched with a mixture of curiosity, awe and bewilderment. The layover had cast an unusual group of characters into Sydney's public eye, from the dashing Jeantot to the stoic Desmond Hampton to the competent if incomprehensible Neville Gosson. No one on Sydney Harbor doubted the racers' courage or endurance.

At 3 p.m. the starting gun sounded and the boats made for the line. Jeantot aboard *Credit Agricole* had been reaching off at the leeward end of the line but when the gun went off he trimmed his sails and accelerated towards the line. He was going to be first across when, suddenly, he had to alter his course. Ahead of him, sailing across the starting line the wrong way, with his spinnaker pole rigged and the sail ready to hoist, was Yukoh Tada on *Koden Okera*. Tada crossed the line heading west just before the gun went off as the rest of the fleet hardened up and sailed east, the right way, out of Sydney Harbor. Jeantot's slight hitch slowed him just long enough for none other than Dan Byrne on *Fantasy* to cross the line first and lead the fleet, ever so briefly, out to sea. For Byrne, it was a proud moment. After Cape Town and his fast passage across the Indian Ocean, he reveled in showing off *Fantasy*'s transom.

At the windward end of the starting line, Richard Broadhead ran through a fire drill of his own. As he cleared the line, the underwater blade on his new Fleming self-steering gear snagged on the starting buoy's anchor line, stopping *Perseverance of Medina* in her tracks with her sails luffing wildly. Frantically, Broadhead leaped to the stern. He climbed down onto the frame that held the gear on the transom and tried first to kick free the orange inflatable buoy that had become his mooring. He then got his knife out and was getting ready to get into the water to cut the anchor line when a friend arrived in a dinghy and did the job for him. Delayed and harried, Broadhead trimmed his mainsail and genoa and chased Byrne and the others toward Sydney Heads.

Byrne's lead did not last long. Gosson's 53-foot *Leda* drove by *Fantasy* and took the lead. To leeward, Jeantot collected himself after Tada's blunder. Once he got *Credit Agricole* moving well, it wasn't long before the powerful 56-foot cutter overtook *Leda* and assumed its usual place at the head of the fleet. In the northeast breeze, the fleet was able to slack sheets a bit as it cleared the Heads on a course for Stewart Island at the southern end of New Zealand.

Dusk fell over the Tasman Sea and one by one the boats sailed into the darkness and out of sight of each other. Behind them lay half of the race. The racers' numbers had been reduced in the most Darwinian way; six sailors had not been able to make the grade, for six different and, on the whole, good reasons. But they were gone. The 11 who continued had proved they had the skill and endurance to prevail in extraordinary conditions of loneliness, poor weather, sickness and injury. They had consistently made sound decisions. They had shown time and again they were able to learn quickly from their mistakes. They were the fit.

As they sailed down the Tasman Sea, the fleet arranged itself more or less in the pattern that had become established during the second leg. Jeantot marched out to a wide lead and was followed by Reed and Broadhead and de Roux. Gosson lagged behind the other Class I boats, sailing just ahead of the knot of other Class II boats led by Francis Stokes. Gradually, Byrne slipped to the rear of the fleet, yet was never very far behind. Only Bernardin chose a radical route. Because *Ratso* was so light and prone to being hurled about by the large seas of the Forties, he chose to sail north of New Zealand before gradually dipping into the higher latitudes. He gambled that the lighter winds and smaller seas would enable him to drive his 38-foot cutter faster to cover the longer distance in less time. The 500 pounds of ballast he added in Sydney (sand bags in the bilge) would help keep *Ratso* upright on the way south. After Cape Horn, he planned to jettison the ballast to lighten ship for the gentler winds along the South American coast.

The first easterly gale hit just as the Class I boats reached New Zealand. Reed in *Voortrekker* got hit the hardest. *Voortrekker*'s mast hit the water and kept going. The sloop did not roll all the way over, but he was nearly upside down before her lead keel began to pivot her upright again. While upside down, most of his drinking water spilled out from his tank, leaving Reed with short rations for the rest of the voyage. But worse than that was the chaos in the interior of the boat.

"The biggest hassle was the mess. There was peanut butter everywhere. In the sleeping bag, on the floor, on the cushions, everywhere. And there were eggs dripping from the bulkheads and ceiling."

Near Reed, Broadhead and de Roux were making it a tight race for third place. De Roux, once again, made remarkable daily runs in his 41-foot sloop *Skoiern III*. By keeping up with the 52-foot *Perseverance* and the 49-foot *Voortrekker,* he was accomplishing the theoretically impossible. To a large extent, waterline length determines a boat's speed. Yet here was a boat with 10 feet less waterline making similar speeds. The difference, as it had previously, lay in de Roux's ability to coax speed out of his boat and his skill at choosing the right course through the weather systems. After the gale, as the four front runners rounded New Zealand's

Stewart Island, they found a good breeze and a cooperative sea. For the next week, Jeantot led the three others eastward as they made for the 100-mile gap between the Bounty and Antipodes Islands, which would be the last hazard on the way to Cape Horn.

But behind the leaders, the smaller boats missed the wind and they lagged behind. For New Zealander Richard McBride, turning the corner eastward around his homeland provided him with an opportunity he could not pass up. During the first week out, McBride once again suffered the migraine headaches that plagued him during Leg II. On the third day out, he opened his bottle of pain killers and left them sitting on the galley bench after taking two tablets. At that moment, *City of Dunedin* lurched on a wave, tipping over the bottle. One after another the tablets streamed into the oily murk of the bilge, lost for good. Without the tablets, McBride could barely function during headache episodes. He had to do something and Stewart Island was his best chance for help.

Via radio, McBride contacted the New Zealand Navy's *RV Acheron* and they in turn arranged for a rendezvous at Stewart Island. In a failing breeze, McBride rounded South Cape and there met the fishing vessel *Arun,* which towed *City of Dunedin* into Broad Bay. After a night at anchor, a helicopter loomed in over the hills and parked in the air over the schooner. Down came food stores, more medicine as requested and two television journalists, who interviewed McBride for the New Zealand Broadcasting Corporation. Taping and interview completed, the two journalists were hoisted off the black schooner's deck and disappeared with a wave back to the mainland, to a hot lunch, a crowded pub and a few tales of excitement. McBride was not sad to see them go. He hoisted anchor and ghosted out of Broad Bay on a light breeze. The fishing vessel *Arun* escorted *City of Dunedin* out of the bay and stayed with her as she cleared the rocky coast. Although *City of Dunedin* was not a fast boat, McBride had shown she was capable of staying with the front runners in Class II during the southern ocean legs. His return to New Zealand, although brief, was in many ways triumphant. He became a celebrity. Even so, it was not hard to leave Broad Bay and New Zealand behind. He had the race to finish and Cape Horn lay ahead.

McBride followed eastward behind Stokes, Byrne and Gosson. They sailed in the high Forties, wanting to avoid the higher winds and colder weather further south. The daily ham radio chat show, or "coffee klatch" as Byrne called it, continued and McBride and Stokes were the centers of conversation. Tada, too, tuned in every day. Not long after the fleet turned the corner at Stewart Island, Stokes found himself trying to explain to Tada, via the radio, how to bake bread. He ran through the recipe—yeast, flour, shortening, salt and so on—and then described the process of kneading the bread and letting it rise. At the other end of the radio signal, Tada tried to take it all in. But when Stokes finished, Tada still had one simple, perplexing question.

"Francis," he asked, "what is flour?"

Despite his limited English, Tada often was able to express his ideas and emotions better than native English speakers. Tada brought a unique attitude to the race. "Hard training," he called sailing in the southern ocean. The training was to improve his mind, enhance his senses and open his understanding of jazz and abstract art.

"I want to hear color. I want to see music," he said.

Oddly enough, it was Tada's interest in jazz that led him to discover sailing. In the early sixties, Tada saw a documentary film about the Newport Jazz Festival that featured a long clip showing boats in Newport running downwind under billowing spinnakers. The pictures were accompanied by a free-flowing Thelonius Monk piano solo. Tada's healthy imagination was captured, and he went back to see the film again and again. It wasn't long after that he purchased a small sailing dinghy and began teaching himself how to sail.

Every morning at sea, Tada sat cross-legged on his bunk and meditated, training his mind and body for the task at hand. During the second leg layover, he spent some time painting abstract pictures and at Pier One in Sydney he held a one-man show by nailing his small, square canvases onto the pier's pilings. He called the show "Fantasy of the Deep Ocean" and each painting was a wild, vibrant swirl of color. While at sea in the first leg, he brought his electric piano—he carried the piano as well as a tenor saxophone on board—and set it up on the coach roof of *Okera*. The tune he played was a kind of Zen exercise in random but studied creation. He held his fingers a fraction of an inch over the keys. As the boat moved with the ocean beneath it, Tada's fingers struck the keys. The tune had the plinking, atonal quality of traditional Japanese music and the composition's title was, again, "Fantasy of the Deep Ocean."

On the third leg, Tada planned to concentrate on his music. Trying to learn to "see music" would be his recreation, his mental escape from the confines of *Okera*'s cabin and the strictures of the race. But the race was foremost in his mind and during the third leg he planned to test himself by sailing as far south as possible to sail the shortest route to Cape Horn. He planned to navigate along the rim of the floating pack ice, in the cold and fog at 60°S. Because of the risk of icebergs, he fitted his boat in Cape Town and in Sydney with a bowsprit or "bergsprit," which would avert a head-on collision by deflecting *Okera*'s bow enough to save the boat. The first sprit had been torn away during the gale the first night out from Cape Town. But the second was engineered a bit better and stood up to the long passage to Cape Horn.

Aside from cutting off hundreds of miles on the voyage, sailing south to the ice had two other practical benefits for Tada. The route carried him into calmer waters than the gale-swept Forties and Fifties. According to his research, the highest average wave heights in the southern Pacific occured between 50° and 55°S. Tada said, "My boat not good for choppy seas, so I choose calmer seas."

Another reason to sail south was to find the Antarctic Circumpolar Current, a warmer "river" in the ocean that runs eastward through a cold sea. If he found the current and was able to stay in it, he hoped to add 25 or 30 miles to his daily average. It was a risk, because ice had been reported at 64°S and the current he wanted to find lay at approximately 62°S, leaving him roughly 100 miles of room for error—not much when a skipper is navigating in fog and strong winds, and is looking for poorly charted currents. But it was a risk Tada sought eagerly; his own personal philosophy dictated such "hard training." Unlike several other skippers, Tada never wore a safety harness. Instead of relying on a tether, he meditated to train his senses to be alert to danger. "No safety harness for me because I am like child. My thinking is very simple. My feeling is very simple. If I have accident, I am like samurai. My heart is like samurai at fight time. My spirit is extension of my training."

Tada was his own man, seeking his own destiny. But he had a strong mentor who had taught him the hard training of adventure. That mentor was working that summer at an Argentine base on Antarctica. Naomi Uemura was a Japanese explorer and adventurer in the same mold as Thor Heyerdahl or Jacques Cousteau. In 1978, Uemura led a Japanese dog sled team on an assault of the North Pole over the Greenland ice cap. It was a long and arduous trip, requiring base camps, food drops and radio coordinations. The man he chose to run the support crew was his friend Tada. Over a period of seven months, Uemura accomplished a remarkable dog-sled run and Tada learned about personal discipline.

Now, Uemura was in the Antarctic at the Argentine base at San Martin and in regular communication with Tada by ham radio. Uemura reported the winter had been mild in the Antarctic and there was less ice than usual. He told Tada how to find the Antarctic Circumpolar Current and how to avoid turbulent upwellings at the Albatross Cordillera (a submerged range of mountains along Tada's route). While Uemura had been driving his dogs across the Arctic ice cap, Tada had been the voice on the radio offering help and solace. Now the roles were reversed. Uemura did not let his comrade down.

After clearing the Tasman Sea and sailing into the windy Forties with the rest of the fleet, Tada began a slow descent into the cold and fog. He sailed through the Fifties and then entered the rarely visited Sixties. Looking for the circumpolar current, he took water temperature readings every day, looking for the two-degree increase that would mean he had found his highway east. Once he reached the Sixties he entered a frozen kingdom, a land of ice smoke and freezing blankets of fog. If there were icebergs to avoid, he could not see them. He did not see the sun or take a sun sight for 50 days. The cold made working on deck difficult and changing sail an ordeal. To remove his gloves to wrestle a shackle or tie a lanyard was to run the risk of frostbite. Down below, the cabin heating system did not work efficiently, so he was forced to spend long hours wrapped in his sleeping bag as *Okera* blundered ahead through the nearly frozen sea in the dense fog. In the cold, Tada became lethargic. Like a child only half awake, he sometimes could not bring himself to leave the warmth of his sleeping bag, and urinated into a small plastic sack. It was hard training for Tada, yet his own strength kept him sailing on. No doubt Uemura's support bolstered Tada's resolve. Uemura promised Tada early in the leg that, when *Okera* rounded Cape Horn, he would be there. The promise was a magnanimous gesture. But there was no practical way for Uemura to carry it out.

While Tada was blowing on his hands and stamping his feet in the moderate breezes and low seas in the Sixties, the front runners faced one easterly gale after another. In the Fifties and Forties, the westerly prevailing winds drive a parade of low pressure systems to the east. In the lows, the wind shifts to the east as the front of the storm passes, only to shift to the west once more as the system moves east. That, at least was the theory. What Jeantot, Reed, de Roux and Broadhead discovered, however, did not match the theory. They sailed east, day after day, into the teeth of easterly winds. After two weeks of struggle, each was exhausted and exasperated.

Early on the morning of the 15th day out of Sydney, during an easterly gale, Jeantot got the worst scare of the voyage. The prior afternoon, the wind had begun to build and he shortened sail quickly. During the evening, the Aries broke and he was forced to engage the automatic pilot before going to sleep. Two hours later, he awoke to *Credit Agricole* accelerating noisily over the tops of waves and crashing heavily into the troughs. Still half asleep, he began to make hot chocolate, when an errant wave picked up *Credit Agricole* and rolled her over. Jeantot fell headlong across the cabin and landed on the edge of the berth, almost knocking him out and acquiring a cut on his right eyebrow. Pots and pans, food stores, books and clothes lay scattered around the cabin in a pitiful mess. On deck, the VHF antenna and the running lights at the masthead had broken off when the top of the mast hit the water. Beyond that there was little obvious damage. *Credit Agricole* suffered the knockdown, picked herself up, and shook herself off. Jeantot did not feel as resilient. Groggy and bleeding, he gave up. He hauled down all sail, shut off the autopilot and went to bed.

But he could not sleep. He felt the boat drifting westward and knew that Reed (especially Reed), de Roux and Broadhead were still sailing hard for Cape Horn, catching him and perhaps passing him. Feeling guilty, he pulled himself out of his warm bunk and went on deck to raise some sail. As he set the autopilot, he felt the wheel and knew at once something was wrong with the rudder. After inspecting the cables and gears inside the boat he realized the damage was under the water, and thereby proportionally more serious. But he was tired and the boat was moving, so again he went to bed. He didn't get up all day.

That night he spoke over the ham radio with his friends in France. He told them about the roll-over and said, "It was a work-related accident, so I think it was okay to take a day to rest."

In the morning, Jeantot felt better and cleaned up the mess in the cabin. The rudder had not mended itself over the night, so he dropped all sail, donned his wet suit, and with a line tied around his waist, he jumped over the side to inspect the damage. In the shockingly cold and pristinely clear water, he saw that the bottom bearing on the rudder had broken, leaving the rudder unsupported along its bottom section. It seemed serious. He did not believe he could carry full sail and run to top speeds. He worried that he might lose steering altogether. That night, via the ham radio, he reached Dumas, his naval architect, in France. After making calculations, Dumas assured Jeantot the broken bearing had been redundant to begin with and that it would be safe to drive the boat up to 15 knots. Above that speed, the forces on the rudderpost might be enough to cause the shaft to bend or break.

Relieved, Jeantot hoisted his genoa and shook a reef out of the mainsail. He had a governor on his powerful cutter now, but the upper limit was still generous enough for him to stay in the lead. Tired and bruised from the roll, Jeantot turned south. With his weather fax he had been charting the low-pressure areas as they marched eastward. The pattern showed he should be either up in the Forties or down in the Fifties, but not right in the main fairway. Still in the lead and able to sail at nearly top speed, he gave in to the battering easterly winds and headed south into the frozen regions Tada was already exploring.

Behind him, de Roux made the same decision after struggling through an easterly gale. *Skoiern III* had handled the storm ably and was making superb daily runs, again leading Class II by a wide margin. But de Roux was exhausted from beating to windward and, like Jeantot, sought the solace of the calmer waters and lighter winds of the high Fifties. The choice to go south was strategic as well as a relief. The great circle course led that way and the reports from Antarctic field stations indicated that icebergs were not drifting into the Fifties at all.

It was a French migration to the south. But the three others who were running at the head of the fleet, Reed, Broadhead and Gosson, had a different reaction to the hard easterlies. They tacked to starboard and headed north out of the path of the gales. They were trying to position themselves on the top edges of the low-pressure systems, thereby missing the full brunt of the east winds. The only trouble with the choice to go north, one Jeantot could not comprehend, was that the English-speaking sailors were steering away from the great-circle course, lengthening instead of shortening their passage to Cape Horn.

But for Broadhead, adding a few miles to the overall distance sailed did not matter as much as staying out of the cold and fog in the deep southern latitudes. He struggled through the cold of the second leg, never getting his boat moving to her potential. On the third leg, *Perseverance* was showing her true speed through the water and Broadhead was giving Reed a battle for second place.

"When the easterlies hit, Jacques said over the radio that he was heading south to look for better winds. But Bertie and I decided to go north. Down south it looked like a bundle of lows. Plus having gotten so cold on the second leg, I knew what it was like. Couldn't work the boat. Maybe you save 200 miles, but what good is it if you can't work the boat? Both Philippe and Jacques found the cold and before long Jacques hit easterlies down there and began to sail north again. He got smart. Where Bertie and I headed, we found warm weather. You could sail in blue jeans and a shirt."

The English-speaking sailors traveled back up to 46°S while de Roux dipped to 58°S and Jeantot descended all the way to 62°S. When the easterlies subsided several days later and de Roux began to head north again, he and Gosson and Broadhead and Reed (who was 200 miles ahead of the others) began to converge, until Broadhead, Gosson and de Roux were within 300 miles of each other once again.

On February 7, three weeks into the voyage and after a week of lumpy seas and contrary winds, the leading boats were hit by the stiffest gale of the leg. The seas rose during the day until they towered against the sky. The wind howled at 50 knots and at times gusted to hurricane force. It began in the east, but quickly veered to the northwest and piped up to full force. For all caught in the fury, survival became the only strategy.

Aboard *Leda Pier One*, Gosson spent the morning lashing down deck gear and securing sails. His boat suffered one breaking wave after another and often the deck streamed with water. The 53-foot cutter strained in the tumultuous sea, but to Gosson she seemed able to handle what was being offered. He went below to heat water for coffee and while the kettle heated, he braced his tired and overworked body between the stove and a cabinet. At 56, this was a rough game for an old man.

The next thing he knew, he was airborne. "It was like someone had pulled a chair out from under me," he said. *Leda* rolled and sent Gosson soaring 10 feet across the cabin. He landed head first against a half-inch fiddle board over the settee. The wood snapped easily under his cheek. The fall knocked him out at once so he didn't feel the jarring blow to his lower back on the table top. It was the first time in his life he had been knocked out cold—despite having played professional rugby football in his youth. All he knew when he woke up was that his lower back throbbed with nauseating pain. Then, as he looked around, he saw he was lying on the deckhead and that *Leda* was upside down and rolling slowly over. Adding insult to injury, the kettle he had been tending began spitting warm water into his face.

Leda rolled again and gained her level footing. Gosson was able to press on slowly under reduced canvas, despite his throbbing head and the shooting pains in his lower back that sent him to the medicine chest for strong pain killers.

Gosson was lucky; he was still sailing. Two hundred miles away, Jacques de Roux was looking death squarely in the face.

16

59 Hours

February 8: 8 p.m. The storm was the worst of the voyage. After shortening sail down to the storm jib alone, Jacques de Roux had nothing more he could do on deck, so he climbed down the companionway ladder, slipped the wood slats that close the companionway into place and lay down on his bunk, fully dressed in oilskins and boots. On deck the wind blew 50 knots and gusted to hurricane force. The barometer, which had been falling for 24 hours, had begun to rise again. But that was not necessarily a good sign. A rapid rise after a long fall was a clear indication of strong winds to come.

De Roux left *Skoiern III* to be steered by the Sailomat wind vane self-steerer, which was not doing the job. The boat often skidded sideways down the steep wave faces, tripping and shuddering each time like a wounded bird.

De Roux waited. The storm would play itself out eventually. Meanwhile, he longed for someone to talk to, a human contact to ease the anxiety of weathering the gale.

The compass over de Roux's bunk had been reading 090°M since he had come below. As he watched it, the compass rose swung slowly to 060°M, meaning a 30-degree windshift.

He was preparing to go on deck to put *Skoiern III* back on her correct course when suddenly he was thrown like a sausage against the top of his bunk. Water flooded in. He found his footing and realized that he now stood on the underside of the deck. *Skoiern* was upside down and stayed

148

that way for an interminable moment. The world was dark and foreign and frightening. De Roux held on. And then his ears popped. A submarine commander, he knew what it meant. He was deep under the water and going down.

But then *Skoiern* began to come up again. The air pressure, compressed under the weight of flooding water, decreased on his eardrums. After a long, slow roll, during which de Roux crabbed his way down the side of the boat, *Skoiern* floated upright again.

De Roux breathed a sigh of relief, but only briefly. The wood slats in the companionway had broken loose during the rollover, leaving the cabin open. The water was up to his waist and only four inches from the companionway sill, the level at which water would flow into the boat freely and sink it. One more wave into the cockpit and he would be lost. De Roux had to bail for his life. He grabbed a plastic bucket and set to work.

There is an old saying that there is no bilge pump like a scared man with a bucket and de Roux proved it true. He bailed without stopping for three hours, until the water level in the cabin was down to the wood floorboards. Around him, the cabin that had been his home for six months at sea lay in ruin. The diesel fuel tank had ruptured, spreading a smelly film over everything. Clothing, books, pots and pans, sails and lines, all rested oddly where they fell. *Skoiern* was strange and cold and dark.

It was 11 p.m. when de Roux finally climbed up the ladder to inspect the damage on deck. He found his mast lying broken over the starboard side, sheared five feet above the deck and held in place by the halyards that ran inside the mast. The starboard lifelines had been smashed along with the stern rail. The situation was critical. To cut the mast free of the boat before it seriously damaged the hull, he began cutting the rope halyards with his knife. In the high wind and seas and darkness, he could hear the mast cruelly smashing against the hull. He cut the halyards and then with bolt cutters he cut the stays away from the mast. Finally, after what seemed like an hour, the mast dropped into the water and the dangerous ram ceased battering *Skoiern*'s hull.

But the damage was done.

When he climbed below again, de Roux found the water rising to his knees. The hole, punched by the flogging mast, was not hard to find. After bailing out the cabin again, he tore out a storage compartment filled with spare line and food. Underneath it he located a one-foot split in the aluminum, gushing freely with seawater. Using rags and wood plugs he managed to slow the flood. He could just stay ahead of it with his plastic bucket.

After emptying the cabin of water for the third time, de Roux sat down in the dark and dampness to consider what he should do. He was exhausted but still able to function. He was scared but not paralyzed.

His boat was mortally wounded but he was very much alive. This was his assessment: He'd lost his mast over the side; the boat required bailing one hour out of every two; the automatic pilot had been destroyed; all electronics were drowned by seawater; diesel fuel lay over everything; the batteries, radios and diesel engine could not be used; all clothing, bedding and food stores were soaked.

De Roux's prospects were bleak. Land lay 2,000 miles away. He had been dismasted in one of the stormiest stretches of water on earth. Although doing so ran against every fiber of his being, he once again climbed the ladder and crab-walked his way forward on the bare deck. Finding the Argos transmitter, he paused for a moment, and then punched the Argos' emergency button. It was 38 minutes past midnight on the morning of February 9, 1983.

Along with *Skoiern*'s position, the electronic message the Argos transmitter sent was simple: Help!

February 9: 3 a.m. Two and a half hours later the Tiros satellite (a United States weather satellite carrying the French Argos equipment) passed over de Roux's head and immediately relayed the distress signal to the Argos headquarters in Toulouse, France. There, Roger Roland received the printout on the Argos computer and within minutes picked up the telephone to call BOC race headquarters in Newport, Rhode Island.

The phone rang at 6:45 a.m. It was a cold February morning. Ice crystals glinted on the windows while the first glimmer of pink broke through the cement wall of the eastern sky. Peter Dunning, who had been named sailing master of the race by BOC, received the call on his home phone. He jotted down the data and proceeded to set in motion one of the largest, most complex rescue operations in yachting history.

Dunning phoned race director Jim Roos and both men hurried to race headquarters at Goat Island Marina. Two orders of business required immediate attention. First, they had to inform all concerned authorities, primarily BOC in London, and did so with a telephone call to Dick Kenny, the BOC race liaison. For the next two hours, both Roos and Dunning sat at separate phones calling a wide variety of agencies, bureaus and foreign governments. Because de Roux was a French naval commander, they called officials at the French embassy in Washington, D.C., as well as naval command in France. Because Chile was the nearest country to *Skoiern* and because the Chileans had promised to have a naval vessel on station near Cape Horn to give the skippers assistance, Roos

called the Chilean embassy, seeking their help. The U.S. Navy, the British
Navy, the Coast Guard, rescue squads in Honolulu, New Zealand and
French Polynesia all were alerted.

In this first round of calls, Roos and Dunning hoped to find out if there
was a ship (naval or otherwise) near *Skoiern* that could be pressed into a
rescue operation. And they wanted to find out if an air search-and-rescue
operation, from Antarctica, Chile or French Polynesia (all approximately
2,000 miles from de Roux's position) would be possible. By 10 a.m., the
official wheels were in motion. But no commitments for official rescue
efforts had been made by any party. The BOC race was an amateur
contest, run by amateurs for the benefit of adventurous skippers and
backed solely for public relations purposes by a British multinational
company. Political and naval officials from governments and agencies
around the world had to consider these details before they could act.
This race, and this type of distress at sea, did not fit their normal emergency modes.

At 10 a.m., the unofficial wheels finally got a spin when ham radio
operator Rob Koziomkowski once more got involved. It was through
Koziomkowski's ham contacts in the Pacific that Roos and Dunning
hoped to accomplish the second urgent item on the morning's agenda.
They hoped to contact the nearest competitor, who happened to be Neville Gosson. If they could reach Gosson soon and divert him to de Roux's
position (the intercept from the morning Argos position was 165 miles at
a course of 149°T), they would be able to move a boat into the rescue
area within 24 hours. It was a big if.

An hour and a half later they were hit with the first real setback of the
day. Rodney Jenkins in Sydney phoned with the news that Gosson had
missed his morning radio schedule with an Australian ham, Bill White.
Gosson had been in contact with White the evening before, and had
reported *Leda*'s knockdown, the injury to his back and the encounter with
the tea kettle. White passed that information on to Jenkins, who, true to
form, began a rumor that Gosson had been badly scalded. Jenkins' noise-
making did not help to clear the airwaves to *Leda*. Gosson, like several of
the other ham operators in the fleet, did not have an appropriate ham
license. White was protecting the special frequency he was using to talk
with *Leda*. At midday on February 9, Roos and Dunning hit a dead end.
It would be another 24 hours before *Leda* again tuned in to White's
guarded frequency.

Roos and Dunning were not stymied. Although several other boats
were within reasonable range of de Roux, the only skipper close enough
to reach *Skoiern* within two or three days was Richard Broadhead on
Perseverance of Medina. He was 317 miles to the northeast of de Roux as
of the morning Argos positions. Broadhead was sailing fast and giving

Bertie Reed a run for second place. He finally had his 52-foot cutter moving well, showing the speeds he had hoped for at the outset of the race. But Broadhead was not a radioman by nature. He had lost the use of his radio during both the first and second legs and was using the set primarily to chat with Reed and de Roux as they all sailed toward Cape Horn. The only long-distance transmitting he had been doing from the southern Pacific was to the South African ham, Alistair Campbell, who was relaying technical information on radio repair through him for Reed, who was once again trying to repair his broken gear over the phone.

Roos' plan was to try to intercept Broadhead during his call to Campbell. At 12:30 p.m., he telephoned Matthew Johnson, a New Zealander who had been very active in the ham net during both the second and third legs. In New Zealand, the time was 5:30 a.m. on the morning of February 10 so the phone call found Johnson asleep and, once awake, grumpy and irritable. But, once Johnson heard the story Roos had to tell, he agreed to listen for Broadhead at the scheduled time three hours later. Where Roos and Dunning had met a stone wall in their attempt to reach Gosson, they now had a hopeful path ahead of them again. If Broadhead came up on schedule, and if propagation was good in the South Pacific, and if de Roux could wait for all of this to happen, then there was hope.

Five hours passed before the next break materialized. During that lull, two new elements appeared in the puzzle. Contact had been made with the U.S. Navy's Fleet Numerical Oceanographic Center in Monterey, California. Lieutenant David Pedeneau agreed to supply the BOC team, Koziomkowski in particular, with classified navy satellite weather data for de Roux's corner of the southern Pacific. Compared to the weather data the ham network had been receiving thus far in the race from the National Oceanographic and Atmospheric Administration (NOAA), the classified weather forcasts from Monterey were extraordinarily accurate and up-to-date. The forecast on the afternoon of February 9 was for moderate winds from the southwest through the next 48 hours, followed by a rising northwesterly gale beginning early on Saturday, February 11. The forecast gave Roos and Dunning a window of calm. After Friday night, the gale would close down the area and de Roux's rescue would become increasingly difficult. They had two days.

Also, early in the afternoon, Roos and Dunning received word that the French Navy had dispatched a destroyer, the *Henri*, from its base in Gambier Island in French Polynesia. The entrance of a search ship and the French navy gave those at Goat Island a glimmer of hope. But it was a faint glimmer. The *Henri* was low on fuel and would be able to steam at only half speed. The French Naval Command in Tahiti estimated that it would be four days before the ship could reach de Roux. Four days in the frigid waters of the southern ocean was an eternity.

At 5:20 p.m. Newport time, Jenkins called from Sydney. He had the first good news of the day. Broadhead had come up on the ham schedule and Johnson had been able to intercept the signal. He passed along the news of de Roux's predicament and the morning Argos positions for boats in the area. Broadhead had done what they had all hoped. He immediately jibed, trimmed sheets and headed off to the south and west. He had 317 miles to go.

Fourteen hours after de Roux had punched the button on his Argos transmitter, a rescue vessel was on its way. There was hope, at last. Yet, the way was not all clear ahead. Broadhead had had trouble with both navigation and radio transmissions throughout the voyage. If Roos and Dunning had to choose one man to carry the burden of finding de Roux, it may well have been some other skipper. But they had no choice. All they could hope was that Broadhead would, in his British way, somehow muddle through.

February 9: 2:30 p.m. Broadhead had just gone to the trouble of raising the spinnaker pole on the mast to brace the jib, when it became time to keep his radio schedule with South Africa. He went below, tuned up the ham set and immediately received a call from Johnson. Broadhead was trying to reach Alistair Campbell and sternly told Johnson to clear the channel. But Johnson persisted. He barked the words, "Emergency, emergency, number 10 pulled Argos."

And then it dawned on Broadhead why de Roux had not come up on the radio chat hour with Reed the evening before. He might be dismasted, and perhaps even had taken to his life raft. The air temperature that morning aboard *Perseverance* was 41°F and the sea temperature 38°F. If de Roux had taken to a life raft, Broadhead knew he would not live long. For Broadhead, no decision was necessary.

He wrote down de Roux's position and the 220°T intercept in his log and altered course. The first thing he did, in inimitable Broadhead style, was to drop the spinnaker pole onto his hand. Only luck prevented it from breaking his fingers. He wrestled the pole back into its holders and then jibed. Grinding the winches, he pulled in the jib and then the mainsail until he sailed hard on the wind. The wind blew 20 knots from the southwest, so he could not make the course directly to Jacques. But on his course of 170°T, he was not far from the 220°T intercept. He was on his way.

Broadhead was diverted from the race at an ironic moment. Throughout the third leg, everything finally was going well for him. He had not muffed the tactics, as he had on the first leg. And he was not having trouble with the self-steering vane nor with the radio, as he had on the second. *Perseverance,* which was a fast buoy racer designed to be sailed by a crew of 12, had begun to show her true speed. Broadhead was beginning to live up to what he saw as his true potential as a skipper.

Tall and slim, Broadhead is a sandy-haired man who stands with a stoop. He tends to swallow his words as he speaks and averts his eyes if challenged. He is shy, but not timid. He has tried just about every adventure he could find. After leaving the Harrow School, one of England's elite boarding schools, he escaped to the Caribbean where he spent a year working at odd jobs.

Twice he tried to settle into a regular life. In 1972, he spent a year in the army, serving in the Guard's Brigade Squad. In 1973 and 1974, he attended the Royal Agricultural College in Cirencester. But between the army and school, he drifted off to Australia for 12 months, during which he worked as a jackaroo, a laborer and a surveyor. None of the seeds he sowed took root. In late 1974, he spent a few months working aboard a commercial trawler plying the English channel and then escaped England again, this time to South America where he stayed for three years, working on a rubber plantation, a cattle ranch and at a number of other odd jobs. It wasn't work he was looking for, but adventure against which he could test himself. One of his adventures in South America was a 3,500-mile trip the length of the Amazon River.

In 1978, he bought a 43-foot sloop, built by the prestigious English boatbuilder Camper and Nicholson. The boat, named *Light Horse,* changed his life. Over the next three years, he sailed alone from England to Rio de Janeiro and back and then from England to the Caribbean and back again. He had discovered a form of adventure that put all his faculties to the test. When the BOC race was announced in 1980, he knew at once this was the challenge for which he had been preparing.

Broadhead immediately began an extensive sponsor-seeking campaign. He believed the effort would cost £200,000, and that it would be a bargain considering the publicity that was sure to follow. He produced an elaborate 37-page brochure outlining his plans and featuring newsclips and advertisements highlighting sponsorship efforts in other races by several prominent British corporations. In the introduction Broadhead wrote:

"This letter is an invitation to participate with me; I have entered my name and that of my boat for the race and I will participate, but my ambition is to win. My competitors are at this moment building boats in foreign yards and with foreign assistance. If I am to meet them on equal terms I need help, I need equipment, I need back up and I need the right boat. I can win this race for England; will you therefore take the time to read what follows. The winning can be for England, for you and for your Company. The winning will most certainly not go unnoticed nor be forgotten."

Broadhead's brochure was the first Nigel Rowe and the BOC Group had heard about the race; it led them to make the inquiries which eventually resulted in their sponsorship of the event. Broadhead himself did not fare as well. There was interest, but no financial commitment.

Ultimately, Broadhead sunk his life savings into the purchase of *Perseverance of Medina*. He felt that his previous boat, *Light Horse,* was seaworthy enough to complete the voyage, but not as the vehicle for a winner. And Broadhead wanted to win.

Before the start, Broadhead spoke about his frustrating efforts in locating a sponsor. "My last penny is in this boat. I may have holes in my trousers but there are none in my sails. I'm not sponsored but maybe that's a blessing—I'm totally independent."

Behind the disheveled appearance was a competent man. Broadhead believed this about himself. It was something he needed to prove to his family (landed gentry from Devon and London), his friends and, especially, to himself. It had taken him two legs of the race and 14,000 miles of sailing to get his feet under him. In that time, Broadhead realized he would not be the winner he had hoped to be. But in the third leg, the pieces had fallen into place. Now, with everything going well, he had to face a challenge tougher than rounding Cape Horn. Three hundred and seventeen miles from him in the wide, featureless expanse of the Southern Pacific, Jacques de Roux was in desperate trouble. Everyone close to the race knew de Roux never would punch the Argos button if his life were not in jeopardy. Broadhead set out knowing he, perhaps, was de Roux's only hope. Broadhead knew the competence was there. All he had to do was prove it.

All day on February 9, he sailed south in the general direction of de Roux. The radio was buzzing with activity about the rescue. During the day, Broadhead spoke with Stokes and McBride. He informed them of his situation and they promised to monitor the rescue closely. That night, he had a long conversation directly with Koziomkowski in Newport. The transmission traveled 10,000 miles, bouncing to the ionisphere four times, but propagation was clear and Koziomkowski's powerful equipment kept it steady. They discussed the latest weather forecasts from Monterey, which called for a high pressure ridge to pass through the area that night, followed by two days of fair weather on Thursday and Friday. A gale loomed ahead for Saturday. Broadhead's time limits were clear. They also discussed the apparent movement of de Roux's Argos.

Broadhead assumed that de Roux was most likely in his life raft. The set and drift information data that Monterey had been able to supply corroborated this view. De Roux was moving at 0.3 to 0.8 knots in a northeasterly direction, riding the surface current and the southwesterly wind.

Broadhead noted all this in his log and scribbled navigational notes and calculations on scraps of paper. He knew he had to be accurate. He had to grasp every detail. Never in his life had such a heavy burden as another man's life rested on his shoulders.

February 10: 7 a.m. Aboard *Skoiern,* de Roux had not panicked or despaired. During the first day after the dismasting, he bailed and rested, bailed and ate, bailed and tried to assemble some type of jury-rigged mast on which he could hoist some sail. The previous night's storm had subsided. The wind blew at 25 knots from the southwest and the waves were subsiding.

His plan was simple and orderly. He wanted to make all possible speed in a northeasterly direction to clear *Skoiern* as quickly as possible from the gale-ridden Fifties. Also, he wanted to send a clear message to those who might be looking for him: He was still alive, still navigating and sailing and still very much worth a rescue effort. He did not want anyone to think he had taken to his raft, which in the cold would sustain him a few days at most.

Working in fits and starts, he arranged a spider web of ropes to one end of the spinnaker pole. Then, with much difficulty, he raised the pole to a vertical position and lashed it to the five-foot stump of the mast. The spider web of lines were then pulled tightly, staying the pole like guy wires. By morning of February 10, he had a mast and hoisted his booster —which he shortened to a third its normal size.

The sight of the sail flying, at last, gave de Roux hope. Even if he was never found, he might, with luck, sail to safety. But what encouraged him more was the knotmeter reading: He was sailing at three knots and occasionally scooting ahead at five knots. No one, now, would think him a castaway in his raft and therefore probably dead from exposure.

He bailed and he rested and then he bailed again. The one hour of work dragged by minute by minute, bucketful by bucketful. His one hour of rest vanished like a fleeting dream. The water continued to flood through the hole in the hull and there was nothing he could do to stop it. By the end of the second day, his back was sore and his shoulders and arms knotted with cramps before each hour passed. It was then he realized what would finish him. He would live as long as he could bail, and he would bail until exhaustion overtook him.

In a matter of days he would not be strong enough to lift another bucket. Then the ordeal would be over.

February 10: 8:30 a.m. Freezing sea smoke rose off the bay around Newport early February 10. Roos and Dunning had been trading four-hour watches at the Goat Island Marina phones through the night. They sat quietly over cups of coffee when the first call of the morning came in. It was a direct call from Bill White, the Australian ham who had been handling Gosson's radio contacts through the third leg. Gosson had missed his second radio schedule in two days. No one knew whether or not he was more seriously injured than he had reported two days earlier. White was worried. Gosson was no youngster and had been driving a big, ornery boat for nearly a month through some of the toughest waters of the world. He could have suffered a heart attack, a stroke, a terrible fall.

For Roos and Dunning, the news was distressing and a disappointment. Gosson was still the closest skipper to de Roux and had *Leda* diverted that morning, two boats would have been on station in de Roux's vicinity before the predicted gale began to blow on Saturday. Now, Broadhead was really the sole potential savior.

The other avenue Roos and Dunning had tried to explore was official search and rescue by a military or scientific group nearby. Late the previous morning, U.S. Army Sergeant Old, at the rescue center in Honolulu, Hawaii, had offered to alert all military aircraft flying to and from Antarctica to the crisis. Army and Air Force C-130 transports passed near de Roux's position several times a week en route from bases in Hawaii to the South Pole. These might be diverted to help an air search effort.

At 1:21 p.m., Captain Stoker from U.S. Flag Plot in Washington, D.C. (a navy department that keeps track of American and many foreign flagships), called Newport to report his efforts to start an air search and rescue. He had contacted commanders in the Pacific and tried to get them to send, first, a C-130 from Antarctica, or second, a P3 from Tahiti. His efforts had failed. The distances were too great and the area of ocean too vast for either group to carry out an effective search and rescue. The idea had to be abandoned. Once again, official channels proved a dead end. There would be no air search for de Roux.

On the evening of February 10, Broadhead came up on his radio schedule with Koziomkowski and Johnson. He was still sailing at six knots to the south and the wind had increased. He asked for the most recent Argos positions and weather reports. Koziomkowski passed on the information. Broadhead worried that he would sail past de Roux. He was having trouble deciding just where to steer and when to stop. Exhausted and barely coherent, he said he was going to sleep and then signed off.

In Newport, the crew at Goat Island could only imagine how tired Broadhead was. Everyone crossed their fingers.

February 11: 8 a.m. Like a music box winding down at the end of its song, de Roux hoisted the plastic bucket ever more slowly. He had not slept or been dry or eaten a hot meal in three days. He was no longer certain of his senses, for they played tricks on him. He saw rescue ships that didn't exist and heard voices in the wind. At dawn, he noticed a change in the weather. Storm clouds had moved in during the night, indicating, as he had learned over the last month, that a northwesterly gale was building. *Skoiern* was holding together, but de Roux did not know how his hull patch would hold up to the battering of high waves and wind. He could only hope the storm center would go by to the south of him.

It was 8 a.m. when he completed an hour of bailing. He climbed on deck to eke another knot of speed out of his jury-rigged boat. His hands were not obeying his brain. He fumbled with the sheets and lines. He was struggling with the headsail on the foredeck, when he looked up and saw *Perseverance of Medina* sail past under Yankee and double-reefed mainsail 50 yards ahead of him. Broadhead was not in the cockpit. De Roux yelled. He waved his arms. And then, seeing no one, he dashed below and found his flare gun. One by one he shot off the parachute flares. The gun reported like a 12-gauge shotgun. Still, Broadhead did not hear the gun, did not see the flares, did not notice *Skoiern* although he had nearly run de Roux down.

As quietly as she had come, *Perseverance* sailed away into the gray morning, the dark blue hull gradually fading into the slate-colored waves that rolled ominously from the northwest. His excitement, his hope, began to wane. When he realized Broadhead would not see him, he sat down in the cockpit of his sinking boat and let his exhausted hands fall limply onto his lap.

February 11: 6:30 a.m. All Friday morning, Broadhead fiddled with the calculations trying to establish once and for all where he should be heading. He had managed to grab two hours sleep at midnight—his only sleep in 24 hours. Scraps of paper lay about the chart table and on them were the figures that would lead Broadhead to the needle in the haystack that was *Skoiern*. But he didn't trust the figures. He had never been a scholar and never had a flare for math. Now de Roux's life depended upon his ability to make the figures add up. He struggled to calm his thinking and to organize his notes.

At 6:30 a.m., Broadhead tuned into his scheduled radio contact with

Johnson in New Zealand and Koziomkowski in Rhode Island. He wanted the latest Argos positions and whatever drift information Roos and Dunning had been able to work up. The wind had shifted from southwest to northwest and the mares' tales running in front of the gale were in the sky. But the most important news from Newport was that de Roux's Argos position showed him moving toward Broadhead at five knots. He was not in his raft after all. With the new position, Broadhead sat down once again with his chart, his scrap paper and his pencil. He knew he was very close as he worked out the intercepts between positions. All night he had felt the two boats were coming together, although he couldn't say why. "Telepathy" he called it. The news that de Roux was sailing again buoyed Broadhead's spirits. A boat with a sail would be much easier to find in the rolling oceanic terrain than a small life raft.

But the rising wind, the threatening sky and the prediction of a gale scared him. He felt an urgency he had never known before. Always in his adventures, it had been his own life at stake. Now, it was another man's and that made all the difference. He must succeed.

He worked out a new intercept that should take him directly to *Skoiern*'s new position. After checking the figures one more time, he altered course to 275°T. He believed de Roux was 7.8 miles away. If that was the case, at his present seven knots they would rendezvous in just over an hour. At the end of an hour and a half, at 8:30 a.m., he planned to heave to and wait for new Argos positions.

At 7:30 Broadhead shortened sail, slowing down the boat to get a better look at the sea around him. He climbed onto the boom and from there he could see a circle of ocean four miles across. No de Roux.

At 7:55 a.m. Broadhead climbed down the companionway ladder to make a cup of tea before his next radio schedule. He lingered by the stove as the water heated and then sat down at the chart table to tune up the crackling ham radio. He did not see the flares or hear the gun shots, though at that very moment de Roux was 50 yards away using every means in his power to get Broadhead's attention.

Broadhead sipped his tea, scanned his calculations, and then lifted the microphone and began his call to Koziomkowski and Johnson. From Newport, Broadhead got a new set of calculations worked up by two teams of professional navigators who had volunteered to help in the rescue. Their mathematics were excellent, but their data was hours old. Ridiculous as it may seem, while Broadhead discussed de Roux's position with Koziomkowski 10,000 miles away, he could have stood up from his navigator's table and seen *Skoiern* fading away into the waves. But Broadhead didn't stand up. He jotted down the new intercepts worked up by the volunteer navigators, which didn't agree with his own figures. Then he proceeded to sail another half hour to his preordained waiting spot.

The Argos system did not provide a continuous position report, but a twice daily update as the satellite orbited over the corresponding section of ocean below. The next satellite pass would not be for six hours and he would have to wait for the new information. Broadhead was worried. The gale was coming early. He had sailed to the "spot" where he calculated he would find de Roux, only to be told by Koziomkowski in Newport that the volunteers had come up with a different solution. What numbers could he trust?

By 9 a.m. *Perseverance* was stopped in mid-ocean with only a scrap of headsail flying. Broadhead was at his intercept position—the position he had calculated himself. He waited full of expectation. The sea around him was a wide gray desert of water, cold and inhospitable. He was full of doubt and the sea offered no relief. He climbed onto the boom again to scan the horizon. Nothing. He walked forward and then aft. He climbed to the galley to heat water for another cup of tea and climbed on deck again. Nothing, only waves and wind and empty sky. And then, out of the corner of his eye, he saw a flash of light. At first he thought it was an iceberg. He looked again. Could it have been the bridge of a ship? He struggled to focus his weary eyes on the image two miles distant, periodically obscured by passing waves. When he did, he saw de Roux standing on the deck of his dismastened *Skoiern,* madly waving a white sailcloth flag in the air.

They had done it. Roos and Dunning and Koziomkowski in Newport, Johnson and the other hams throughout the Pacific Basin, and Broadhead on *Perseverance,* had won a stunning two-and-a-half day treasure hunt. Professionals had offered help, but none ventured to take on the rescue. Inexperienced, against all odds, the amateurs had stepped in.

The prize they won was de Roux's life.

As soon as he sighted de Roux, Broadhead dove below, switched on his ham set and broadcast to the world through Matthew Johnson that de Roux was found. It was a marvelously generous gesture to share the triumph with all who had been involved. It was the gesture of a man happy with himself and content with his own competence.

Finding de Roux had been the great test. But getting him aboard *Perseverance* proved more difficult than Broadhead imagined. As Stokes had said after managing, awkwardly, to get Tony Lush aboard *Mooneshine* in the Indian Ocean, no skipper gets much practice at open sea rescues. Once Broadhead transmitted his good news to the ham network, he released the backed headsail and ran slowly downwind toward *Skoiern.* As he approached he could see de Roux wildly waving his arms in the air. Broadhead saw why: *Skoiern* was floating low in the water, her mast was gone and her skipper looked as if he had been sharing his berth with Death itself over the last 59 hours. The wind was building and the gray sky threatened. The rescue would have to be made quickly and as efficiently as possible. Every moment counted.

As he sailed in next to *Skoiern* for the first time, Broadhead in his characteristically understated wit shouted to de Roux, "Hello, Jacques, do you want to come aboard?"

The French skipper's jaw dropped. He stared at Broadhead as though he were a moron. "Yes, I'm sinking."

Broadhead lowered his mainsail and under jib alone made a pass at *Skoiern*. But he was sailing too fast and all de Roux managed to pass over was his sextant. On the second pass, Broadhead slowed *Perseverance* as much as possible. But again he was going too fast and the two boats collided, without much force but hard enough to prevent de Roux from throwing his kit bag aboard or jumping over himself. Broadhead swung the 52-foot sloop around and tried to make a third landing on the bobbing figure of *Skoiern*. The two boats collided badly. *Skoiern* was almost full of water, so she behaved more like an iceberg than a boat, sending a fearful shudder the length of *Perseverance*.

The waves and wind were building. It had been blowing a steady 20 knots when Broadhead first sighted de Roux and 25 when the two boats first came together. Now, as he came in for his fourth pass, the wind was up to 30 knots and the waves were breaking. As he approached, Broadhead tried to slide alongside *Skoiern* so de Roux could jump easily aboard. But, fearful of another collision, he stopped the boat too far away. The wind began to blow the boats apart. De Roux panicked. With a look of wild abandon on his face, he leaped from his sinking deck, almost reaching *Perseverance*. His leap fell short, but he managed to grab *Perseverance*'s rail at deck level, his feet just above the water.

Broadhead immediately ran forward from the wheel and grabbed de Roux, first by the shoulders and then by the seat of the pants. As he did, *Perseverance* swerved over a wave and headed up into the wind bringing her directly against the bow of *Skoiern*. De Roux's legs hung between the boats and Broadhead just managed to hoist the exhausted Frenchman aboard before they collided. De Roux's legs would have been crushed. No sooner was de Roux aboard than Broadhead had to dash to the stern to fend off the marauding *Skoiern*, which was trying to commit one last assault by ramming the brand new and absolutely essential Fleming self-steering gear. Broadhead pushed the sinking boat away, grabbed the wheel of *Perseverance* and with a hard turn altered course once and for all toward the east. Ahead lay a planned rendezvous with the French destroyer *Henri* and then Cape Horn.

De Roux lay on the deck where Broadhead had deposited him, his mouth moving at top speed. Oddly, the Frenchman who spoke but broken English during the race, now spluttered non-stop in English. De

Roux's excitement at being alive was unquenchable. He told Broadhead his story and then retold it. He was ecstatic.

Broadhead gave de Roux dry clothes and prepared a hot meal. After they had eaten, the exhaustion that had been creeping into Broadhead's bones from the past three days overtook him. He left de Roux babbling happily over the ham radio with Reed and the others nearby and drifted into his bunk. Listening to the wonderful sound of de Roux telling his tale once again, Broadhead drifted off into a long and well earned sleep.

During the 59 hours of the rescue, one life had been saved, another had acquired new meaning.

February 11: 7:30 p.m. In Newport, the news of the rescue arrived via telephone from Johnson in New Zealand. The cheers filled the little Goat Island Marina office, which was crowded with helpers and members of the local press who were on hand. They had done it. The men and women involved, Dunning and Roos especially, hugged each other and shook hands. And then, from the bar at the Marina Pub right next door, the bartender arrived with arms loaded with cold bottles of champagne. A stack of plastic cups hung from his finger. Corks popped across the room, cups were filled and then hoisted in a well deserved cheer of congratulations for Broadhead, for the hams, for Roos and Dunning and for all who helped. The amateurs had prevailed.

Three hours later, the latest Argos position report chattered up on the teletype. It gave the latest positions for the BOC fleet. There was no signal for number 10. *Skoiern* had sunk.

17

Turning Point

PHILIPPE JEANTOT SAILED gradually northward from 62°S as he approached Cape Horn. On the afternoon of the thirty-second day out from Sydney, the clouds parted briefly, the fog lifted and there before him stood the barren gale-swept cliffs of the island of Diego Ramirez. *Credit Agricole* was sailing fast under the booster headsail that Philippe had braced on the spinnaker pole. Jeantot had built a solid lead over Bertie Reed, who had not dipped as far south, and was poised to be the first to Cape Horn, which lay 50 miles to the north of the island in front of him. He wanted to sail south of Diego Ramirez Island, leaving Cape Horn far out of sight as he turned the corner northward for Rio de Janeiro. But the wind did not cooperate and swung into the southeast, forcing him to sail north and between the island and Cape Horn. That afternoon, the wind picked up to storm force and the seas mounted. The waves that ran unobstructed across the Southern Pacific for three thousand miles rolled up on the shoal waters around the Horn and became huge and uneven. Jeantot sailed on through the portal between the cape and the island in weather straight from the legends that he had read and heard so much about. That was the way he wanted it.

Cape Horn, the most southern extremity of South America, juts into the tumultuous seas at 56°S. When David White and his fellow drinkers first conceived the race, it was on Cape Horn that they focused their imaginations. Among the BOC skippers, each had proven himself a capable offshore singlehanded sailor, a member of the singlehanded elite. They had faced calms and gales, they had worked until they were blinded by tiredness and then worked another hour, they had done things that set them apart from other sailors and other men. They had served their apprenticeships and done their hard training. One great challenge remained.

In 1982, prior to the BOC race start, only 30 men and women had sailed alone around Cape Horn, starting in 1934 with a Norwegian, Al Hansen. Many others had tried and failed. Some had died in the quest; most had been driven back by terrible weather, poor planning or the simple enormity of the task. Those who had bested the cape had become sailors of a different standing—even heroes for those who would use the word. Sailing around Cape Horn led first into the calmer waters of the southern Atlantic. But it also led into the pantheon of the greatest single-handed sailors.

Ahead of Jeantot past the Horn stood Bernard Moitessier and Alain Colas. Ahead of Tada—who was at the moment running a remarkable third behind Jeantot and Reed—and beyond Cape Horn stood Akoi, Kenichi Horie and Ushijima, all national sailing heroes of Japan. In front of Richard Broadhead stood Francis Chichester, Alec Rose, Robin Knox-Johnston, Nigel Tetley, Chay Blyth and Naomi James. Oddly for Americans Stokes and Byrne, only Webb Chiles led the way, and his accomplishment was tainted by the fact that it was not a true antipodeon circumnavigation, that is, it did pass through two opposite points on the Globe. (Chiles' voyage, which started and ended in San Diego, was some 10,000 miles shorter than an antipodeon circumnavigation.) Yankee whalers and Forty-Niners were the men to first tame the Horn for commerce, yet America still awaited a true singlehanded Cape Horn circumnavigator.

Jeantot passed Cape Horn later that night in a full gale. The sea was rough, the night inky. Hand-steering to relieve the uncertain autopilot, he was in the cockpit of *Credit Agricole* when he first saw a red light approach. It was the Chilean naval vessel *Maipo,* which the Chilean navy had volunteered to keep on station in the event any of the racers should need assistance. Jeantot didn't. And he did not particularly welcome the intrusion of another boat into his private adventure. *Maipo* called with her signal light, splitting the night with the high-powered beam. Finally, Jeantot turned on his VHF radio and assured the Chilean skipper he was well and knew his position. *Maipo* followed Jeantot for several hours and then, after rounding the Horn, the naval ship flashed her light one last time and altered course for the Beagle Channel in the archipelago of Patagonia. Jeantot was not sad to see them go. He savored the moments here at Cape Horn. A dream had been achieved, a symbolic victory won. The gallery of singlehanded Cape Horners quietly shifted to make room for the newest member.

Jeantot was a sailor first, however, and a noter of legends second. He did not celebrate right away. He sailed on through the night and did not sleep until he rounded the eastern cape of Staten Island (which the race committee had designated the turning mark due to the hostilities between the Argentinians and British over the Falkland Islands). Finally clear of land and headed on a northerly course, he slept. When he awoke, he trimmed sails, cleaned the galley and took photographs of the boat and the land off to the north. Only then, when all that ought to have been done had been done, did he pop the cork on the bottle of champagne friends had given him and toast Cape Horn and *Credit Agricole,* "my brave boat," as he called her. He knew his life would never be quite the same again. The French Imperative was calling.

Ahead lay another 2,000 miles of sailing along the Argentine and Brazilian coasts to Rio de Janeiro. The way through the Southern Atlantic promised to be riddled with fickle winds, currents and contrary weather systems. It would not be all smooth sailing. But, somehow, after rounding Cape Horn, the leg seemed over. Jeantot felt a natural letdown, a relaxation of vigilance as he turned north and prudently he fought the urge to sleep, to dawdle. Reed was close behind and in the Southern Atlantic, none of the skippers knew how to sail faster than Reed. This was his ocean.

Two days after Jeantot slogged his way around Cape Horn in a nighttime gale, Reed arrived to find the legendary waters as "calm as a millpond." It was a lucky break because Reed needed to make an emergency stop. Ever since *Altech Voortrekker* was rolled over just before rounding New Zealand, Reed had been seriously short of fresh drinking water. He was reduced to cooking and washing in saltwater and had to ration his drinking water. By the time he neared the Horn, his water tanks were almost dry and he had decided to make a forced stop at Port Stanley in the Falkland Islands before turning north toward Rio.

All the way across the Southern Pacific, Reed had sailed on the edge of real trouble. Had he been slowed down by broken gear, had he lost the use of his mainsails or had *Voortrekker* suffered keel or rudder problems, he could have faced a long slow sail to Chile and almost certainly run out of water before reaching land.

"I decided not to say a word about the water," he said. "It would have started everybody worrying and the media would have built it up all out of proportion."

But now at the Horn he could not tough it out any longer. Reed contacted the *Maipo* and arranged to pick up water at Deceit Island just beyond the famous turning mark. "I had spent about six weeks there a few years ago," Reed said, referring to an assignment while in the South African Navy. "You know, the people in the settlement remembered me.

They came out in their fishing boats and offered me water, beer, cigarettes, chocolate, anything I wanted."

Reed anchored for two hours under the island's stark, windswept cliffs. The wind was calm and for the first time in a month *Voortrekker*'s decks ceased their violent rolling. The scene was quiet and cold and overhead the sky hung like a gray tarp over the mountains of Patagonia. Working quickly, Reed got the water and beer aboard and, waving goodbye to those who had helped him, he once again hoisted sail and prepared to sail north toward warmer climates and gentler seas. As he got the anchor aboard and got his sloop's bow pointed in the right direction, a light snowstorm began that made the water hiss faintly and cast an eerie white light across the black hills. The snowstorm lasted only half an hour, but it gave Reed a beautiful memory of his interlude at Cape Horn.

Soon after the storm ended, Reed caught a fair southeast wind that sent him northward at a fast clip. He was once again on Jeantot's heels. Although two days behind, he wanted to trim that margin as much as possible before Rio. Reed had made *Voortrekker* sail remarkably fast across the Pacific; but his competitors, Jeantot in particular, expected no less from the tough South African in this part of the race course.

The next Cape Horner in the fleet, surprisingly, was Yukoh Tada in his Class II *Koden Okera*, which had not been a front runner in the prior two legs. Tada's cold journey to 62°S between New Zealand and the Horn, the route Naomi Uemura had helped to plot, had served him well. When he reached the Horn, he led Gosson by nearly 300 miles and was more than 600 miles ahead of Francis Stokes, his nearest competitor in Class II. Sailing into the frozen reaches of the high latitudes brought Tada up on the southern side of Diego Ramirez Island. The northeast wind he found there forced him to turn south of the island to miss a chance to sail close to Cape Horn. "The chart for Diego Ramirez is not right," Tada said. "I pass two miles from island and find bad water. Had to escape to south."

The northeast wind built as he rounded the island and he continued east sailing into a 45-knot gale, *Okera* pounding hard in the steep waves as she charged ahead. Cape Horn was Tada's final test following his southern ocean training. It was a test that held a deep symbolic importance for the Zen sailor—who emulated the discipline and singleness of purpose of the Japanese samurai. His goal was to open his mind to embrace the fundamental contradictions of life. Yet arriving at such a goal never would be as concrete as arriving by boat at the Horn. The gales and cold that Tada suffered to sail to Cape Horn had tested him sorely, but he had proved he could succeed. As he sailed past Cape Horn, he was given a sign that his other, less tangible goals also might be within his grasp.

Out of the high rolling waves of the gale, Tada caught sight of a ship steaming northward. It was an icebreaker and it was flying the Argentine flag. Still in Chilean waters, where the Argentine ship was not welcome, Tada knew he would not be able to use his radio to contact the skipper to find out if his old friend and mentor Uemura had been able to live up to his promise. The ship passed two miles from *Okera,* steaming steadily into the wind. Despite the distance, Tada did not doubt that Uemura was aboard. They did not speak, nor did they need to speak. The promise had been kept and the sign given. This gale and this encounter were the reasons Tada had journeyed so far. And then the ship was gone.

If Tada's rounding was sublime, Richard Broadhead's was characteristically ragged. A gale had been forecast for the region of the Horn as *Perseverance of Medina* approached from the north. As Broadhead tried to see the land before the Horn, he was hit by 50 knots of wind and tossed by the confused seas that mounted the underwater shelf. Running before the rising wind, he had to perform a slow controlled jibe to stay clear of the land. But when the main boom swung across the deck, the mainsail detached itself from the mast and flogged free. Broadhead pulled it down. With just the small staysail jib flying he was still making eight knots toward shore.

When the rugged coast finally did come into view, Broadhead realized his navigation had been off by several miles. He was coming in on Isla Hoste, which lies north and west of Cape Horn. It was a windswept, lee shore. Under jib alone, he quickly turned seaward again. Working frantically, he mended the mainsail, hoisted it with four reefs and began to claw his way into the teeth of the gale. Luckily the new Fleming self-steering gear he had installed in Sydney was up to the task of steering in the horrible conditions. Over the radio he raised the Chilean navy ship *Maipo* to report his position and his struggle. The Chilean skipper replied sardonically, "I feel very sorry for you."

Typically, Broadhead had the distinction of finding the worst weather at the Horn. The wind had blown 55 knots for two days and the seas near the shore had built into careless, breaking monsters. "This is what I had expected Cape Horn to be like," Broadhead said. "What I hadn't expected was to be beating into it instead of running before the westerlies. It was bloody hell."

Ever since he had turned back on his course to begin the rescue of Jacques de Roux, Broadhead had stumbled over one weather hazard after another. First, he had had to deal with the gale that built the night he hauled de Roux on board. Then he was faced with a long beat away from his course to the Horn in order to rendezvous with the French Naval vessel, *Henri,* which had been dispatched from French Polynesia to aid in the rescue. The sailing was difficult, wet and cold. What made it worse was that the intransigent skipper of the *Henri* insisted, in his most obstinate Gallic tone, that Broadhead detour from the race, instead of offering to rendezvous on or near the race route. Broadhead was furious, but he obeyed the skipper's order and sailed north. While listening to the conversation between the *Henri* and Broadhead, de Roux pointed to the radio, which was barking the skipper's demands, and said, "That is why I am resigning from the French Navy!"

As if the detour wasn't enough of a slap in the face, when *Perseverance* finally did rendezvous with the *Henri* and de Roux was transferred (while the *Henri* "just buggered on"), Broadhead was left drifting on a calm sea. He had sailed north for four days and now he found himself in a zone of variable and light winds. To the south, Jeantot and Reed were streaking toward Cape Horn. Broadhead's chance to finish close to them was rapidly evaporating. For six days he crept back into the region of the westerlies, yet the wind remained light and *Perseverance* sailed forward as if running in manacles.

"If nothing had happened," Broadhead said, "I would have been 100 miles behind Bertie with a fair chance to catch him. You know, when you are alone you think about these things. You can compensate for lost time by sailing harder. But how do you compensate for bad weather?"

After the calms that carried him ever so slowly southeast toward Cape Horn, his weather, naturally, changed for the worse. The wind backed around to the southeast and increased to 55 knots as he made his landfall. It was not easy or comfortable sailing. Sailing *Perseverance* into the wind in a storm, Broadhead said, is "to be avoided at all costs." But that was what the Horn dealt him and, in a very real sense, Broadhead was not disappointed. The Horn was living up to its legend. Sailing under the small jib and the quadrupled reefed main, he edged his way off the rocks and then turned east to round the Horn. He never saw it, but he felt its presence. He could hear the voice of Chichester in the wind and feel the restless energy of Blyth and Knox-Johnston in the waves under his keel. He had passed the portal and had joined the small circle of English sailors who had known that wind and those waves.

But, as seemed to be true of his entire voyage, Broadhead had to work harder than the others to earn his traditional gold earring. Soon after rounding Cape Horn, he found himself sailing close-hauled with the Fleming in control of the helm. He was below, on his hands and knees working with a bucket to bail the bilge, when *Perseverance* slipped off the side of a very steep wave and began to roll. The boat pivoted in air and descended into the deep trough. Broadhead said, "I think we went over to about 120 degrees. She must have turned over on the top of a very big wave. But, because we were at the top of the wave, the mast did not go into the water."

At the time, he did not know what had happened, being only aware of the roll and then of the vast amount of water entering the cabin. He thought after the boat righted herself and as he bailed furiously with the bucket that *Perserverance* had hit something or broken a hull fitting and was sinking. He bailed and he bailed, uncertain whether he was sinking or not, until the water level receeded.

When he had emptied the boat, he climbed on deck to discover that the stainless steel frame of his spray hood had broken and was hanging off the stern rail. The cockpit was full of water and one of the hatches in the cockpit was open. That was where the water in the cabin had come from. Lines and gear hung over the boat's side, but the mast stood, the sails were in place and there was no hole in the hull. He had made it through a nightmare similar to the one that had nearly finished de Roux. He had turned the corner. After the rescue and after Cape Horn, a new, more confident Richard Broadhead sailed on into the Atlantic.

In his understated way, he said, "I was a bit regretful not to actually see Cape Horn, but just Isla Hoste in the murk. But when you go around, I suppose you don't want to cheat, do you, by going in light winds. It was Cape Horn weather I came looking for and it was Cape Horn weather I found."

Implicit in the journey around the world to Cape Horn was the threat that a skipper might die. Tony Lush had lost *Lady Pepperell*, Desmond Hampton had lost *Gipsy Moth V* and Jacques de Roux had lost *Skoiern III*. But through three-quarters of the race, no one had perished at sea. At Cape Horn, three Class II skippers stepped very close to the fatal line and in doing so, earned special passages around the Cape and into the honored hall of singlehanders.

Francis Stokes approached Cape Horn in the most inconceivable condition—he was partially lost. In Sydney, he had installed an NCS satellite navigator that should have given him accurate position reports anywhere on the globe. But the machine worked only sporadically. Not being sympathetic to electronics in the first place, Stokes had developed only a polite relationship with the device. Of more concern was the overcast sky that had dropped over *Mooneshine* during the two days preceding landfall. Stokes had not been able to use his sextant to fix his position with observations of the sun and stars. He was making his landfall with no more than his dead reckoning position to go on and he knew, in that region of the world, that dead reckoning had a cruel double meaning.

In his log, on the 42nd day from Sydney, Stokes wrote: "It's hard to resist counting the miles before they are run today as Diego Ramirez and Cape Horn both appear on my plotting sheet. If I can keep the pace, we should pass Diego Ramirez in the morning and perhaps see Cape Horn by evening twilight."

He did not mention his concern regarding his position, partially be-cause he was yet to learn how far off his reckoning was. He sailed on through the night under a starless sky and across a rolling, black sea, interrupted only by the white crests of the occasional breaking wave. Dawn broke, gray and ominous. A light rain fell, a rain that changed from time to time to snow. Fog banks lay like huge soft landmasses around him. It was an inauspicious beginning, but it was to be as Stokes wrote in his log, "A long day, but ultimately the most rewarding of this voyage or even my life."

Soon after daylight, Stokes set a course of 050° magnetic for the north-ern tip of Diego Ramirez. But after sailing for three hours, he could not see land where he thought it ought to be, so he changed course a bit to the south. His depth gauge was flashing, but it refused to show the depth of the water beneath *Mooneshine* and that, too, confused Stokes because he was sure he had sailed into the shallow waters close to the Horn. After four more anxious hours of sailing, he changed course again to the north. He had decided, after much work at the chart table that he might be sailing right past the island and the Cape without being able to see either. It was baffling.

"With no change in conditions," he wrote, "I had no thought of actually seeing anything. So, I was totally surprised when the mists parted at 4:45 p.m. local time and there I was five miles due south of Cape Horn—close enough to see details on the rock. I don't know whether excitement or confusion was greater. I was 20 miles ahead of my DR position and found it hard to believe I was there."

It was exhilarating to finally reach Cape Horn. Yet, with a 20-mile error in his navigation, he easily could have run smack into the promontory without having seen it at all. Or he could have wandered blindly into the warren of reefs and islands that surround the Cape and lost his boat and his life. Stokes fumbled with his camera to take a photograph of the scene to the north of him and he managed to take one photo of himself with the automatic timer. The photo, developed later, showed just how ex-hausted and how concerned he was. He looked old and worn and his damp hair hung limply in his face. In the midst of the achievement, he did not radiate the look of one who was experiencing "the most reward-ing day of his life." He had worked so hard to get there, had taken so many risks, puzzled through so many navigational problems, that he now was very nearly at the end of his strength. It was largely good luck that brought Stokes safely up to and around Cape Horn.

Yet that piece of luck, three-quarters of the way through the race, was entirely just. Stokes had shepherded other skippers all along the way. He had saved Lush's life and taught Tada how to speak better English. At the Horn he was rewarded, for the thoughtfulness, the seamanship and the goodness he had spread among the skippers of the BOC fleet. Although the low key, self-effacing Stokes never would openly make the connection, the "reward" in "the most rewarding day" had been his life.

Closing behind Stokes and the others in Class II was Richard Konkolski, who had started seven days late from Sydney. Konkolski was making the most remarkable passage of his life. He had sailed his 44-foot *Nike III* (he had changed the numeral from II to III in Sydney) faster than many of the larger boats. Had he started with the fleet, he would have been leading Class II by a wide margin. During the run across the southern Pacific he managed to sail *Nike III* 247 miles during one 24-hour period. It was a new speed and day's run record for boats in that size range. Even Jeantot in his 56-footer never sailed that fast or that far in one day during the entire race.

But Konkolski's headlong rush to catch up almost came to a swift end shortly before Cape Horn. Relying on electrical power from his diesel generator for the power to drive his autopilot, Konkolski had to run the generator regularly. After the terrible knockdown in the Indian Ocean that had driven him to Fremantle for repairs, he had installed a new generator, rigged a new exhaust system and installed an alarm on the exhaust manifold to warn him of malfunction. The device had given him trouble during the leg from Fremantle to Sydney and in Sydney, before starting out, he had to repair it once again.

The autopilot worked satisfactorily across the Pacific, steering a steady magnetic course. But the exhaust system on the generator continued to give him trouble. One night he switched on the generator and lay down on his bunk for a rest. As he dozed, he heard the air-cooled engine slow down and then speed up again, so he got up to see if there was a problem in the fuel line. The next thing he knew, he found himself lying on the cabin floor. He struggled to breathe and with a burst of adrenalin, he managed to haul himself up the steep companionway ladder and into the fresh air on deck. His head ached terribly and he knew, as he lay sprawled over ropes in the cockpit, that he had almost been asphyxiated by the generator's exhaust fumes. The alarm system had not shut off the engine, so he had to force his way into the cabin once again and switch off the engine.

Once the boat had been ventilated, he could see that the exhaust pipe had broken. "I was very lucky," he said. "First, I was lucky to wake when I did. And then I was lucky that it was good weather and I didn't have to change any sails. Afterwards, I had pains in my muscles for a week and headaches."

The incident almost spelled the end of Konkolski's voyage, but he was barely slowed down. His voyage around the world had been riddled with adversity—calms in the Atlantic, gear damage in the Indian Ocean and generator trouble in the Pacific—yet he had proved time and again that he was able to get remarkable speed out of *Nike III*. He was not to be denied Cape Horn and the finish of the race. His ambition and his motivation were too big to permit him to quit. At the Horn, he found calm weather and comfortable seas. It was foggy when he came up on the south side of Diego Ramirez but the fog lifted at twilight, giving him a look at the island. He passed the Horn in darkness and sailed into the Atlantic at a fast clip, riding a fair wind. After struggling from the moment he left Czechoslovakia nine months before, he finally had a triumph handed to him on a platter. At the end of the earth, he found a moment of justice.

Guy Bernardin was the last of the 10 skippers still in the race to round Cape Horn. For Bernardin, the Horn was imbued with mystique. He looked upon the dangers of the ocean as an arena in which strong men could struggle toward new limits of endurance, achievement and self-awareness. In that arena, Cape Horn was the ultimate test. The Indian Ocean, when he was washed overboard and miraculously found a handhold, had taken him right to the edge. In Sydney, he had pondered the trip into the Pacific. His little 38-foot *Ratso* was too small and too light for that ocean, but he was determined to go on. With his wife helping, Bernardin loaded 500 pounds of ballast in the form of sandbags, intended to make the little boat more stable in the crashing seas of Cape Horn. Bernardin's strategy was to jettison the ballast as soon as he sailed north into the lighter winds along the South American coast. Hedging his bet with the weather, Bernardin chose to sail north of New Zealand after the start in Sydney, and was the only boat to do so. After crossing the Pacific at a higher latitude than the rest of the fleet, he came upon Cape Horn and there came face to face with a challenge greater than any he had yet experienced at sea.

His course for Cape Horn brought him southward along the coast of Patagonia, a forbidding coastline of ragged, mountainous islands that jut up from the sea, their steep shores pummeled by southern ocean surf. When he was barely 15 miles from the cape, he suddenly heard the sails up on deck flapping. Rousing himself from his bunk, he climbed on deck to find that the wind had changed. Instead of heading for the Horn, *Ratso* was sailing ashore onto Cape West, which was now less than 1,000 yards ahead.

"That boat started luffing and I knew something was wrong," Bernardin said. "My boat was talking to me. I had three reefs in my mainsail, a small storm jib, and only a small genoa so I couldn't tack away until I changed the sails. I was almost aground."

He managed to get the sails changed and turn *Ratso* seaward again, with only a couple of hundred yards to spare. Sea spume and the sound of surf filled the air. But he made it out unscathed and the experience served only to heighten his passage around the Horn two hours later.

"Passing the Horn was the best day in my life," he said. "It was somewhat like waiting for Christmas so you can open your presents. I have been waiting for Cape Horn and when I saw it it gave me new life. I feel very young and happy."

For Bernardin, a large part of the meaning of Cape Horn and the race was to try to penetrate the mysteries of such a struggle. He spoke for all the skippers when he talked about the Horn after earning his gold earring.

"The problem now," he said, "is to come back. I don't want to go on too long, and I don't want to die in my boat. Maybe it is time to find another challenge, to go higher and higher.

"It is funny how some people say, 'You are so courageous, you have done a fantastic thing.' For me, sailing singlehanded around Cape Horn is the most natural thing to try to do.

"To work a regular day at a regular job, now that would take real courage."

18

The Human Factor

DICK MCBRIDE IN *City of Dunedin* rounded Cape Horn in pure Cape Horn weather, a 50-knot northwest gale. For McBride, this was how it should have been. He had sailed to a place of legend and would have been disappointed to have found it ordinary; it would have diminished the effort he had spent to get there. But he was not disappointed. The legend lived up to the songs and stories and fables.

"Gradually, the wind backs to the west and increases until the gusts are hitting well over 60 knots. This feels like the real Cape Horn I have read about so often. The tiller kicks in my hand as breaking seas try to poop us; but we race on, still reasonably under control.

"All is black to the north, but the presence of the great cape can be felt in the particular quality of the sea and wind. A number of birds keep me company; storm petrels and prions dancing through the spray and foam while a sooty albatross wheels overhead, sometimes riding the updrafts from my sails. Two dolphins appear almost alongside, surfing on the face of a great sea. Their presence fills me with joy and as I watch my eye is drawn beyond the dark wall of cloud.

"And there out of the murk materializes the stark magnificence of Cape Horn. I am spellbound. The mood, the atmosphere is everything I have ever imagined. We are about four miles off and closing. The cape is a wraith in the mist."

McBride's voyage to Cape Horn had been a long one, stretching over the five years since he had first sat down with naval architect Colin Childs

174

to discuss the plans for a steel boat that was capable of cruising to Cape Horn. He had built his boat and then learned to sail it on the southern ocean. He had overcome the limitations of inexperience, limited finances and the constraints of time. He had contended with the effort of sailing a cumbersome staysail schooner against a fleet of light, modern sloops. His moment at Cape Horn was the culmination of all that effort.

But, like many who reach goals they have desired for a long time, McBride suffered a let down after the jubilation of success, a dark moment at the opposite end of the emotional spectrum. It was the human factor he had worried about toward the end of the second leg when confronted by the Bass Strait. Then, he mastered his frailty. This time he did not.

He was on his way north the next day. He rounded Staten Island and had the Falkland Islands ahead of him. Stokes and Konkolski had sailed inside the Falklands through the Falkland Passage, which was the shorter route, while Tada had gone east of the islands. McBride planned to follow Stokes and set his course west of the Falklands. During the day, he climbed the foremast to check the headstays. A week before arriving at Cape Horn, he had discovered that one of his twin headstays was held by only two strands of the wire. Now, he was surprised to find that both stays were broken and that his foremast and entire rig was in jeopardy. At the least, the damage would mean that he could not press *City of Dunedin* hard to windward. And, it meant he would have to replace both stays in Rio.

That night he spoke on the ham radio with Konkolski, who was ahead of him and almost clear of West Falkland Island. Konkolski, by coincidence, had lost his forestay as well and was sailing slowly under his mainsail and staysail. Konkolski had chosen to avoid the southerly currents that flow between Argentina and the Falklands by hugging the shore of West Falkland Island. When his forestay collapsed on deck, he found himself close to shore and unable to tack effectively to windward. The waters around him were littered with small islands, but he did not have a detailed chart so he called McBride asking him to raise Dan Byrne, who did have charts for the north end of West Falkland Island. It was a round-about paper chase, but very much in keeping with the spirit of cooperation that the skippers had fostered throughout the race.

McBride relayed Konkolski's request to Byrne and then relayed back the chart information. As it turned out, *Nike III* was clear to tack close to the shore in order to stay out of the current.

During the radio communications, McBride had grown concerned about taking *City of Dunedin* into the Falkland Passage. Konkolski had met strong head winds and McBride would more than likely encounter the same winds within 12 hours. With damaged headstays and a boat with a disinclination for windward work, he could find himself slowed down dramatically and possibly with serious rig troubles.

"To have stopped and hove-to until the repair (on the forestays) was complete may have been advisable but we were still racing, and *Fantasy* and *Ratso* were still behind and *Mooneshine* was within striking distance."

McBride mulled the problem through the night as the northerly wind gathered force. After spending most of the night changing and handling sails, he decided to go east of the islands. It was the prudent decision. The day was clear, so after setting his new course he shot several sun sights with his sextant to get a good position fix. Later that afternoon, he sighted Cape Meredith at the southern tip of West Falkland Island, confirming his position at 40 miles south of the island. The way was clear to sail eastward past Sea Lion Island and East Falkland Island. The wind blew a steady half-gale from the northwest and *City of Dunedin* romped along on a broad reach at six knots. It looked as though McBride had a pleasant night of sailing ahead.

At 11 p.m., he checked his course and his position and then made a cup of coffee and sat down at the chart table to drink it. On the chart in front of him he could see exactly where he was and the ample room he had between his boat and the islands. Feeling weary, he put his head down onto the crook of his arm for just a moment.

Two and a half hours later, he awoke to an awful crash. As soon as he heard the collision and then the grinding of the hull, he knew what had happened. He dashed on deck. The boat was lying on her side on top of a rocky ledge 50 yards from the dark silhouette of an island. The wind had shifted from northwest to south, driving the boat off course and onto the island. The ocean swell was increasing. As he struggled to haul down all his sail, waves broke over the hull. The noise of the surf and of the hull being dragged by the waves over the ledge was deafening.

After tying down as much equipment as possible to keep the surf from carrying it away, he dashed to the stern of the boat to switch on the Argos emergency transmitter. Moving quickly and purposefully, he went below, where water was beginning to rise over the cabin floorboards. Tuning up his ham radio, he broadcast "Mayday, Mayday." His call was answered at once by a ham in Hawaii, and his emergency message was relayed to the race headquarters in Newport. In the exchange McBride's position was passed along incorrectly by one of the hams, but his batteries were so low that he did not want to deplete his reserve to correct the error.

With contact made and the hope of help not far off, McBride had to begin doing whatever he could for the boat and for himself. *City of Dunedin* lay hard over on her side and was half full of water. McBride believed at the time that the ledge had punched a hole in the steel hull. As a precaution, in case he had to abandon ship, he managed to struggle off the boat and through the breaking surf on the beach to carry a long rope ashore. He pulled the rope taut and tied it around a rock. The boat was tethered and he had a lifeline if he needed to get ashore in worsening conditions. He knew from his encounter with the gale at Cape Horn that the wind and the breaking surf could increase quickly and ferociously.

But he hung on through the long night as the waves pushed the hull toward the beach. Within a few hours of the unexpected landfall, Mc-Bride was in touch directly with race headquarters in Newport, via ham Rob Koziomkowski, and had been given the most recent Argos update. He had, as suspected, come ashore on the southern tip of East Falkland Island, on Craigylea Point on Bull Peninsula.

Among the rugged individualists who set out from Newport at the start of the race, McBride, at 39, may have been the most rugged—rugged looking anyway—and the most ardently individualistic. In a race that demanded extraordinary seamanship, he arrived with very little sailing experience, having learned only basic lessons in piloting and navigation from magazines and books. And, in a race dominated by powerful, light-weight sloops that had been designed for racing, he brought a doughty steel schooner with an unusual name that was so heavily rigged, she could "be picked up by a crane from the top of her mainmast."

All McBride's life he had run across the mainstream, marching always to the beat of his own drum. As a young man he first tasted the hard outside life stalking deer in New Zealand's Southern Alps with his father, Kaye. When he was 17, he attended the inaugural session of New Zealand's Outward Bound school and from then on the lure of hard challenges beckoned him.

But he didn't heed the call right away. A capable writer and a talented photographer, McBride went to work for the New Zealand Broadcasting Corporation as a copywriter after graduating from school. But the NZBC was too mainstream and too tame. He needed to go his own way. McBride launched a career as a photographer in the South Island city of Christchurch. But he was never cut out to run a modest little studio or to drag his camera bag around to weddings and graduations. He set out on a freer road. He worked stringing wire fencing across the green hills of the South Island. He spent time as a bushman, or logger, in New Zealand's Southland and took up crayfishing in the Southland fjords.

In 1972, he signed on to a New Zealand Antarctic expedition as photographer and spent the southern summer photographing the fantastic, surreal landscape on the southern continent. At the end of his tour, when the expedition was preparing to return to New Zealand, McBride was offered the job of staying behind in the long winter's darkness to take care of the huskies in the dog team. He took the job and spent the next six months cohabitating with huskies and the night. During that winter, he discovered his penchant for solitude. After returning to New Zealand, he took up work as a bulldozer driver at the site of New Zealand's largest earth dam. For the next five years, he drove the Caterpillar during the day and worked on his steel schooner at night. In boat-building, McBride's big, creative hands finally found a task that suited them.

His plan always had been to sail his schooner to the Antarctic ice and then to the archipelago of Patagonia and Cape Horn. When the Around Alone race was announced in the sailing press, it became a goal to shoot for. He never really dreamed he actually would be in it.

But, in the last year of building the boat, he realized that he could get it done in time, if only he had money to continue. What McBride needed was sponsorship and bit by bit local companies in the city of Dunedin—where he was finishing the hull—began to offer help. The *Otago Daily Times,* Dunedin's daily newspaper, became a major supporter in exchange for regular stories from McBride. A steel supplier furnished materials to finish the boat in exchange for sewing the company's logo onto McBride's huge green "gollywobbler" sail. Other companies supplied cash and services and each got its name somewhere on the boat. McBride had been waiting to name the boat after one major sponsor. But no such sponsor came forward, so he chose the name *City of Dunedin* and made a deal with the city's recreation department. In exchange for a cash advance, he would run when he returned a small sail-training program for the children of Dunedin.

"I want to do something useful when I get back," McBride said. "I think television has taken away the necessity for kids to use energy in their own leisure time. I am hoping that the boat can become a social asset to the city."

Finally, the boat was finished and McBride made his first offshore passage, a 1,000-mile qualifying run into the Southern Ocean. It blew a gale. But McBride discovered that his boat was able and he enjoyed singlehanding. However, he had run out of time and would not be able to sail the boat to Newport in time to start the race. One evening, he explained his predicament during an interview televised over the NZBC. By happenstance, Mr. M. North of PACE shipping was watching the interview from his hotel room in Auckland, New Zealand. North immediately picked up the telephone and contacted his agent in Dunedin, Tapley Swift of the ACT shipping company. North instructed Swift to do whatever he could to help McBride. The result was a free ride for *City of Dunedin* to the United States. As had happened in the past, at the moment of greatest crisis, someone stepped forward to lend McBride a hand. McBride and his boat arrived in Newport a month before the start.

Throughout the final months of preparation, during which McBride was in the press regularly, he had to face the difficult question of why he would choose to sail alone around the world. "I'm a bit unsure of the answer to that question," he said. "But like most singlehanders and adventurers I believe I'm more 'self curious' than I am courageous."

Had McBride chosen a spot near Cape Horn to shipwreck, he could not have picked a better place than East Falkland Island. It was the one spot where a New Zealander would be welcomed as family. The Argentine-British conflict over the islands had concluded only a few months before and East Falkland was still heavily populated with British soldiers and sailors. Soon after dawn, the air-splitting sound of a helicopter alerted Dick to his rescue. Not six hours after sailing ashore in one of the most remote islands in the world, McBride found himself swept off the beach in a modern military helicopter and deposited aboard the British frigate *HMS Penelope,* where he was given a hot bath in a well-lighted stateroom. Besides breakfast and dry clothes, McBride was given a waterproof survival suit and high-volume pumps. With the help of the *Penelope*'s chief engineer and the bosun, he managed to empty *City of Dunedin* of approximately eight tons of water. He discovered the hull had not been badly split; the leak was via a small pipe fitting that led into the ballast keel. Once the pipe was plugged, the water ceased flowing into the boat.

That was the first step. But getting *City of Dunedin* off her rocky perch at Craigylea was a major engineering problem. How to get the boat off the beach in time to sail for Rio for the next start—McBride's main concern—was a question whose answer was not immediately apparent. He never doubted that something would happen soon—his luck had held in the past.

The appearance that afternoon of General David Thorne, commander in chief of the British forces in the Falklands, was a good sign. General Thorne, by chance out inspecting his ships that day anyway, promised to give McBride whatever help he needed. Being a New Zealander, McBride was something of a country cousin to the British troops holding the Falklands. The joke running around the fleet was that New Zealand's expeditionary force in the Argentine conflict finally had arrived.

Also in the vicinity of Bull Peninsula, as it happened, was the British Navy's largest oceangoing tug, aptly named *Salvageman.* After discussing the salvage problem with *Salvageman*'s skipper, Capt. John Bolds, McBride realized that the shallow run to the beach where *City of Dunedin* sat prevented any of the large ships from simply towing her off. The next step was to fly, via helicopter, to Port Stanley, where he began to organize a rescue scheme with the gents from "Nav Ops," or naval operations. Nav Ops was at the time the local military bureaucracy. After discussing his situation with the officers, McBride was told somewhat vaguely, that he should return to the settlement at North Arm, near Craigylea Point, to await "developments."

For the next two weeks, McBride stayed with New Zealanders Tony and Lyn Blake, who managed the huge sheep farming operation at North Arm owned by the Falkland Islands Company. Although he could have landed on less comfortable ground, it was two weeks of delay when what McBride wanted most was action. With the boat on the rock and the race all but over, McBride had known better days.

But, at the end of two weeks, Nav Ops had a plan and they had a man to carry out the operation. In Port Stanley, attached to the Royal Navy, was the ship TEV *Rangatira*, a New Zealand Maori name for a British ship. Nav Ops thought it a good idea to get a crew from "a New Zealand-named ship to salvage a New Zealand-owned yacht." Coincidentally, the Chief Officer aboard the *Rangatira*, J. R. Webber, had previously worked for the company that shipped *City of Dunedin* to the states, and had been involved in those arrangements.

The plan to haul *City of Dunedin* off the beach, in what the sailors had nicknamed "Dick's Bay," required a five-ton anchor, approximately 100 meters of cable, a heavy, three-part block and tackle and three of the farm tractors from the North Arm settlement. Webber had assembled a team of men from the *Rangatira* as well as two scuba divers. On Saturday, March 26, a huge navy Chinook helicopter hoisted the bulky cargo of anchor and gear and men from the rugby field in Port Stanley and ferried it to the inhospitable bluffs above Dick's Bay. Then, using a heavy cable strop, the Chinook's pilot deftly positioned the huge anchor 150 yards from the shore in about 15 feet of water. That afternoon, the divers rigged the block and tackle from *City of Dunedin* to the anchor offshore and then back finally to the three tractors stationed ashore.

At 5 p.m. all was attached. Webber and McBride were ready to give the salvage a try. The tractors revved and moved forward, tightening up the cable. But before *City of Dunedin* had moved an inch, the cable parted at the anchor. The divers went back into the water and by 6:30 the block and tackle was reattached. The tractors hauled again. This time, *City of Dunedin* moved toward deep water. Dick held his breath. But again, the salvage was frustrated by gear trouble; the cable jumped off a block and had to be forced clear again. Half an hour later, in total darkness, the exhausted men throttled up the tractors one last time, and this time hauled *City of Dunedin* over the bumpy rock ledge, into water deep enough for her to float free on her own bottom.

McBride led the cheer. After 23 days as a castaway on a remote beach, he and his boat were almost ready to sail again. *City of Dunedin* was moored that night to the five-ton anchor and, elated, the men made the three-hour overland drive to North Arm. The salvage had taken far less time than Webber or McBride had contemplated. But their elation did not last long. During the night a strong southwest wind picked up, building steep ocean swells. Before dawn, *City of Dunedin* snapped her mooring lines and once again washed up on the beach at Dick's Bay.

As McBride stood on the tilted deck of his beached boat in the first light of a gray dawn, life seemed bleak. Yet the weather quickly cleared and, after a day of reorganization Webber and his men returned to Dick's Bay to give the salvage another try. The boat was 150 yards from her original grounding position, so McBride and the sailors from the *Rangatira* spent most of the day rerigging the cable and strops to fit the new situation. Then, at 1:15, the tractors began to pull and within five minutes *City of Dunedin* had made the trip yet again over the rocks. Again, a cheer from McBride and the men ashore went up. But the work was not finished. Another southwest gale was forecast for that night, so McBride and Webber's volunteers spent the afternoon rowing anchors out to sea in a small rowboat. When the anchors were set, McBride would haul *City of Dunedin* out to them and then the process—called kedging—was repeated. Bit by bit, McBride managed to move the schooner three-quarters of a mile out to sea, where she lay at anchor in a position that would permit him to escape a gale, no matter the wind direction. Twenty-five days after he had first put his head down on his arm for a catnap, McBride was once again back in the race. That night, as he rerigged *City of Dunedin* for sea, he found the damage his boat had sustained was remarkably light. The hull was dented along the waterline and her paint was badly chipped, but she was still seaworthy and safe. McBride knew that only a steel boat such as his could have survived the ordeal. A wood or fiberglass yacht would have been destroyed by the rocks and the pounding surf.

The gale that had been forecast did not arrive, so after a quiet night on his anchors off Dick's Bay, McBride hoisted sail and rejoined the race. He steered east, continuing his course around East Falkland Island, and then turned north for Rio. But, he found during the afternoon that his generator was not working properly. Without it he would lose his radio and without the radio he would lose his direct link with rescuers, should he run into trouble on the 2,000-mile passage to Rio. He decided to stop in Port Stanley to have the generator repaired. That evening he sailed into Port Stanley harbor, playing "hide and seek" with blacked-out ships lying at anchor. Within three days he had repaired the generator, with the help of the mechanics from the tug *Salvagemen,* repaired a broken headstay and made the drowned cabin a bit more livable.

On April 6, McBride hoisted sail yet again and tacked out of Port Stanley for the open sea. Ahead lay Rio and the rest of the race around the world. Behind him in the barren Falkland Islands were a group of volunteers, officers and civilians who had rallied to his aid. The British had committed men, machines and money to the salvage of *City of Dunedin,* but deferred their right to make a salvage claim against McBride. It was a magnanimous gesture, yet very much in keeping with the spirit that the BOC race and the lone skippers stirred in people around the world.

McBride's quest was not an ordinary one. His quiet determination to sail his schooner alone around the world evoked admiration in the sailors in the Falklands, who had known the hardship of war and could appreciate the rigors of battling the southern ocean. At this far corner of the world and at a time of serious trouble, McBride had found kindred spirits who were ready and willing to help him on his way. The human factor had put him on the beach. But his own resiliency and the generosity of a band of strangers got him off again.

In the end, he was the only skipper in the race to have a piece of real estate named after him.

19

Light Winds and Lazy Days

FOR EACH SKIPPER it was tempting, after sailing north of the Falkland Islands, to assume the worst was behind him. No one had considered Sydney the halfway point of the race, though it certainly constituted half the total distance. The turning point, both in a real and spiritual sense, was Cape Horn. So it was only natural that after putting the Horn astern, there would be a drought in the reservoir of vigilance and willpower.

It was not the screeching winds and barreling seas of the Roaring Forties that demanded their patience and poise as they sailed along the South American Coast. Instead, the light winds and sultry skies turned the days into long, lazy, sluggish affairs; after weeks and weeks of sailing in the rugged southern ocean, the tedious routine of searching for every steamy puff of air while inching toward port was almost too much to take. The Rio landfall characterized the entire layover: It was much too hot and much too long.

Philippe Jeantot and *Credit Agricole* continued the remarkable monopoly on first place by arriving on the evening of March 5 after a voyage of 48 days. The storm that Jeantot battled one week before finishing did not prepare him, however, for the gale of journalists that mobbed him as he stepped ashore. Reporters, at this point, were nothing new to Jeantot, who had become quite adept at handling the hullabaloo. But this batch, for the first time, was decidedly French. They had come to Rio to see for themselves if Jeantot was real. They were going nowhere until they found out.

Bertie Reed tied up *Altech Voortrekker* two nights later. Always the bridesmaid, he once again had succeeded in accomplishing the near impossible in his classic wood sloop. Reed and Jeantot brought far different methods and motives to the task of lone voyaging, although both attained similar results. But Reed's tenacity was revealed in one amazing statistic. By staying north of Jeantot between Sydney and Cape Horn, he chose a longer route on that portion of the voyage. (Over the entire course he sailed a total of 8,473 miles to Philippe's 7,941.) Yet, though he sailed more than 500 more miles than the Frenchman during Leg III, he arrived only two days behind.

Richard Broadhead finished in third place, six days after Reed. He had been nipping at *Voortrekker*'s stern when the call from Matthew Johnson sent him on his search for Jacques de Roux. The remainder of the voyage Broadhead brooded about what could have been and almost was. But upon landing in Rio, he was greeted by Jean Louis and Vera de Roux— de Roux's brother and sister-in-law, who had flown in especially for the occasion. He did not need a second reminder about the success of his mission. Broadhead was later granted a six-day allowance for the time he lost during the rescue.

Yukoh Tada was fourth into Rio, and probably not a moment too soon. Although he had made a fast voyage to the Horn, Tada's vast supply of good luck began to deteriorate soon after. North of the Falklands, he lost his second bergsprit, though thankfully not while fulfilling the use for which it was intended. That it lasted as long as it did was a minor miracle. Before leaving the dock at Pier One in Sydney, the boat had bounded forward on its mooring the morning of the restart and broke its bobstay, the metal support that helped secure it to the boat. It snapped once and for all along the coast of Argentina ("Maybe during sleeping time," Tada said), leaving four small holes in its absence. Tada was able to stuff the holes with a sail, but it took 40 bucketfuls of water in a one-man fire brigade to dry out *Okera*.

If that incident was a fire drill, Tada's arrival in Rio was a three-alarm fire. Tada crossed the line just before 8 p.m. in 30-knot winds and a driving rainstorm that limited visibility to less than 50 yards. The race committee radioed Tada they would have a tow boat waiting for him at the mouth of the harbor and to wait there after crossing the line. Once across, Tada could not spot the boat, but elected to continue even though he had no chart for the area and his color radar was a blur because of the heavy rain.

Within two miles from the sanctuary of the plush, luxurious Rio de Janeiro Yacht Club, sailing fast but sailing blind, *Okera* deposited herself

ungraciously on an area of flat rocks on Ilha da Laje, a small, low-lying
island in the shadow of famous Sugar Loaf Mountain.

"On the rocks, on the rocks!" Tada screamed into his microphone,
though he was unable to say exactly what rocks. But by the time the
towboat had located the Japanese sailor, *Okera* lay flat on her side like a
fatally beached whale as the surf lapped at her hull.

Standing at the bow of the towboat as it arrived at the club, Tada
looked like an Oriental Ahab in his white foul weather gear and bright
orange southwester hat. Two friends from Japan were waiting for him.
There were hugs and handshakes and champagne all around when Tada
clambered off the boat. Then two large Brazilian women—dressed to the
nines and smiling broadly from beneath a month's supply of rouge and
mascara—decided that Tada was the cutest thing they'd ever seen and
began buying more drinks. Everyone involved with the race, except
Tada, was concerned about *Okera* on the rocks. The most frantic of all
was Rear Admiral Roberto Monnerat (Ret.), rear commodore of the club,
who felt that a boat aground when it was supposed to be moored at his
club was both a disgrace and an embarrassment.

On his way to dinner with friends, Jeantot was informed of the predicament and immediately offered his help. Meanwhile, Tada was convinced of the gravity of the situation. Soon, a volunteer team of local
yachtsmen, Jeantot and a former diving buddy, Tada and others set off
in three boats. When they reached the island, everyone went silent. *Okera*
was now completely out of the water, a victim of the outgoing tide. Worse,
she was being guarded by three armed soldiers, for Ilha da Laje is no
ordinary island, but the foundation for a pillbox-like concrete fortress.
The soldiers refused to let the rescue team ashore. The race committee
member aboard the tow boat, radioed Admiral Monnerat, who in turn
telephoned a colonel friend to see what he could do. The colonel told the
admiral that permission to go ashore was granted. The rescue team told
this to the soldiers, who said no one was going to set foot on any part of
the rock until they were told so directly by the colonel. The entire link-
up was rearranged again. Finally, one of the soldiers stepped aboard the
tow boat to speak with the colonel.

"Who do you think they are, communists?" the colonel screamed. "I'll
see *you* in the morning."

Jeantot suggested setting two anchors well offshore with the boat's
spinnaker halyards to secure the boat, while another line was made fast
between *Okera* and the two boats. When the tide began to fill in, the
anchors held the yacht in place, while the tow boat slowly eased *Okera* off.
By 1:30 a.m., *Okera* was once again in her natural element with only a
nasty scrape on her port side. Tada thanked everyone profusely. "I am
lucky man," he said. Later, when retelling the story, he took to calling the

fort "Okera Rock." He also theorized that the onshore mussel beds had cushioned *Okera* against serious damage.

Richard Konkolski, Neville Gosson and Francis Stokes all arrived on March 16. The trio had been becalmed for days on end, and tied up their boats in 90-degree weather. Konkolski, although finishing several days behind Tada, won Class II even though he had restarted seven days after the fleet in Sydney. (The rules allowed a seven-day grace period for sailors who finished after the restart; thus only Konkolski's elapsed time —the time he was at sea—was counted.) Konkolski had been a pre-race favorite in Class II along with de Roux. But the Czech sailor did not rise to his potential until after de Roux's sinking. Despite Konkolski's good Leg III showing, Tada and Stokes, while not winning any individual leg, were running first and second in the standings on overall elapsed time.

Leg III saw Gosson, once again, nursing home a damaged boat. The knockdown he suffered on the night de Roux flipped his Argos switch had pulled out the starboard chain plate aboard *Leda*, allowing the deck to actually rise and fall during high winds. The damage worsened as the leg wore on until, after rounding the Horn, a gap almost 18 inches long and a half-inch wide existed. Because of the weakened hull, Gosson was afraid to put the boat on starboard tack. Because he had no radio, he could tell no one of his problem. As he closed Rio, he religiously kept the boat on port tack. But while nearing the coast, the wind shifted from north, to northeast, to east-northeast. Gosson followed the wind in a wide arc, at one point actually sailing in the opposite direction from the city. Race followers plotting the Argos system updates thought that Gosson might have gone a little daft from the bump on his noggin.

Dan Byrne, aboard *Fantasy,* finished last, not counting Dick McBride, arriving just after daybreak on March 23, four days behind Guy Bernardin and *Ratso.* Byrne's landfall was slow torture due to healthy portions of adverse currents and shifty winds. For part of his last week at sea, Byrne was lucky when he was able to hold his own against the current rather than being swept backwards. His cause was not helped by a severe storm north of the Falklands that ripped the lower piece of his mainsail track off the mast, leaving him with a double-reefed sail for the remainder of the voyage.

Twenty-four hours before landing Byrne battled a violent thunder and lightning storm, with 30-knot rainsqualls and intermittent patches of totally calm air. The next morning Byrne's wife, Pat, along with Stokes, Tada and several race officials, boarded a boat to rendezvous with *Fantasy* at the finish line. An earlier expedition had returned to port after Byrne had been becalmed several miles from the line. When they met a second time, Byrne, who had slept little in the previous days at sea, was just rousing himself from a short snooze. *Fantasy,* meanwhile, was slowly drifting near the rocky shore along the southern end of Copacabana Beach. It seemed an alarming situation to everyone but Byrne, who was happy to greet his company.

"Dan, I've got some new slacks for you," Pat said.

"Uh, Dan, maybe you ought to think about jibing," offered Stokes.

"Too much talk, too much talk. Very dangerous." screamed Tada, who was now well versed in the problems of sailboats nearing rocks.

Byrne, who had his back to the shore, looked over his shoulder and calmly said, "Oh yes, the rocks."

As he spoke, a light offshore wind sneezed in *Fantasy*'s direction. Byrne trimmed his sails, reached away from the rocks, purposely crossed the finish line from the opposite direction, then turned again and crossed the right way on the last gasp of the fading northerly.

It was a fitting end to the longest, hardest leg.

Sitting on the deck of *Ratso II* in the heat of one brilliant Brazilian afternoon—when most living things in the area had used what good sense they had and found a patch of shade—Guy Bernardin raised both hands up high as if he were balancing a large pumpkin on his shoulders. "I do not know about Philippe," Bernardin said. "Maybe he is getting the big head."

The opinion, though not a singular one, was in part due to the relentless heat that makes irritability in the tropics a stable frame of mind, and partly due to the fact that, from the press particularly, Jeantot was treated a far cry differently than the other sailors. It was not a situation that Jeantot sought; the simple fact was that in the eyes of the media there were two priority interviews. The first was with Jeantot, and the second was with anyone else. An easy attitude for the other skippers to strike was: Why him? We didn't sail in different oceans.

But Jeantot was different, and the pressure of being a winner continued to work its changes. In the six months before the race began, he had secured sponsors and built the fastest boat in the fleet. It was something that David White could not do in two years. Then he took that boat and sailed it as hard and as fast as he could. He built a big lead early but never became complacent. He wanted to win every time he set sail and through three legs he had done just that. With overall victory within his grasp, people who knew not the smallest tidbit about sails or boats or oceans were beginning to take notice of Jeantot. And they wanted to be on his train when it pulled out of the station.

There was much work to do on many of the boats before the final leg began, but somehow it just didn't seem to get done. Something the racers called the "Brazilian factor," set in. Lethargy became the order of the day. Because of the large gap between the end of the third leg and the April 10 start of the fourth, it was easy to behave as the locals did and put things off for *"amanha."* The regal surroundings of the Rio de Janeiro Yacht Club made it especially easy to wave at the waiter and order another round.

Of all the skippers, Konkolski and Tada were the busiest. Konkolski had a long list of projects, but topping it off was the matter of his recalcitrant engine. On *Nike* there was barely enough space, above or below-deck to set a coffee cup. Gears, tools and sails lay everywhere. Tada, once again, had taken on a special project. To maximize performance in windward conditions for the final leg, Tada was adding a half-inch layer of foam and fiberglass to his bulbous steel keel. The theory, Tada maintained, was that the rounded and faired padding would enhance the keel's hydrodynamics and give him more speed and pointing ability. Tada had one other job, of course, which was to repair the deep scar along *Okera*'s port side.

In Rio, Tada also held the last of his popular "seaweed parties," which he had hosted in Cape Town and Sydney as well. Generous complements of beer and saki flowed at each of the gatherings and guests were served bountiful helpings of rice balls, raw fish and, usually, one or more dishes featuring some style of kelp. Tada provided the entertainment, singing and playing his electric piano and saxophone. At each of Tada's parties, everyone was invited, including all the racers, yacht club staff, PR and press people, and anyone who happened to be wandering along the dock. It was a generous gesture offered freely from a man with a generous heart.

As the time neared for the racers to set out one final time, it was difficult for them not to look ahead, beyond the finish of the race. Some, like Bernardin and Gosson, had given up their businesses to race and knew not what lay ahead. Others, like Byrne and Stokes were, for the most part, retired and prepared to take it all one step at a time ("I guess I look forward to sitting around the swimming pool at home this summer," Stokes said). Konkolski was nervous about his United States citizenship application. Broadhead had spent his life savings, and wished only to sell his boat and then "maybe get a fishing trawler in the Falklands or somewhere." Reed, who had risen from the stature of hero to superstar in South Africa for his performance, said, "I'm glad to have finally sailed around Cape Horn but now all I want to do is finish the race and get home so I can get on to other things."

Each racer had, of course, sailed alone. But in many ways they had been together all the way around. Just as entering the race had changed each man's life, so would finishing it. Journalist Barbara Lloyd, who covered the race all the way around the world, summed up what waited ahead in the April 7, 1983 edition of *The Washington Post*.

"The weather is improving north of the equator, and the hurricane season is months away. The myths of Cape Horn are put to rest. And the unforgiving waves of the southern ocean, the bitter cold and the icebergs are behind them.

"It is life that is the obstacle now. The checkbooks, the car repairs and the leaky roof—all are phantoms ready to come alive."

The start of the homeward leg, on April 10, began as lazily as Leg III had ended, in sweltering weather and light winds. Before the fleet reached Newport, they had to face one last crisis that underscored what the BOC Challenge had become.

After the start, nine of the 10 remaining boats sailed out from Rio and turned sharply north. Only Tada on *Koden Okera V* chose to follow the advice of *Ocean Passages* by sailing first east into the southeast trade winds before setting his course northward. The rest, led by Jeantot, Reed and Konkolski, clung to the Brazilian coast, seeking shore breezes and trying to stay clear of the contrary Brazilian current.

It was a risky choice because of the threat of being run down by the heavy ship traffic in the area and because of the risk of sailing ashore, as Hampton and then McBride had done. Nonetheless, in light headwinds, the fleet inched homeward on what seemed an easy last slide to the finish.

Then, two weeks into the leg, an incident occurred that unlocked the darkest door of imagination for everyone involved. Richard Konkolski's Argos stopped transmitting. Since the devices had been installed in Cape Town, no one else's had failed. Then, Konkolski missed a scheduled radio contact with ham Peter Thuridl in Brazil, the first he had missed since leaving Rio. Finally, that night, Konkolski failed to come up on the evening "chat hour" with the other skippers, another ominous first.

So close to the end, the other skippers and those at race headquarters in Newport feared the worst. There were two terrible possibilities for the silence. *Nike III* could have been run down by a ship that was innocently steaming through the shipping lanes. Or, in the eleventh hour of the race, Konkolski could have been run down by a Russian or East German trawler in the retribution he and others had feared in the eight months since his defection.

Peter Dunning and Jim Roos immediately went into what Roos called "our emergency mode." Ham Rob Koziomkowski, who was in daily contact with the fleet and the Atlantic Marine ham network, went into action. Through the night and next day, Koziomkowski passed the alert to hams in South America and the Caribbean. Their hope was that Konkolski was having only radio trouble—perhaps he had been struck by lightning—and they might be able to hear a call for help on an unprescribed frequency.

Also, as concern for Konkolski mounted, Roos and Dunning reached Neville Gosson on *Leda Pier One*, who was nearest *Nike III* and asked him to turn around and stand by for a search. Guy Bernardin on *Ratso II* was trailing *Nike III*, so Bernardin altered course to intercept with the Czech's last known position.

Within hours of the failed Argos transmission, the ears of the hams were cocked and the first step of a search and rescue had begun. The lessons learned during Tony Lush and Jacques de Roux's rescues had been rehearsed well and could now be applied without hesitation. As the rest of the skippers sailed north during that night and next day, each kept a radio vigil. One of their own was in danger. The brotherhood was threatened.

Luckily, the emergency was a false alarm. Twenty four hours after his Argos had stopped working and after he had failed to come up on his radio schedules, Richard Konkolski contacted the ham network. He had had electrical trouble, putting his radios out of commission and he knew nothing about his Argos. He had been sailing north at a good clip the entire time and the only difference aboard was that he had stored a wet genoa on top of his Argos transmitter, which was mounted on the foredeck.

Gosson continued north as soon as he heard the news and later would be given a time allowance for his efforts. Although Konkolski's Argos did not begin transmitting again when the sail was removed, race officials learned after conferring with Argos headquarters in France, that occasionally a wet sail will block the Argos signal.

It was the last scare, but it reminded everyone involved just how closely knit the skippers, hams, and race officials had become.

All that remained was the finish.

20

Closing the Circle

On the evening of May 8, 1983, a crowd began collecting at the Marina Pub on Goat Island. The chatter among the men and women lounging at the bar and eating sandwiches at the tables was lively and decidedly foreign-sounding. Many spoke French. The excitement among the crowd was evident. Outside, a steady rain fell on the pavement and a cold fog shrouded Narrangansett Bay and Rhode Island Sound.

At midnight, the word went out from the trailer that served as the temporary BOC Challenge office. The time had come. Race committee members, the press and volunteers from the host Goat Island Yacht Club boarded the fleet of 18 chartered boats and set out from the piers. Above Newport, the white spire of Trinity Church stood illuminated. Flood-lights on several piers along the waterfront showed the 12-Meter racing boats that had come to Newport to vie for the America's Cup later in the fateful summer. The small armada of powerboats, with their red and green running lights glistening in the rain, cut smooth wakes through the moored boats of the harbor. Like a task force bound for naval action the armada pointed seaward and steamed purposefully into the darkness.

Out there, beyond the city lights and beyond the flashing light on top of Brenton Tower at the mouth of Narrangansett Bay, Philippe Jeantot and *Credit Agricole* were sailing toward the finish line. After eight months of racing 27,000 miles, Jeantot was about to close the circle. His estimated finishing time at Brenton Tower was 2 a.m. The flotilla was going to be there to welcome him, time him and then tow *Credit Agricole* to shore. The most remarkable and most successful singlehanded race ever run

191

from the United States, or anywhere else for that matter, was set to climax. The champagne bottles were ready.

Beyond the bay, the open sea rolled in steep swells and the rain pelted hard against the windshields. A few of the French photographers, who wore their cameras like bandoliers, sidled to the rails to ease their stomachs. Yet, despite the weather and the seasickness, the radios on the boats crackled with excited chatter. "Where is he?" and, "When will he cross the line?"

And then out of the darkness and from beyond the horizon, Jeantot performed his first royal act as race winner and as conquerer of the world. He radioed all who were listening that he was five miles from the finish line and was going to drop his sails and sleep for the rest of the night. He had arrived in each port of call along the route at night and in bad weather, he said, and this time he wanted to arrive in daylight, at least. There was nothing he could do about the weather.

He did not mention his sponsors over the radio. But nobody doubted he had been made aware during the previous day at sea that it would be to everyone's commercial advantage to have clear, sharp, daylight film footage of the finish. He was 30 hours ahead of Bertie Reed, so the delay would in no way affect the outcome. The press could wait. At race's end, the thunder of sponsorship was being heard around the world. So, Jeantot dropped his sails and went to bed.

While Jeantot slept, the rest of the fleet sailed on toward Newport. Behind *Credit Agricole,* the boats were strung out single file well back into the Atlantic. Dan Bryne, after a slow trip through the doldrums, was still in the tropics and bringing up the rear. Right behind Jeantot, Reed was charging for home and making remarkable speed.

When the fleet left Rio 28 days before, Reed was a full 10 days behind Jeantot on elapsed time. He had no hope of winning his class or claiming the cash prize. But that did not stop him from pressing at every opportunity and making his best showing. In fact, in his slower boat he had no business being right on Jeantot's heels. But he had led for the first half of the leg and had stayed close to Jeantot in the northeast trade winds. By pressing hard, he was making Jeantot work for his victory and making an exciting finish to a lopsided victory. It was the only way Reed knew how to sail. His excellent performance was something for those behind to emulate.

The real race of the last leg belonged to the boats of Class II. After 22,000 miles of racing from Newport to Rio, only 2 days, 2 hours and 2 minutes separated leader Yukoh Tada and Francis Stokes. In the first two weeks after the start in Rio, it seemed Stokes might be able to make up the time and steal the victory. Tada, always enigmatic if not downright crazed at the start of a leg, sailed with the fleet as it crept northward along the Brazilian coast. But, at Cabo São Tomé, a day north of Rio, Tada suddenly turned east to split tacks with the rest of the fleet and with Stokes in particular. Tada sailed east out of the contrary Brazilian Current for two days before he again tacked to sail northward for Newport.

Like the "bergsprits" Tada had built in Cape Town and Sydney, his Rio project, the keel modifications, were not a success. By radio, Tada reported sluggish performance aboard *Okera* when going to windward. It appeared it might be the break Stokes needed.

"By the time I got to Recifé," Stokes said, "I was as much as 180 miles ahead and I was entertaining delusions that I might be able to continue to extend that lead right through to Newport and win the whole shooting match."

But Tada's different course proved to be at least as direct as the route Stokes and the fleet chose. *Okera* and *Mooneshine* passed through the doldrums and hit the northeast trade winds at about the same time. Gradually, day by day, Tada's longer, lighter boat gained on *Mooneshine* in the fresh trade winds. The keel work apparently did not affect the boat off the wind. By the time they had passed the halfway point of the leg, with 2,000 miles remaining to Newport, Tada and Stokes were less than 75 miles apart. The gap continued to close as the two boats sailed north past Bermuda and through the Gulf Stream. By the time they were within 48 hours of Newport, their Argos positions showed they had nearly identical distances to sail to reach the finish line.

The competition between the two skippers was spirited. At the end of the course lay a $25,000 prize. But the money was not foremost in their minds. They had sailed virtually together around the world. Tada said of Stokes, "He is best sailor. He is my English teacher and cooking teacher." In the end, they had become kindred spirits sailing in company, each determined to sail as well as possible, to perform at his maximum and to absorb the lessons and pleasures of the race to the fullest. The rivalry and the race to be first across the line in Newport was as much an expression of that relationship as it was of their desire for victory.

At 5 a.m. on May 9, the flotilla of powerboats once again left the Goat Island docks and steamed out of Newport Harbor. The pelting midnight rain had stopped and the breeze and seas were calmer. But the fog was worse. It hung over Rhode Island Sound like a wet blanket, obscuring sight, muffling sound and disorienting the powerboat navigators. By 6:45 a.m., 22 boats had gathered around the base of Brenton Tower, where the tenor horn pierced the fog once every minute. Although the sun had come up behind the fog, the light was dim and, for cameramen in the flotilla, things were no better than the previous night.

Then, soon after 7 a.m., the sound of boat horns filled the air. As if on cue, the fog lifted to reveal *Credit Agricole*'s black hull sailing at seven knots toward the finish line. As he passed Brenton Tower and headed for the mouth of the bay, Jeantot was joined by the flotilla, which circled him enthusiastically. Friends and family waved and bottles of beer and champagne were hoisted in Jeantot's honor. Watching this lone man handle his 56-foot boat in the confusion and rough, wake-tossed water, it was plain to see how he had managed to sail around the world so competently and at such a record-breaking pace. He moved about the deck of *Credit Agricole* with an unconscious athletic grace, always finding footholds and handholds on the pitching deck while managing the huge sails and heavy ropes. And, *Credit Agricole* was fast. She shot along in the mild morning breeze keeping abreast of the steaming powerboats. Her black hull, with its sharp, vertical bow and wide, flour-scoop stern, showed immense power and startling speed. This boat and this man, which set a new record of 159 days for a singlehanded circumnavigation, beating Alain Colas' record by 10 days, proved they were the forerunners of a new age of singlehanded offshore sailing.

A Coast Guard 44-footer escorted *Credit Agricole* into the calm waters of Narragansett Bay with her fire nozzle describing a feathery arc in the sky. When his sails were furled, the guardsmen threw Jeantot a line. After 5,300 miles of sailing from Rio, *Credit Agricole* was towed into "B" dock at Goat Island, where it all had begun eight months before. A jubilant crowd welcomed Jeantot at the dock. Bottles of Moët popped open and, following tradition, Jeantot shook one bottle after another and sprayed the expensive champagne into the air and over the crowd. Friends and relatives jumped down onto *Credit Agricole*'s decks to hug and congratulate the young Frenchman. Among them was his mother, Genevieve Jeantot, a demure, gray-haired woman whose eyes sparkled as she planted a kiss on her son's cheek. Later she said in her limited English, "He ees goood skipper." Right behind her, clamboring to give the young man a hug, was Jeantot's banker, representing the Credit Agricole Bank, which had given Jeantot half of the money needed to enter the race. The broad grin on the banker's face was a clear indication that the bank's investment had been superb.

After giving a number of interviews from the deck of his boat, Jeantot was swept away in a whirlwind of public relations representatives and race organizers. It was a whirlwind that would very rapidly launch the 31-year-old Frenchman to international fame. A formal press conference was staged at the nearby Sheraton Islander Hotel. Jeantot showed remarkable poise under the heat of the television lights and the assault of questions from the approximately 40 reporters on hand, considering he had just arrived from a solitary and peaceful 28-day passage. In the hour after he stepped ashore, Jeantot became a proud public figure, but not an arrogant prima donna. He was modest and charming and accessible. And, as always, the women in the crowd found themselves staring when they meant to be just watching.

That afternoon, Jeantot was escorted to New York by BOC and Credit Agricole's PR representatives. That night, 16 hours after finishing the race, he appeared on ABC television's *Nightline*. The next morning, he was awoken early so he could appear with Tom Brokaw on NBC television's *Today* show. Also that morning, Jeantot's face appeared on the front page of *The New York Times*, *The Washington Post*, *The Providence Journal* and a number of other metropolitan daily newspapers. Within a week, *Sports Illustrated* magazine had run a four-page profile of the new French sports hero, including an account of the race around the world and a photograph of Jeantot in a tank suit.

The young, rebellious diver who had run from one dangerous occupation to another—from paratrooper to record-setting deep-sea diver to singlehanded sailor—had at the end of the BOC Challenge become a matinee idol on both sides of the Atlantic.

Despite the sound and fury, despite the $25,000 he won in the race and the promise of much more to come in endorsements and fees, Jeantot was not spoiled by his instant fame. In the aftermath, he had to ward off toadies and sycophants, he had to assess each new situation with more care than he would have a year before. But behind his first perimeter of defense, the essential Jeantot remained intact. That became evident to those close to the race upon his return from France, where he had jetted for a quick public relations tour. He walked into the BOC office at the Goat Island Marina and saw an issue of the French newspaper *Le Monde* lying on the table. Translated, the headline asserted in bold face type that Jeantot was a greater hero than Eric Tabarly. Jeantot picked up the paper, read the headline and the lead of the story and then threw the paper down again in disgust. "That newspaper is not true," he said. "This is just one race. Tabarly is Tabarly. Jeantot is Jeantot."

By the time Reed crossed the finish line on the morning of May 10, just over 24 hours after Jeantot, the whirlwind had left Newport. He was greeted at the line by a small flotilla of boats, taken in tow and brought into Goat Island. There was no frenzy, no triumphant arc from a Coast Guard fire hose, no throbbing crowd or television producers on the dock. Instead, Reed was greeted by the hard-core race fans and they appreciated his every quip. He was handed a bottle of champagne during his tow in and he made a good show of opening it, tilting it to his mouth and so forth. But, the job done, what Reed really craved was "a beerie, please, mate." And once he arrived at the pier, the towboat placed *Voortrekker*—which Reed called the "fastest, most uncomfortable, prettiest 50-footer around"—right in front of the moored *Credit Agricole*. After four long legs of following Jeantot into port, this coincidence was too good for Reed to pass up. As he tossed mooring lines to helpers on the dock he quipped, "This is the only time in the race *Credit Agricole* has seen *Voortrekker*'s transom."

At the dock, Reed obliged the crowd by spraying them with champagne from his victory bottle. He grinned with impish pleasure as the foamy jet doused the familiar faces of the race organizers and the press who had followed the race around the world. That playful pose was the quintessential Reed: His eyes were swollen from a long night of competitive sailing; his hair was tousled like a little boy's after a long night's sleep. The race over, he was delighting in transforming all his competitive energy into a frolic with friends. He had spent eight months racing in a boat that gave him little chance of winning. Yet he had squeezed every ounce of speed out of his "old girl". Of the last leg, he said, "I had a little chance but not very much. Philippe shot away at the corner of Brazil. If it had been a light upwind beat all the way, I might have been able to hold him."

But he was hardly sad or wistful at the outcome. He made no excuses. That was not "Biltong Bertie's" straightahead style. He preferred to make light of his achievements and of the dangers of the sea. Responding to a question from someone at the pier about the dangers of offshore sailing, he said, smiling, "Well, you have to accept the good with the bad. On the way up here a whale tried to mate with me—but he didn't know what sex I was. He started to dive down into the phosphorescence and the only thing I could think to do was to turn on the engine and try to drive him away. At the same time, there was this ship bearing down on me. . . ."

That night, the Goat Island Yacht Club and the BOC threw a simple American-style barbecue of beer and hamburgers for Reed. (They had thrown one for Jeantot the night before, but he was in New York contending with his fame.) The party was low key and unpretentious, which fit Reed to a tee. Although he would have preferred to win the race and the cash prize, Reed was pleased to celebrate by eating and drinking with friends. But his achievements on the voyage around the globe were not overlooked by the race committee. At the official awards ceremony, held on May 28, Reed was awarded the Konkolski Bell, which Richard Konkolski had donated for the skipper who got the best performance out of his boat. Although he had finished second, Reed had driven harder and sailed closer to his boat's maximum performance than anyone else, including Jeantot. It was the only way Reed knew how to sail.

A week later, as a northeast storm lashed the U.S. East Coast, the battle for overall first place in Class II ran right down to the wire. Richard Konkolski had already finished, to once more take line honors for Class II. But he was not a contender for the top prize for his class. All eyes remained on the duel still going on. On the bulletin board at race headquarters the pushpins for Tada and Stokes stood dead even, both 271 miles from the finish. But out on the storm-tossed Atlantic, Stokes and Tada had chosen different approaches to the finish and gradually, through the night and last day of the race, Stokes managed once again to open a lead.

"It usually is pretty disastrous to make your plans according to what the weatherman says," Stokes said. "But this time I listened to what the local forecasters were saying and took their advice."

Stokes steered east of the rhumb line in the last few days expecting the northeaster and then when it filled in he had the wind on his beam as he reached for the finish line. Tada, listening to his own private weatherman, went looking for the prevailing westerly breeze and found himself too far west. He had to tack into the storm to reach the finish. For a few hours it seemed the storm might delay Tada long enough for Stokes to win overall. But it was unlikely.

In the driving rain on the night of May 16, 209 days after departing Newport on that sunny August afternoon, Stokes sailed across the finish line.

"It was pretty neat," he said, "to see the light of Brenton Tower through the rain." At the tower several boats and the race committee boat stood by to greet the first American finisher. They took *Mooneshine* in tow and brought the 39-foot cutter into the pier at Goat Island. In the pouring rain, more than 100 people gathered to welcome Stokes. He was "surprised and overwhelmed by the welcome." Two of his children, his wife, Nancy, and several other friends and relatives—who had brought balloons and, of all things, potted plants for their hero—waited at the dock.

As always, Stokes arrived in port clean-shaven, freshly washed and dressed in clean clothes. His face was tanned from the three-week sail through the tropics and he looked youthful. At 57, he was the "elder statesman" of the fleet. But that had not stopped him from making what the other skippers characterized as a "letter-perfect voyage" around the globe. Nor did it stop Stokes from becoming one of the linchpins in the community. He was the skipper who helped Tada when the Japanese sailor's English let him down. He pulled Tony Lush off the sinking *Lady Pepperell*. And he had provided a ready and willing radio link whenever communications became difficult between the boats. The race would have been very different and possibly less of a success without him. For Stokes, the race had been "the happiest year of my life, and at 57, that's saying something."

Tada arrived at the finish line the next morning, 14 hours behind Stokes, to win the Class II trophy and the check for $25,000. He managed the victory without winning any of the individual legs. He remarked after his tow into "B" dock at Goat Island, that winning the race was the "biggest fluke" in his life.

From the beginning, Tada had sailed his own style of race. He had forged into areas of the ocean the others had shunned, and tested himself against his own personal goals as much as the obvious hurdles of the race. He was innovative with his unusual "bergsprits" in Cape Town and Sydney and with the keel modifications in Rio. Although neither was a success, the enthusiasm of the experiments seemed to carry him along. In port, he generated laughter and goodwill wherever he turned, and often left his fellow skippers scratching their heads in wonderment at his bizarre behavior; seeing music and hearing color are not normal wharfside conversational topics.

That he won his class was not as much of a fluke as it may have seemed. Both Konkolski and Jacques de Roux were favorites to take the small-boat trophy, but both men encountered adversity that held Konkolski back and stopped de Roux altogether. Tada endured and that, in the long run, was the difference. His Oriental "hard training" paid off in a most Occidental way—hard cash—but also in the pure achievement of negotiating the oceans' toughest tests with skill and humor.

On the evening Tada arrived, the yacht club fired up the barbecues again to welcome both Stokes and Tada. Beer flowed. Many of the other skippers—who already had arrived and who had already celebrated in the same yellow tent—came to join the "odd couple" of the race. The camaraderie among the skippers after experiencing such an adventure together turned the party riotous.

"My friends are my treasures," Tada said. "That is all I need."

Four days behind Stokes and Tada, Dan Bryne made yet another difficult landfall. He hoped to finish two days earlier. But when he got within 100 miles of the coast, the wind dropped and he lay virtually becalmed for 24 hours. Finally, the west wind gathered steam and he rode across the finish line on a 25-knot breeze. As he tied his mooring lines around a piling at the dock, Byrne remarked, "These finishes are driving me crazy."

Byrne was met again by his wife, Pat, whose ardent support had been one of the main factors contributing to his success. Stokes was on hand for Byrne's finish as well, having driven to Newport from his home in Moorestown, New Jersey. It was a sweet landfall and a proud end to a long race. He had accomplished his dream and overcome the high hurdles of three oceans. Moreover, when he crossed the finish line, he became only the second American to complete a singlehanded circumnavigation via Cape Horn. Webb Chiles was the first. The voyages of Slocum, Pidgeon and others were circumnavigations via Panama or the Strait of Magellan. And Stokes' circumnavigation was not completed singlehandedly because he was accompanied by Tony Lush most of the second leg.

The company of sailors Byrne joined was a rare one. But the gray-bearded sailor, who looked more like Ernest Hemmingway everytime he sailed into port, did not really care about the records as much as he cared about completing the race itself. Soon after arriving, Byrne ran into David White (who had sailed back to the states from South Africa earlier in the year, and had flown up from Florida to see the end of the race), at Goat Island. Byrne said, "That was one hell of an idea you had."

By May 20, when Byrne arrived, nine of the 10 skippers still in the race were in Newport. A week later, BOC hosted the awards ceremony at the Sheraton Islander Hotel. Lots of silver was passed out. Everyone involved with the race—from Jim Roos and White who got it off the ground, to Byrne who finished at the end of the pack—won something and most won a duffle bag full of trophies to take home with them. It had been that kind of a race. The sense of community was stronger among the nine skippers present than was the competition. The race was the first of a kind, a rare and unique adventure in which every skipper felt lucky to have participated.

In the short speech Jeantot gave upon being awarded the overall winner's trophy, he said what all the others felt. "It was the friendships that made this race special to me. I hope that it will not change for the next race."

But it wasn't quite over.

Still, 1,000 miles at sea and sailing for Newport was Dick McBride and *City of Dunedin*. After his month on the beach at South Falkland Island, and then a restart from Rio on April 28, McBride was once again in the race. *City of Dunedin* sailed steadily through the northeast trade winds and then inched her way through periods of calms and storms north of the

Gulf Stream. The steel schooner was battered from her encounter with the Falkland rocks, but the repairs in Rio held the boat in one inelegant but solid piece. Down below, McBride's accommodations were ragged. The boat had filled with water and everything inside had drowned. He had not replaced or repaired much of the interior and the high water marks stained the interior bulkheads.

It had been a long, hard trip around the world in a boat that was not well suited to the job at hand. So when he finally saw Brenton Tower ahead of him on the morning of June 7, the sense of victory was especially pleasant. A small flotilla of boats rushed out to meet him at the line. Once he was tied to the pier at "B" dock, a small group of press and race organizers gathered to give McBride a rousing welcome.

McBride's was the signature arrival. It capped the adventure. That evening the Goat Island yacht club threw one last barbecue. As the evening fog rolled in over Narragansett Bay, the party grew into a wild finale. Many of the other skippers were still in Newport, living on their boats, pausing after the year-long effort. They all came to hoist a beer to the last finisher.

They had become a tribe. In the month since Jeantot had first closed the circle of the race, the tribal bonds grew stronger and stronger. They tended to cling together, to rely on each other. They shared the quick understanding of an in-joke, knowing nods at the mention of money troubles and encouraging slaps on the back when new plans of action were hatched. They were different from the rest, not better or worse, not heroes, even—but men apart who had ventured to the farthest reaches of human experience to look their own fates squarely in the eye. It was not something most people on the piers of Newport could grasp. And that only served to drive the tribe closer, to make them more dependent on each other. Now it was really over.

BOC sent representatives from the race committee to the barbecue to award McBride his prizes and to wave the company's flag one last time. The party under the yellow tent raged into the night until the food and beer were gone. And then, without saying goodbye, the skippers disbanded into the fog, never to reassemble in quite the same way again.

Epilogue

CLASS I

RICHARD BROADHEAD returned to England after the race where he refitted *Perseverance of Medina* and then set out for a winter's cruise of the Caribbean. No longer singlehanded, he sailed in the company of a lady friend he'd met in Newport. He returned to London in January, 1984, to receive an award as British Yachtsman of the Year in recognition of his rescue of Jacques de Roux. He also won a seamanship award from the British Navy.

NEVILLE GOSSON spent the summer after the race living aboard *Leda Pier One* in Newport, Rhode Island, and writing a book about his life and sailing experiences. He sold *Leda* in the early fall and returned to Sydney to tie up the loose ends of his construction business and complete his book.

DESMOND HAMPTON returned to London and his business interests.

PHILIPPE JEANTOT returned to France where he went on a personal appearance tour for Credit Agricole that lasted nearly a year. He received a multi-year racing contract from the bank, along with 6 million francs ($1 million) to build an ocean racing catamaran and a new 60-footer for the 1986–87 BOC Challenge.

TONY LUSH moved to Newport, where he bought a house and began searching for sponsors for the 1984 OSTAR and the 1986–87 BOC Challenge.

BERTIE REED returned to South Africa, retired from the South African Navy, went into private business, and began seeking sponsorship for the 1986–87 BOC Challenge.

PAUL RODGERS sailed singlehanded from Cape Town to Newport to England and then back to Cape Town, where he began work on a non-sailing novel. Meanwhile his first book, *Loner*, an account of his attempt to complete a double circumnavigation, was published.

201

DAVID WHITE sailed from Cape Town to St. Petersburg, Florida, where he began extensive renovations on *Gladiator* in preparation for the 1984 OSTAR.

CLASS II

GUY BERNARDIN moved to New York, New York, where he sought and found sponsorship for the 1984 OSTAR and the 1986–87 BOC Challenge.

DAN BYRNE put *Fantasy* aboard a truck in Newport and hauled her cross-country to California, where he made personal appearances at most of the major fall boat shows. He completed work on his movie about the race, commissioned the design of a new 60-footer and was the first official entrant for the 1986–87 BOC Challenge.

GREG COLES remained in Cape Town and returned to his job as an employee of yacht designer Richard Glanville.

JACQUES DE ROUX briefly returned to France, and then took a position with a cannery firm in Indonesia. He also began seeking sponsorship for the 1986–87 BOC Challenge.

RICHARD KONKOLSKI and his family were granted political asylum in the United States in November, 1983. Konkolski bought a duplex in Newport, Rhode Island and found work as a contractor, and in the maintenance department of a Providence hospital. His wife, Miki, began a business called Mighty Miki's Home Maintenance. His son, Richard Jr., entered the Newport public school system.

TOM LINDHOLM returned to California and then went cruising with his wife in the South Pacific.

DICK McBRIDE spent the summer in Newport, where he was joined by his father, Kaye. At summer's end, he took a job skippering *Outward Bound,* a New Zealand entry in the 1980 Whitbread Race, from Newport to New Zealand. He then returned to Panama, where his father and a crew had sailed *City of Dunedin,* for the trip to New Zealand. He also began seeking sponsorship for the 1986–87 BOC Challenge.

FRANCIS STOKES returned to his home in New Jersey and to his yacht brokerage business in Annapolis, Maryland.

YUKOH TADA was given a hero's reception upon returning to Japan in *Koden Okera*. He renewed a sponsorship agreement with Koden, an electronics firm, for the 1984 OSTAR and the 1986–87 BOC Challenge. He also began work on a book about the race and gave a one-man show of his abstract paintings in Tokyo. In the winter of 1983, he was informed that his friend and mentor, Naomi Uemera, was killed in an avalanche while attempting a solo ascent of Alaska's Mt. McKinley.

Appendix I—ROUTES AND WEATHER

The course around the world from Newport via Cape Town, Sydney and Rio de Janeiro involved two transits of the Atlantic and two long runs through the southern ocean. The Atlantic legs involved strategy as well as boat speed. Choosing the right route through the prevailing weather systems made a difference of hundreds of total miles sailed, saving many days for those who found the best wind. The southern ocean legs were flat-out boat races through the Roaring Forties and Screaming Fifties. Down south, the trick was to position themselves on the correct side of passing storm systems to get a following wind and at the same time avoid being lashed to ribbons.

Technology, in particular the weather facsimile machines eight of the racers carried, (including class winners Philippe Jeantot and Yukoh Tada) played an important role in solving the navigation riddles. And perhaps the most interesting outcome of the race was the realization that close-winded modern boats, whether sailed singlehanded or not, can sail routes quite different from those common just a generation ago. Although it is too soon to throw the old sailing bible, *Ocean Passages For The World*, overboard, Philippe Jeantot and the others proved that the traditional way to sail the oceans is no longer the only way, nor the fastest way.

LEG I—NEWPORT TO CAPE TOWN
Distance: 7,100 miles
Start: August 28, 1982

The Atlantic Ocean provided the racers with the toughest weather riddle of the race, for they had to negotiate the North Atlantic high, then cross the northeast trades, the doldrums, sail into the southeast trades and then skirt the South Atlantic high before making the last dash to Cape Town. They had to stay clear of the high-pressure systems because ridges of high pressure are notorious for being windless, so the choice, both in the north and south, was either to go east or west of the system. *Ocean Passages* recommends the easterly pass in the north and the westerly pass in the south.

Along this course, de Roux, who many considered the best sailor in the

204

fleet, sailed 7,941 miles, which is approximately 800 miles more than the rhumb-line course. De Roux won Class I for the leg and beat his closest rival, Francis Stokes in *Mooneshine,* by two days, two hours. Stokes also sailed the traditional route.

It is surprising then, to see that Jeantot sailed only 7,314 miles on the route, 600 less than de Roux and more than 700 less than his nearest competitor in Class I, Bertie Reed. Jeantot chose the route not recommended by *Ocean Passages.* He sailed west of the North Atlantic high, close reached through the northeast trades, crossed a narrow band of doldrums at about 10°N and then entered the southeast trades several days ahead of the rest of the fleet. When he hit the equator, he was leading by 200 miles. A week later, as he reached through the trades, his lead grew to 600 miles. Cutting the corner to the west of the South Atlantic high, he extended his lead at Cape Town to an amazing 1,200 miles.

This was a new way to approach the route from the East Coast of the U.S. to the Southern Hemisphere. Most of the racers agreed that what Jeantot did will change the thinking of many racers and cruisers setting out to sail the route.

The alternative route to Cape Town was to go east of the North Atlantic high and then stay east and try to skirt the South Atlantic high by tacking down the African coast. It is the route used by crewed ocean racers sailing from Europe, the Whitbread Round The World Race, in particular, and both Richard Konkolski and Guy Bernardin had used the route successfully on previous voyages. Konkolski sailed straight through the Cape Verde Islands and then along the African coast until he hit the equator where he headed south for Cape Town. Bernardin went even further east into the crook of the coastline. For both it was a disastrous move, as they never found the breezes that were supposed to be there. Konkolski was nearly becalmed for 17 days and Bernardin sailed into Cape Town at the tail end of the fleet calling the leg "the most frustrating sail of my life."

LEG II—CAPE TOWN TO SYDNEY
Distance: 6,900 miles
Start: November 13, 1982

Although all the racers expected to find heavy going in the southern ocean, none was ready for the hammering they received in the first two weeks out of Cape Town. The first night, they were scattered by a gale. *Okera* was rolled, *Fantasy* was knocked down, Byrne's engine and other gear were damaged so badly he had to turn back. *Moonshine* was knocked down and Stokes damaged his back in the fall. In the next 14 days, five more southern ocean gales swept over them. The last one pitchpoled *Lady Pepperell,* forcing Tony Lush to abandon ship. He was rescued by Francis Stokes.

The route from Cape Town to Sydney, according to *Ocean Passages,* is a straight run south to 40°S and then east along the parallel until it is time to make for the Bass Strait between Australia and Tasmania. Only Neville Gosson and Jeantot dipped well below the rhumb line, and Gosson sailed all the way to 56°S as he sorted out headstay trouble that prevented him from sailing to windward. It is interesting to note that de Roux sailed 6,658 miles, while Jeantot sailed 6,488 and Gosson sailed 6,229 miles.

The danger in sailing the great circle course, as Gosson did, is ice, which has been known to drift as far north as 35°S but is common below 55°S. What makes sailing through the Screaming Fifties even more interesting is the fog that shrouds the ice. Gosson made it back in one piece, however, finishing third and recording his best showing of the race, despite the broken forestay.

The other decision skippers had to make was to use the Bass Strait or sail around Tasmania. In Cape Town, Gosson, the only Australian in the race, pointed out at the skippers' meeting that the Bass Strait and the east coast of Australia leading to Sydney was a dangerous stretch of water, mired by islands, foul currents and head winds. But the fleet as a whole used the strait, with only Gosson and Dick McBride sailing around Tasmania.

As the leaders cleared the strait, Gosson's warning suddenly rang true. Tired from the tricky coastal navigation, Desmond Hampton slept through his alarm while *Gipsy Moth V* sailed headlong onto the rocks of Gabo Island.

LEG II—SYDNEY TO RIO DE JANEIRO
Distance: 8,250 miles
Start: January 16, 1983

Cape Horn. If there was one reason for the race, it was that rocky promontory deep in the southern ocean. It is the Everest of sailing. The route leading to the Horn is similar to that of Leg II. *Ocean Passages* recommends that skippers sail south into the Roaring Forties and then settle onto an easterly course at a latitude between 47°S and 51°S until reaching the meridian of 115°W where they should dip gradually for the Horn. From the Horn, the natural route, with the current, leads between the Falkland Islands and the mainland.

Naturally, once the boats had rounded South Cape in New Zealand, the shortest route would have been the great circle course, but again, that led through the ice. Jeantot and Tada were the two who came closest to the great circle, sailing 7,941 and 7,958 miles respectively. Bertie Reed, on the other hand, stayed further north out of the ice and fog and had to sail a total of 8,473 miles. Reed said, "In the Roaring Forties and Screaming Fifties, gales steam eastward like freight trains, churning the sea into tall, breaking waves (some are 50 feet and more) that roll from two and sometimes three directions at once."

In the cross fire, de Roux's 44-footer *Skoiern III* was rolled and dismasted. Holed by the loose spar and sinking, de Roux pulled his Argos emergency switch setting off a frantic 59-hour sea rescue in which young

Richard Broadhead was the hero. He plucked de Roux off *Skoiern*, which was lying awash and sinking.

The Horn was not a disappointment. Richard McBride got the best view of the famous landmark. He wrote of that day, "Cape Horn in sight! Massive. Magnificent. If one wanted a day with all the soul of Cape Horn, this is it—wind gusting to 50 knots—huge seas—albatross and storm petrels—and two dolphin." After the thrill came the letdown. Three days later, McBride put *City of Dunedin* on the Falkland Islands, where she stayed for nearly a month before he refloated her.

Light winds prevailed during the sail north to Rio. Those who sailed close to the coast found they had to turn seaward at the mouth of the River Platte in order to avoid a contrary current and keep the wind. Those who stayed offshore had to contend with maddening calms. After the longest and most arduous leg, the sight of Sugarloaf Mountain was a relief to every skipper.

LEG IV—RIO DE JANEIRO TO NEWPORT
Distance: 5,300 miles
Start: April 10, 1983

Once in Rio, the long battle for the skippers seemed behind them. The last leg promised to be one of light variables and trade winds, the kind of sailing you can do in shorts and a T-shirt. From Rio, *Ocean Passages* recommends that the skippers briefly sail southeast into the trades, avoiding the Brazil current that runs southward along the coast, before turning north. Only Tada and McBride took this advice. The rest of the fleet, exploiting the windward ability of their boats, snuck northward along the coast trying to stay inside the current and picking up whatever shore breezes they could find. The next obstacle was the doldrums between the belts of trade winds, which was long the nemesis of commercial sail. *Ocean Passages* recommends crossing in a section between 27°W and 32°W, but again, none of the fleet stayed that far offshore.

Appendix II—RESULTS AND STANDINGS
THE BOC CHALLENGE: OVERALL POSITIONS ON ELAPSED TIMES
TIMES GIVEN IN DAYS, HOURS, MINUTES AND SECONDS

Position	Yacht/Skipper	Elapsed time, legs 1, 2, 3 & 4	Total elapsed time
CLASS 1 YACHTS			
1	**Crédit Agricole** Philippe Jeantot	47d 00h 01m 02s 35d 09h 14m 16s 47d 23h 59m 08s 28d 17h 11m 35s	159d 02h 26m 01s
2	**Altech Voortrekker** Bertie Reed	53d 15h 54m 54s 37d 03h 50m 53s 50d 03h 26m 55s 29d 17h 38m 39s	170d 16h 51m 21s
3	**Perseverance of Medina** Richard Broadhead	56d 18h 51m 19s 50d 05h 05m 18s 50d 09h 26m 11s[1] 35d 00h 44m 00s	192d 10h 06m 48s
4	**Leda Pier One** Neville Gosson	62d 17h 14m 50s 45d 21h 08m 24s 58d 11h 11m 11s[2] 35d 00h 44m 00s[3]	202d 02h 18m 25s
	Gipsy Moth V Desmond Hampton	57d 05h 05m 32s 2nd leg, wrecked on Gabo Island, 18 December 1982	
	Lady Pepperell Tony Lush	57d 21h 47m 10s 2nd leg, pitchpoled and sank, 28 November 1982	
	Spirit of Pentax Paul Rodgers	58d 23h 30m 23s 2nd leg, retired after knockdown, 18 November 1982	
	Gladiator David White	76d 20h 42m 00s 2nd leg, retired with self-steering problems, 21 November 1982	

CLASS 2 YACHTS

	Yacht / Skipper	Leg 1	Leg 2	Leg 3	Leg 4	Total
1	**Koden Okera V** Yukoh Tada	59d 2h 52m 00s	53d 02h 23m 12s	56d 19h 47m 24s	36d 20h 53m 09s	207d 13h 55m 45s
2	**Mooneshine** Francis Stokes	60d 21h 29m 51s	52d 04h 54m 28s[4]	59d 16h 39m 45s	36d 06h 28m 45s	209d 01h 32m 49s
3	**Nike III** Richard Konkolski	65d 16h 38m 50s	63d 06h 42m 18s	52d 06h 12m 00s[5]	32d 11h 13m 20s	213d 16h 46m 28s
4	**Ratso II** Guy Bernardin	68d 17h 06m 14s	52d 23h 11m 35s	62d 07h 55m 05s	37d 11h 38m 04s	221d 11h 50m 58s
5	**Fantasy** Dan Byrne	65d 12h 24m 15s	56d 22h 34m 23s	66d 06h 42m 35s	39d 16h 17m 40s	228d 09h 58m 53s
6	**City of Dunedin** Richard McBride	73d 09h 50m 47s	55d 10h 52m 47s	96d 14h 58m 05s	38d 17h 08m 11s	264d 04h 49m 50s
	Skoiern III Jacques de Roux	55d 19h 38m 08s	46d 01h 30m 08s	3rd leg, pitchpoled and sank, 11 February 1983		
	Datsun Skyline Greg Coles	1st leg, elapsed time not available				
	Driftwood Thomas Lindholm	On completion of leg retired with self-steering problems				
		1st leg, retired with engine and self-steering problems, 30 August 1982				

1 Allows for Race Committee deduction of 145 hours for rescuing Jacques de Roux.
2 Allows for Race Committee deduction of 21 hours for turning back to aid rescue of Jacques de Roux.
3 Allows for Race Committee deduction of 25 hours 18 minutes for turning back to rescue Richard Konkolski.
4 Allows for Race Committee deduction of 12 hours 30 minutes for rescuing Tony Lush.
5 Allows for Race Committee deduction of 168 hours for time spent in port after late completion of second leg.